P9-CEJ-669

THE COMPLETE ITALIAN COOK BOOK

EXPERTS' CHOICE COOK BOOKS

André Simon's French Cook Book
by André Simon and Crosby Gaige

Complete Chicken Cookery
by Marian Tracy

The Complete Italian Cook Book
by Rose L. Sorce

Delectable Desserts
by Ann Seranne

Favorite Regional Recipes
Selected by Marian Tracy

The Fish and Sea Food Cook Book
by Cora, Rose and Bob Brown

The Burger Book
by Louis P. De Gouy

The Illustrated Book of Hors D'Oeuvres
by Lucy G. Allen

The Joy of Chinese Cooking
by Doreen Yen Hung Feng

Smörgåsbord and Scandinavian Cookery
by Florence Brobeck and Monika Brilioth Kjellberg

The Viennese Cookbook
by Irma Rhode

THE COMPLETE
ITALIAN COOK BOOK

[LA CUCINA]

By ROSE L. SORCE

NEW YORK

GROSSET & DUNLAP, *Publishers*

Copyright, 1953, by Rose L. Sorce
[Under the title: *La Cucina*]

By arrangement with Twayne Publishers

ISBN: 0-448-01364-9
1978 PRINTING

MANUFACTURED IN THE UNITED STATES OF AMERICA

FOREWORD

That geological display of mountains, volcanoes, wastelands, and marshes which forms the spine of Italy has made it a picturesque and varied nation but has also left it land-poor. Those towering columns and impressive hillsides inspire the eye with awe, but they do not make good farm land. In consequence, the Italian has had to struggle against unyielding soil for his sustenance, and when he has brought it to harvest he has naturally known a sense of personal victory. The food he has wrested from nature is not only food but an affirmation of the joy and goodness of life. For the Italian tradition lies close to the soil, and there is both a sacredness and a celebration in the Italian's use of good things from the soil.

At the same time, those who know poverty are always most ready to rejoice in plenty. Italian feast days are feasts indeed. In many Italian homes preparations for Christmas and Easter begin weeks and even months in advance. **Abbondanza** (plenty) is an idea that delights the Italian's soul and is even part of his religious feeling. Thus the Italian saying: **Buon pasto loda Iddio.** ("Good food praises God.") And thus the classic reply of the Italian host to the guest who protested that the former had put himself out too much in loading his table: **Non è troppo, è semplicemente abbondante.** ("It is not too much; it is simply plentiful.")

Above all else then, the native ingredient of Italian cookery is gusto. Whether it is a matter of a snack or a feast, the Italian has brought to his eating habits **la gioia di vivere,** the joy of living.

Unfortunately for many Americans who know Italian cookery only through the common run of Italian restaurants, this joy in a good table is not an ingredient that lends itself readily to commercial success. Thus for every Italian restaurant worthy of the name, scores of so-called Italian restaurants continue to serve boiled flour and sour tomatoes as "spaghetti," or something very like boiled cardboard and limp cheese as "pizza." The good Italian restaurant is a joy indeed, but one is not always easy to find. And unless you do find one, there is only one way to get a good Italian meal—you have to prepare it at your own or someone else's home.

Miss Rose Sorce has had the good fortune to be born the joyous daughter of a joyous mother, and to learn at their source the celebrations of the true Italian home kitchen. In this book she has compiled her learning for all to share. As the son of an

Italian mother who must have been very much indeed like Miss Sorce's, I may be pardoned for thinking that such a compilation is a basic contribution to civilization. What can possibly go wrong with a civilization that starts its evenings with a good minestrone and moves through a properly prepared scallopine to a zabaione or a biscotto Tortoni, and thence to black coffee, never forgetting the wine by the way?

Here's how it's done.

E buon appetito!

JOHN CIARDI

Table of Contents

CHAPTER ONE

Antipasto

People exercise so little in this modern age that they need the spicy, piquant appetizers to stimulate their appetites. Every country has its own name for appetizers. In Italy, they are called antipasto, and may be served formally or informally, either at the table with a cool glass of red or white Italian wine, or in the friendly atmosphere of the living room.

Luncheon starts with antipasto, as it opens the appetite for spaghetti or heavier foods. The antipasto, arrangements of which are numerous, includes salami, a curl of well-aged ham, and the inevitable anchovy in its many guises: wrapped around capers, tuna, pickled mushrooms, artichoke hearts, green or black olives, cold veal, fish mayonnaise, radishes, fenocchio, or red and green peppers. Each tidbit of antipasto must be served in a small, separate dish, drenched with the delicate, emerald green olive oil. Even raw vegetables, such as celery and fenocchio, are dipped in oil, salt and pepper to improve their relish. Use your own ingenuity in arranging an attractive plate according to color.

The secret in serving antipasto tastily and effectively is to serve the cold foods crispy cold, and the hot foods piping hot. Any combination of the following recipes may be used according to taste. Try all of them at some time or other; your close friends will become closer, and your family will look at you with a new respect.

Anchovies

PLAIN ANCHOVIES

(Acciughe)

Soak several anchovies about 2 hours in cold water; rub off skin and strip fillets from bones. Mash anchovies to a paste and mix with melted butter. Fry rounds of bread brown on both sides; cover with anchovy paste, sprinkle with chopped green olives and grated Parmesan cheese. Brown under grill, and serve hot.

ANCHOVY FILLETS

(Filette d'Acciughe)

Place anchovy fillets on finger-length strips of toasted bread that have been rubbed in garlic.

ANCHOVY SALAD

(Insalata d'Acciughe)

1 lb. anchovies, salted
1 onion, chopped fine
½ green pepper, chopped fine
1 pickled beet, diced
1 tblsp. capers
2 hard-boiled eggs, chopped

Soak the anchovies in cold water overnight, rub off skin and remove bones by stripping each anchovy carefully down the center. Dry anchovies and place in salad bowl with other salad ingredients.

DRESSING:

1 cup Italian olive oil
⅓ cup red wine vinegar
¼ tsp. sugar
freshly ground pepper

Thoroughly beat above ingredients together and pour over anchovies; let stand 30 minutes, turning now and then to make sure all anchovies absorb as much dressing as they can take.

GARNISH:

3 eggs, hard-boiled and quartered
lettuce leaves
watercress
2 pickled beets, diced
1 tblsp. capers
1 green pepper, chopped fine
1 onion, chopped fine
1 tblsp. oregano

Criss-cross anchovies on a platter and pour remaining dressing over them with a little clear olive oil; garnish with eggs, lettuce and watercress. Pile beets, capers and peppers in contrasting colors around the anchovy. Serve with crusty Italian bread.

NOTE: If anchovies-in-oil are available it will be that much easier.

ANCHOVY SALAMI

(Salami all'Acciughe)

Roll a slice of salami around a stuffed caper anchovy. Serve on toothpicks.

Rocca Cheese and Anchovies (see under Cheese Antipasto).

Vegetable Antipasto

ANTIPASTO AUGUSTINO

1 leek, chopped	1 onion, chopped
2 tblsp. parsley, chopped	1 tomato, chopped
1 green pepper, chopped	3 tblsp. olive oil
¼ cup Parmesan cheese, grated	1 tsp. salt
1 tsp. paprika	rounds of bread, toasted

Cook vegetables slowly in hot olive oil until tender; add cheese, salt and pepper, and serve on toasted rounds of bread.

ANTIPASTO PLATTER
(Vassoio di Antipasti)

Arrange any of the following on a platter:

Salami strips, several Italian cheeses, green and ripe olive mix, celery stuffed with anchovy paste and cheese, eggplant mix, sliced tomatoes, sharp peppers and radishes, all arranged on a bed of endive. Serve with bread sticks, or garlic bread that has been toasted and sprinkled with Parmesan cheese.

* * * * *

Lettuce, fennel (finocchio), radishes, pickled beets, salami and anchovies.

* * * * *

Sautéed mushrooms, sliced hard-boiled eggs, tuna fish, roe, slices of Italian ham, arranged on a bed of lettuce.

* * * * *

Small green peppers, artichoke hearts, pepperoni sausage, celery and anchovies.

* * * * *

Artichoke hearts, lettuce, sliced tomatoes, sliced smoked pork, hard-boiled eggs, green peppers and ripe olives.

ARTICHOKE ANTIPASTO
(Carciofini per Antipasto)

Parboil artichoke hearts and set to cool. Mix together olive oil, oregano, salt and pepper, lemon juice; add artichoke hearts and let marinate 1 hour before serving.

PICKLED ARTICHOKES

(Carciofini al Salamoia)

4 lbs. artichokes, sliced
¾ cup salt
1 qt. wine vinegar
3 tblsp. mustard seed
2 tblsp. whole cinnamon
¼ cup tiny dried red peppers
½ gal. water
3 med. onions, sliced
4 cups sugar
2 tblsp. whole allspice
2 tblsp. whole cloves

Soak artichokes in a brine for 3 hours, covered. Combine vinegar, sugar and spices; bring to a boil, stir until sugar is dissolved. Pack artichokes, drained, with onions in hot, sterilized jars and pour in hot vinegar syrup just to top of jars; seal at once. Makes 7 pints.

EGGPLANT RELISH

(Caponatina)

4 eggplants, cubed
1 peck tomatoes, cooked
1 lb. seedless raisins
¼ lb. pinenuts
4 bunches celery, cut up
salt and pepper
1 cup sugar
2 cups olive oil
1 lb. green ripe olives, pitted and halved
1 bottle capers (2 ¼ oz.)
2 cups vinegar wine

Fry eggplant in deep hot olive oil; drain. Strain tomatoes and combine with olives, raisins, pinenuts, capers and celery; boil and add seasoning, cooking until tender. Add vinegar wine, sugar and cook until well blended: combine with eggplant and, while hot, fill hot, sterile jars and seal. You will find this an enjoyable relish.

FENNEL

(Finocchio)

fennel
salt
olive oil
fresh ground pepper

Soak fennel in ice water until crisp; cut into serving lengths. Make a dressing of olive oil, salt and fresh ground pepper. Serve with the dressing. Just dip fennel into dressing, bite off, and what a pleasant surprise!

YELLOW FLAT BEANS

(Lupini)

Yellow flat beans now come in jars and can be obtained at any Italian store. Remove the wax-like outer shell from the beans, sprinkle with salt and serve with any antipasto arrangement.

STUFFED CELERY

(Sedani Ripieni)

Wash tender celery stalks, or fenocchio, in cold water until crisp; spread with anchovy paste, Rocca cheese or liver paste. Serve with dry red wine.

STUFFED CELERY RINGS

(Anelli di Sedani Ripieni)

1 large bunch celery (or fennel)
3 oz. blue cheese
pinch of garlic salt
salt and pepper
3 tblsp. butter
2 tblsp. tomato paste
⅛ tsp. red pepper

Work together tomato paste, butter and cheese; add seasonings. Separate celery stalks and fill each stalk with filling; reshape stalks to original form and wrap in wax paper. Chill for 1 hour; slice crosswise into rings and serve. Serves 6.

PICKLED MUSHROOMS

(Funghi alla Salamoia)

No. I

1 lb. mushrooms
1 tsp. oregano
1 tblsp. capers
½ cup wine vinegar
3 tblsp. olive oil
salt and pepper

Cook mushrooms until tender; strain. Make a brine of the wine vinegar, oregano, olive oil, capers, salt and pepper; add mushrooms and marinate for 1 hour. Chill and serve mushrooms on toothpicks. These will keep for some time.

No. II

1 pt. mushrooms
1 tsp. peppercorns
1 clove garlic, quartered
1 tsp. salt
1 blade mace
vinegar

Wipe mushrooms clean with a cloth dampened with vinegar; cut off stems and pack in a glass jar. Add remaining ingredients, filling jar with vinegar; cover jar and set away for 2 days. Serve with Italian antipasto.

STUFFED MUSHROOMS

(Funghi Ripieni)

Peel caps and remove stems of small mushrooms; sauté in hot olive oil, and stuff with anchovy paste. Serve on toothpicks while hot.

OLIVE AND CLAM MIX

(Olive con Vongole)

½ cup ripe olives, pitted
⅓ cup celery, diced
2 tblsp. catsup
dash of tabasco sauce
¾ cup whole clams with liquid
3 tblsp. chili sauce
juice of ½ lemon

Quarter olives and combine with remaining ingredients; chill. Serve in cocktail glasses. Serves 4.

GARLIC OLIVES

(Olive con Aglio)

1 lb. ripe black olives
1 clove garlic, sliced
1 part vinegar
½ lb. green olives
1 small onion, sliced
2 parts olive oil

Split olives slightly to allow juices to marinate; place in a jar with garlic, onion, vinegar and olive oil, cover tightly and shake well. Let stand 2 or 3 hours before using. Will keep for weeks.

OLIVE MIX

(Olive Miste)

½ lb. green olives
½ lb. black olives
3 stalks celery, cut up
salt, pepper, oregano
¼ cup olive oil
1 green pepper, cut fine
1 red pepper, cut fine

Mix ingredients together and let stand in a cool place at least an hour before serving. Will keep a week or two.

STUFFED OLIVES

(Olive Farcite)

Stuff green or ripe olives with anchovies, almonds or tiny onions. Serve on toothpicks.

TOMATO WITH CHEESE

(Pomidoro con Formaggio)

tomatoes, sliced thick
white bread
butter
onion, grated
Parmesan cheese, grated
salt

Toast small rounds of bread on one side; butter untoasted side. Place a slice of tomato on untoasted side of bread, flavor with salt and a speck of onion, and pile cheese on top; broil until brown.

Cheese Antipasto

GORGONZOLA SPREAD

(Pasta di Gorgonzola)

1 thin slice Gorgonzola cheese
2 tblsp. brandy
1 tsp. chives, chopped
⅛ lb. butter
2 tblsp. cream
1 tsp. Worcestershire sauce
1 2-oz. package cream cheese
rounds of toast

Mix above ingredients and blend well. Serve on rounds of toast.

ROCCA CHEESE FINGERS

(Formaggio "Rocca")

Spread fingers of toasted garlic bread with Rocca cheese, and serve.

ROCCA CHEESE AND ANCHOVIES

(Formaggio "Rocca" con Acciughe)

6 anchovies
6 oz. Rocca cheese

Mix anchovies and cheese to a smooth paste; spread on toasted garlic bread and serve.

Meat Antipasto

CHICKEN LIVERS AND MUSHROOMS

(Fegatini di Pollo con Funghi)

1 lb. chicken livers
3 tblsp. olive oil
1 tsp. onion juice
¼ lb. fresh mushrooms, chopped
1 tblsp. lemon juice
salt and pepper to taste

Cook chicken livers in hot olive oil a few minutes; drain and strain through sieve. Sauté mushrooms and mix with chicken livers, lemon juice, onion juice and seasoning. Spread on bread disks and serve.

TOASTED CHICKEN LIVERS

(Fegatini di Pollo con Crostini)

12 chicken livers
2 tblsp. fat ham, minced
1 scallion, minced
½ tsp. parsley, minced
½ small carrot, minced
½ stalk celery, minced
fingers of dry bread
3 fresh mushrooms
1 tsp. breadcrumbs
1 tsp. lemon juice
olive oil
meat broth, heated
salt and pepper

Mix ham and vegetables with olive oil and seasoning; simmer. Clean chicken livers carefully, and with mushrooms lay on top of vegetables; simmer 5 minutes, then remove mushrooms and liver; mince and return to pan with enough broth to moisten well, and simmer 2 minutes, stirring once or twice. Mix in breadcrumbs, lemon juice and more broth, if needed. Serve on bread fingers.

NOTE: Delicious served with soup in place of crackers.

CHOPPED LIVER

(Fegato Tritato)

1 slice fried liver, chopped fine
½ small onion, chopped fine
mayonnaise
1 egg, hard-boiled and chopped fine

Marinate the liver, egg and onion in mayonnaise for at least 1 hour before serving.

BROILED SALAMI

(Salamini Arrostiti)

Cut salami into strips; place under broiler a few minutes. Serve on toothpicks, while hot.

WINE-FLAVORED SAUSAGES

(Salsiccini al Vino)

1 lb. small Italian sausages
½ cup white wine

Prick sausages with a fork, place in a hot skillet, cover with wine; cook slowly, covered, until wine is absorbed and sausages are well browned. Serve hot on toothpicks.

Egg Antipasto

EGG AND SHRIMP ANTIPASTO

(Uova con Granchiolini per Antipasto)

Place thin slices of hard-boiled egg on crostini (croutons) or ordinary toast; spread with a thick salad dressing that has garlic salt added, then top with a shrimp and finely chopped watercress.

EGGS MARIA

(Uova alla Maria)

4 eggs, hard-boiled
8 anchovies
3 tblsp. olive oil
1 tblsp. parsley, chopped fine
tomatoes, sliced
½ cup catsup
1 clove garlic, grated

Cut eggs lengthwise and place each piece on a slice of tomato with 2 anchovies criss-crossed on top. Combine catsup, olive oil, garlic and parsley and pour over eggs. Serve on toast. Serves 4.

Seafood Antipasto

MACKEREL ON TOAST

(Sgombro con Crostini)

1 mackerel, cooked
½ tsp. mustard
1 ½ tblsp. butter
1 small onion, grated
½ tsp. paprika
rounds of toast

Rub meat of mackerel through sieve; mix with remaining ingredients to a smooth paste. Serve on rounds of toast.

OYSTERS IN BLANKETS

(Ostriche in Coperta)

1 doz. oysters
6 slices bacon

Wrap half a thin slice of bacon around each oyster; fasten with toothpicks. Arrange on wire rack in baking pan; bake in a hot oven (425°F.) about 20 minutes, or until bacon is crisp and brown. Remove toothpicks and serve. Serves 4.

DRIED ROE

(Caviale)

Since caviar is potent in flavor, it is always served in small quantities. Italian caviar can be purchased in brick form. It stimulates appetites when served in this fashion:

¼ lb. dried sliced caviar
1 small onion, minced
3 tblsp. olive oil
juice of 1 lemon
1 hard-boiled egg, chopped
butter
toast
1 tblsp. parsley, minced

Arrange caviar on serving dish with olive oil, sprinkle with minced onion and juice of lemon. Let marinate for 1 hour. Serve on squares of buttered toast, garnish with chopped egg and parsley.

SARDINE AND HARD-BOILED EGG SPREAD

(Pasta di Uova e Sardine)

1 small can sardines, mashed
1 small onion, chopped fine
toast
2 eggs, hard-boiled, chopped
mayonnaise

Combine sardines, eggs and onion; mix well, add mayonnaise and marinate ½ hour. Serve on rounds of toast.

PIZZA

See BREADS, page 307.

See also PIZZA HAMBURGERS, page 104.

CHAPTER TWO

Wines

It is probable that more wine per square meal is drunk in Italy than anywhere else in the world. In an Italian restaurant a minimum of a quarter liter of wine is assumed to be part of the meal, and the normal menu carries the simple notation "red or white," which means you have your choice of colors. If you want beer, you may occasionally find a restaurant that will provide it on request. Bottled, slightly sparkling water is almost universally available, but ordinary tap water stays in the kitchen and is used for washing dishes.

At the bars and cafés (the Italians have borrowed the English word for "bar" and have used it to indicate a place where you may stand at the counter to be served, or pay a slight extra charge for table service), wine is not normally sold. These places serve beer—and Italians drink a good deal of beer—warm milk, coffee, liqueurs, cognac, soft drinks, and small snacks. Wine, aside from what is served with meals in the restaurants is sold at special shops called vinerie, and may be bought by the glass, bottle, or cask. The wine itself, unless you are dealing with an international restaurant de uxe which has a special cellar, is usually local. Some of the white wines of central and northern Italy have great reputations, foremost among them Lachrymae Christi, Est! Est! Est!, and Orvieto. Unfortunately, the only one of these Italian whites which will bear shipment is Orvieto. All the rest have to be drunk within a few miles of where they are made. That is, they can be shipped and drunk elsewhere, but the result is usually disappointing, the motion incidental to transportation destroying the delicate flavor that makes these great wines.

Italian reds, on the other hand, bear shipment very well indeed and have been shipped all over the world, particularly Chianti, Rufina, and Barolino. No wines are more proper with lamb, beef, stews, or spaghetti; they lend a fillip to the meal that nothing else can equal. It is not, of course, necessary in all cases to follow the Sicilian custom of slipping a piece of ice into the glass of Chianti, a practice at which epicures must shudder. Red wines in general should be served at room temperature, and this is especially true of Chianti.

For veal, fish, and white meats generally, a chilled wine is needed. The rule is simple; red meats, red wine; white meats, white wine. Since Orvieto is not always available, and when available is expensive, it is probably better to use an American white. This is not to say that there is anything wrong with the French white wines of great reputation. They are still the epicure's wines; but they are not the wine for a normal dinner at home. They cost too much.

Among American white wines, the best are those from New York State and Delaware. The others tend to lack that elusive quality called "body"; that is, they are thin. Wines like Lake Delaware, Lake Niagara, Widmerheimer Green, and Taylor Rhinewine would not disgrace the table of a nobleman. It is perfectly possible to drink any one of these whites (or a Chianti where the meat is red) all through the meal, remaining in the best of taste. California produces very superior red wines, especially Claret, but California whites are almost without exception inferior.

Before a meal, Italians almost never take cocktails. In fact, gin, whiskey, and all liquors are customarily treated as liqueurs to be drunk in very small quantities with the after-dinner coffee. The usual aperitif is either a preliminary glass of wine, or, better, a mixture of equal parts of sweet and dry vermouth with a dash of bitters, preferably Fernet-Branca. While on the subject, it may be mentioned that Fernet-Branca, available almost anywhere, can be used for any purpose that bitters serve, and is an excellent change-over from the usual brands.

For an extra-festive occasion, sparkling Asti, the Italian champagne which had its origins in the foothills of the Alps, can be served with the antipasto and fish. It is decidedly sweet and people used to drinking champagne (how many are there?) should probably be warned in advance, but there is nothing whatever wrong with either the taste displayed in serving it or with the taste of the Asti itself.

After dinner, beginning with the dessert, the proper wine is amber-colored Marsala from Sicily, an absolutely perfect wine for cooking purposes also. (It will do anything that sherry does in cooking, and generally do it better.) It belongs in the same general class as port, sherry, and Tokay, being a "fortified" wine, i.e., one reinforced with brandy, and therefore not to be taken as a light table wine with a meal.

There are three distinctively Italian liqueurs: Strega, an orange-colored, heavily herbed liquid of pungent flavor; Maraschino, the very sweet liqueur made from the cherries of the same name; and Fiore d'Alpi, an anise-flavored liqueur with a white branch of crystals running up through the bottle. Fiore d'Alpi, it should be noted, must be taken with caution: it is

150 proof, which means that it has one of the highest alcoholic contents of any liqueur in the world. It is well to remember that, like all liqueurs, it is designed for sipping rather than drinking in any quantity.

SUGGESTED WINES AND LIQUEURS FOR DINNER OR LUNCHEON MENUS

Courses	Wines and Liqueurs	Glasses Used	Temperature of Wine
ANTIPASTO	Dry Sherry Mixed Vermouth with Fernet-Branca Dry Vermouth with peel of lemon Sparkling Asti Champagne	Hollow-stem, wine or cocktail 2½ to 5 oz.	Champagne should be chilled 24 hours
SOUP	American White Wine Dry Red Port	5-oz. stem	Chill 1 hour Room temperature
FISH and SEAFOODS	American White Wine Orvieto White Muscatel	5-oz. stem	Chill 1 hour before serving
SPAGHETTI and RAVIOLI	Chianti Barolino Claret Rufina Sparkling Burgundy	5-oz. stem	Room temperature, except Sparkling Burgundy, which should be chilled 24 hours
MEATS and GAME	Red and White Wines Zinfandel	4-oz round bowl	Room temperature
SALAD	Dry White or Red Wines	5-oz. stem	Chilled
DESSERTS	Oloroso Sherry Marsala Port Madeira Tokay	2½-oz. thin stem	Room temperature
AFTER DINNER COFFEE	Strega Fiore d'Alpi Creme de Menthe Maraschino Chartreuse Benedictine	1-oz. stem	Room temperature

CHAPTER THREE

Soups

Soups and their innumerable "trimmings" (such as ravioli, gnocchi, spaghetti, noodles, etc.) are very popular in Italian cookery. Each Italian province, city, small town, and even village seems to boast of its own particular soup or of some characteristic accompaniment to it.

Perhaps the most typically Italian of all soups is the **minestrone,** so called from the Latin verb **minestrare,** "to put food on the table." And a good minestrone is, indeed, a meal in itself, especially when sprinkled with grated cheese, and served with plenty of toasted Italian bread, and a mixed green salad, and topped off with fruit and a glass of wine or a cup of strong coffee.

Like so many Italian foods, minestrone is not only delicious but economical. It is also easy to prepare. A good minestrone can be concocted from almost any refrigerator leftovers—simply drop them in the pot and give them plenty of time to simmer. Beef tops, celery tops, the outside leaves of head vegetables, and many other such items commonly discarded by Americans do excellently for a minestrone. So do marrow bones. And the good cook will not overlook the combs and feet of chicken as a supreme source of delicious gelatin. Fish them out and throw them away before serving, but not before they have simmered out their gelatin in the soup pot.

SOUP STOCK

(Base per Zuppa)

¼ lb. salt pork, sliced
1 large onion, sliced
4 stalks celery
salt to taste
cold water
1 lb. beef, cut up
1 carrot, diced
butter
pinch of clove
3 quarts hot water

Lay slices of salt pork on bottom of pot, cover with vegetables, dot with butter and top with lean meat, season and cook until onion turns brown; turn meat and cook until done on both sides. Add 1 cup of cold water and, as it evaporates by slow boiling, add more water, then cook again until water has evaporated; add hot water and cook slowly about 5 hours; strain. Keep in refrigerator for soups and gravies.

VARIATIONS FOR SOUPS

(Variazioni per Zuppe)

Use 2 quarts soup stock of any meat flavor:

Stir 3 beaten eggs vigorously into stock until eggs are cooked. Serves 6.

. . . OR . . .

Beat 3 eggs, 4 tblsp. grated Parmesan cheese, and 4 tblsp. breadcrumbs together; add to soup stock and cook 5 minutes, stirring constantly to make it fluffy. Serves 6.

. . . OR . . .

Add any left over, wilted lettuce or romaine to soup stock; sprinkle with grated Parmesan cheese, and serve.

BLACK BEAN SOUP

(Zuppa di Fagioli Neri)

2 cups (1 lb.) black beans
2 stalks celery, diced
1 tblsp. salt
1 ½ tsp. vinegar
slice of lemon
1 ham bone
6 cups water
1 large onion, sliced
½ tsp. pepper
1 tsp. salt
1 egg, hard-boiled, chopped

Soak beans overnight; drain. Combine beans, ham bone, water, celery, onion, 1 tblsp. salt, pepper, and bring to boil; cover and simmer 3 hours or until beans are tender. Remove ham bone and put soup through a coarse sieve; return to saucepan, add vinegar, 1 tsp. salt and heat. Serve piping hot sprinkled with egg and topped with lemon. Serves 8.

KIDNEY BEAN SOUP

(Zuppa di Fagioli)

1 lb. kidney beans, cooked
½ small red cabbage
½ pint tomato sauce
2 or 3 onions
brown bread, sliced
1 or 2 leeks
2 or 3 stalks celery
1 clove garlic
few sprigs of thyme
rosemary

salt and pepper
1 cup stock
4 or 5 tblsp. olive oil

Combine all ingredients, except brown bread, and bring to a boil; simmer gently for 1½ to 2 hours, adding more stock or tomato sauce, as stock boils down. Serve hot with slices of brown bread floating on top. Serves 6.

BEEF BROTH WITH SPINACH

(Brodo di Bue con Spinacci)

2 tblsp. pastina
⅔ cup spinach, strained
2 cups hot beef broth
salt to taste

Cook pastina and broth together until tender; stir in spinach and season. Serve when thoroughly heated. Serves 4.

BEEF VEGETABLE SOUP

(Zuppa di Bue con Legume)

2 cups water
4 tblsp. raw beef, chopped
2 tblsp. cooked peas
2 tblsp. pastina
4 tblsp. cooked carrots, diced
salt to taste

Cook pastina in boiling water until tender; add beef and vegetables and heat through. Season and serve immediately. Serves 4.

CELERY SOUP WITH CHEESE

(Zuppa di Sedani alla Parmigiana)

1½ cups celery, sliced thin
1 tblsp. onion, chopped
2 tblsp. concentrated beef and vegetable extract
1 tblsp. parsley, minced
1 tblsp. olive oil
4 cups water
grated cheese

Cook celery, parsley and onions in olive oil until onions are soft (approximately 10 minutes). Add concentrated extract and heat thoroughly. Serve hot, sprinkled with cheese on each serving. Serve with toasted garlic bread (see page 311).

CELERY ALMOND SOUP

(Zuppa di Sedani e Mandorle)

2 qts. chicken broth
1 cup celery, diced
¾ cup almonds, ground
¼ cup flour

½ cup onion, chopped
1 tblsp. parsley, chopped
¼ cup butter

Cook celery and onion in chicken broth 30 minutes; strain. Melt butter, mix in flour gradually, add broth and cook until thickened, stirring constantly; add almonds. Serve sprinkled with parsley. Serves 6.

CHICK PEA SOUP

(Zuppa di Ceci)

2 cups chick peas
4 tblsp. olive oil
2 onions, chopped
1 clove garlic, chopped
1 tsp. paprika
salt and pepper
1 green pepper, chopped
4 cups meat stock
4 slices salami, cut up

Soak peas overnight; do not drain. Sauté onions, garlic and green pepper in hot olive oil 5 minutes; add peas and meat stock; simmer 1½ hours. Add salami to soup with seasoning. If a thicker soup is desired, remove ½ cup of beans, mash and return to mixture. Serves 6.

CHICKEN SOUP

(Zuppa di Pollo)

1 4-lb. chicken
½ cup rice
1 cup okra
½ cup tomatoes, strained
1 onion, chopped
2 stalks celery, cut into ½-inch lengths

Cook chicken until nearly tender; remove from liquid and cut into small pieces. Return chicken with all ingredients to stock; boil gently for 30 minutes. Serves 8.

CHICKEN, EGG DROP SOUP

(Zuppa di Pollo all'Uova)

4 tblsp. pastina
½ cup chicken, minced
2 eggs, beaten
3 cups hot chicken broth
⅔ cup watercress, chopped
salt to taste

Cook pastina in broth until tender; add chicken and bring to a boil. Stir in eggs, stirring vigorously about 2 minutes or until egg separates into shreds; add watercress. Season and serve immediately. Serves 6.

NOTE: The young leaves of spinach may be used in place of watercress.

CHICKEN IN A HOOD

(Cappelleti)

breast of capon or chicken, cooked
1 cup sour cream
salt and pepper
pinch of mixed spices
3 qts. soup stock
½ cup Parmesan cheese, grated
4 whole eggs
1 egg yolk
2½ cups flour

Chop breast of chicken fine, and mix with cheese, sour cream, 1 whole egg and 1 egg yolk, seasoning; mix well. Mix flour, 3 eggs and salt to a stiff dough, using a little water if necessary. Roll dough paper-thin, and cut into 2-inch rounds. Place a little of the chicken mixture on each round, dampen edges slightly and fold over; press edges together lightly, dampen folded ends, turn back and press. The chicken is now wrapped in its hood. Add the hoods to boiling soup stock and cook about 15 minutes. Serves 6 to 8.

COOKED WATER

(Acquacotta)

3 or 4 large onions
2 or 3 stalks celery
1 lb. tomatoes
3 or 4 sweet peppers
olive oil
slices of bread
eggs, beaten
water
salt and pepper

Chop or slice vegetables, season and cook in hot olive oil until slightly browned; add hot water gradually, sufficient to give the consistency of a thick soup. Serve over slices of bread brushed with egg. Serves 6.

EGG NOODLE SOUP

(Zuppa di Uova)

1 qt. beef stock, seasoned
¼ cup Parmesan cheese, grated
3-oz. pkg. egg noodles

Heat beef stock, add noodles and cook until tender. Serve sprinkled with cheese. Serves 4.

ESCAROLE SOUP

(Zuppa di Lattuga Arriciata)

2 soup bones (marrow)
1 tsp. salt
2 tblsp. tomato paste
1½ quarts water
¾ lb. chopped soup meat or chuck beef
1 clove minced garlic
few sprigs parsley
1 egg
salt and pepper
3 tblsp. Parmesan cheese, grated
1½ lbs. chopped escarole
1 chopped onion
1 cup diced celery
1 chopped carrot
1 diced potato
1 tblsp. minced parsley

Simmer bones, salt, tomato paste and water ½ hour. Mix together chopped meat, garlic, parsley, egg, seasonings and cheese. Form into small meat balls, add to soup. Simmer 10 minutes longer, add escarole and remaining vegetables and simmer 30 minutes longer. Serve with grated Parmesan cheese and garnish with sprigs of parsley. Serves 6.

FROG SOUP

(Zuppa di Ranocchi)

1 doz. frogs
3 tblsp. olive oil
1 clove garlic, minced
1 small onion, minced
1 small carrot, minced
1 sprig parsley
fingers of toast
1 sprig basil
1 stalk celery
1 tomato, chopped
2 mushrooms, chopped
2 tblsp. breadcrumbs, fine
salt and pepper
3 pts. cold water

Cut up edible parts of frogs, including livers, but not the hind legs, which are the tenderest part. Sauté garlic, onion, carrots and herbs in hot olive oil until slightly colored; add tomato, mushrooms and cut-up portions of frogs, together with cold water; bring slowly to boil, simmer until meat is falling from bones; remove bones, season with salt and pepper, add hind legs and simmer until tender. Sprinkle with breadcrumbs and serve with fingers of toast. Serves 6.

GARLIC SOUP

(Zuppa all'Aglio)

4 cloves garlic, sliced
2 tblsp. butter or olive oil
1 qt. chicken broth
4 squares bread, toasted
4 tblsp. cheese grated
2 tblsp. parsley, minced

Sauté garlic in butter until soft but not brown; add chicken broth and simmer 20 minutes. To serve, place a square of toast in each soup bowl, pour in the soup and sprinkle with cheese and parsley. Serves 4.

THICK GREEN SOUP

(Zuppa Gruesa di Verdura)

- 1 cup spinach
- 1 cup green peas
- 1 cup shredded lettuce
- 2 lbs. leeks, cut in large pieces
- ½ cup olive oil
- 1 quart water
- 1 tblsp. mint leaves
- 1 tblsp. celery
- juice of 1 lemon
- salt and pepper

Heat olive oil in large saucepan and add the leeks, salt, pepper and lemon juice. Simmer slowly for 20 minutes. Add spinach, peas and lettuce. Stir about 2 minutes, add water and cook 10 minutes. Press this entire mixture through a sieve. If it is too thick, add a little milk before serving. Serves 6.

LENTIL SOUP

(Zuppa di Lenticchie)

- 2 cups cold water
- 1 qt. ham stock
- ¼ cup celery, diced
- 1 cup Tubettini,* cooked
- ½ lb. lentils
- 2 tblsp. olive oil
- ¼ cup chopped onions
- salt and pepper to taste

Soak lentils overnight. Combine lentils and ham stock; simmer 1 hour and purée lentils. Sauté celery and onion in hot olive oil; add to lentils with Tubettini. Serve hot. Serves 4 to 6.

* See table of spaghetti and macaroni, pages 51-56.

MINESTRONE

No. I

- ½ lb. salt pork
- 2 qts. water
- 2 tblsp. parsley, chopped
- 2 cloves garlic, minced (optional)
- 1 tblsp. butter
- 2 or 3 bouillon cubes or 1 tblsp. meat extract
- ½ small head cabbage
- 2 or 3 carrots, cut up
- 1 cup canned lima beans
- 1 cup peas
- 1 cup rice
- Parmesan cheese, grated

Cut salt pork into 1-inch strips, ¼-inch thick, add water and bring to a boil; add parsley and garlic. Trim out core of cabbage and add leaves, carrots, lima beans, peas and butter to soup; cook 2 hours and add well washed rice. When rice is cooked, add dissolved bouillon cubes or meat extract for added strength; mix well. Serve sprinkled with cheese. Serves 6.

No. II

¼ lb. bacon, chopped
¼ lb. ham, chopped
(ham bone may be used)
1½ quarts meat broth
1 large onion, chopped
1 large tomato, chopped
½ cup navy beans
(soaked overnight)
Parmesan cheese, grated
1 stalk celery, sliced
¾ cup rice
¼ head cabbage, chopped
1 cup green vegetables, mixed
(peas, lima beans, green beans, asparagus tips, etc.)
salt and pepper

Fry bacon, ham, and onion slowly until brown; add meat broth, tomato, celery, beans, rice, and seasoning; simmer until beans are tender, skimming occasionally. Add cabbage and vegetables, simmer until cooked and minestrone is thick. Serve sprinkled with cheese. Serves 6.

NOTE: The addition of skinned and cut-up Italian sausages adds a fine zest.

No. III

1 lb. shin beef with bone
3½ qts. water
2 tblsp. salt
½ tsp. pepper
1 cup kidney beans
1 tblsp. olive oil
2 cloves garlic
½ cup onion, chopped
½ cup parsley, chopped
1 cup fresh green beans, cut up
¾ cup celery, diced
1 cup peas
2 cups cabbage, chopped
1 cup carrots, diced
1 can tomato sauce
½ cup spaghetti, broken into small pieces
Parmesan cheese, grated

Combine beef with water, salt, and beans; cover and bring to boil; skim, cover, and simmer 4 hours. Brown garlic in hot olive oil, remove garlic, and sauté onion and parsley until onions are tender. Remove meat from stock, add onion, parsley, and remaining ingredients, except spaghetti and cheese; cover, and simmer 30 minutes; add spaghetti and cook 10 minutes. Serve sprinkled with cheese. Serves 10.

No. IV

½ cup dried lima beans
½ cup kidney beans
1 clove garlic, minced
½ cup salt pork, diced
½ cup leeks, minced
¼ cup parsley, minced
½ cup carrots, diced
1 cup tomatoes, peeled
Parmesan cheese, grated
1 tsp. basil, minced
2 cups cabbage, shredded
1 cup turnip, diced
1 cup zucchini, diced
½ cup short spaghetti
½ cup celery, diced
2 potatoes, diced
2½ qts. meat stock
salt and pepper

Soak beans several hours; drain, and add to boiling meat stock. Fry salt pork with minced garlic until well browned; add onion, parsley, carrots, and potatoes, cook 10 minutes and add to stock with tomatoes and herbs; cook 30 minutes, and add cabbage with other ingredients, except cheese; cook 30 minutes. Serve in soup plates generously sprinkled with cheese. Serve with chunks of Italian bread. Serves 8.

NOTE: The above makes about 3½ quarts. If not all used at first meal, it tastes even better reheated. Canned lima beans may be used in place of the dried, as second-best but adequate.

No. V

3 pts. meat stock
¼ lb. salt pork, cut in 1-inch lengths
½ lb. fresh kidney beans
½ lb. peas
1 or 2 stalks celery, diced
1 small cabbage, chopped
½ lb. spinach, chopped
3 or 4 carrots, diced
1 small onion, chopped
pinch of sage
½ cup rice
parsley, minced
1 clove garlic, minced
3 or 4 tblsp. Parmesan cheese, grated
salt and pepper
½ lb. tomatoes, chopped

Bring meat stock to a boil and add all ingredients, except cheese, stir well; simmer until vegetables are tender and stock nearly absorbed. Stir in cheese, and serve soup very thick, either hot or cold. Serves 6.

ONION SOUP

(Zuppa di Cipolla)

No. I

1 cup red onions, sliced
1 clove garlic, chopped
1 tsp. thyme
1 tsp. celery salt

1 tblsp. olive oil
6 bouillon cubes
6 cups water
6 slices bread, toasted
4 eggs
salt and pepper

Sauté onions and garlic in hot olive oil until golden brown; add water, bouillon cubes, and seasonings; bring to boil and simmer 5 minutes. Break eggs into simmering soup, cover; cook until eggs are set. Cut bread into quarters and serve floating on soup. Each portion of soup should contain one egg. Serves 4.

No. II

6 large red onions, sliced thin
6 tblsp. olive oil
¼ tsp. white pepper
½ tsp. salt
Parmesan cheese, grated
1 tblsp. flour
6 cups beef stock
6 slices Italian bread cut ½-inch thick

Sauté onions in hot olive oil to a golden brown; season, stir in flour, and blend; add beef stock, cover, and simmer 20 minutes. Toast bread a light brown and sprinkle with cheese. Ladle soup into bowls, place toast on top and serve at once. Serves 6.

OYSTER SOUP

(Zuppa d'Ostriche)

1 doz. raw oysters
2 bouillon cubes
2 cups hot water
¾ cup soft breadcrumbs
1 onion, sliced
1 sprig parsley
1 bay leaf
1 tblsp. olive oil
1 tblsp. flour
2 cups milk, scalded
2 stalks celery
salt and pepper

Clean and pick over oysters, reserving liquid; cut firm part of oyster from soft part and chop separately. Dissolve bouillon cubes in hot water, add breadcrumbs, onion, celery, parsley, bay leaf, and firm part of oysters; simmer 3 minutes, and rub mixture through sieve. Stir flour into hot olive oil, and with oyster liquid add to sieved mixture; bring to a boil, add milk, chopped soft part of oysters, and seasoning. Serve hot with salted crackers. Serves 6.

SOUP OF PARADISE

(Zuppa Paradiso)

4 eggs, separated
4 tblsp. breadcrumbs
2 qts. soup stock
4 tblsp. Parmesan cheese, grated
nutmeg

Beat whites of eggs stiff, add yolks, and beat until well blended; add cheese, breadcrumbs, and nutmeg to taste, and mix. Bring soup stock to boil and slowly add egg mixture a spoonful at a time; boil 5 to 8 minutes. Serves 6.

PARMESAN SOUP

(Zuppa alla Parmigiana)

2 lb. beef shank, cut into small pieces
1½ qts. water
3 tblsp. carrots, diced
3 tblsp. celery, diced
3 tblsp. onion, diced
3 tblsp. parsley, chopped
3 tblsp. olive oil
1 tsp. salt
2 whole cloves
1 bay leaf
½ tsp. oregano
½ tsp. marjoram
¼ cup Parmesan cheese, grated

Brown meat well, add water and bring to boil; cover, and simmer about 3 hours, skimming from time to time. Add vegetables and simmer 1 hour. Serve hot with cheese. Serves 6.

PASTINA CREAM SOUP

(Zuppa di Crema con Pastina)

2 cups milk
2 tblsp. pastina
2 tsp. olive oil
⅔ cup vegetable pulp
2 tsp. flour
salt to taste

Heat milk in double boiler, stir in pastina and cook 15 minutes, stirring frequently for first 5 minutes. Blend olive oil and flour, add to milk and stir until soup thickens; add vegetable pulp and seasoning. Serves 4.

SOUP OF POTATO BALLS

(Zuppa con Polpettini di Patate)

1 lb. potatoes
1½ oz. Parmesan cheese, grated
nutmeg
1½ oz. butter
2 qts. soup stock, boiling
3 egg yolks

Boil and peel potatoes, strain through fine sieve; add egg yolks, cheese, butter and nutmeg, and mix well. Place mixture on floured board, roll into long strips, and slice the size of peanuts; shape into balls and fry in hot olive oil. Place fried balls in soup bowls and cover with boiling soup. Serves 6 or 8.

PUMPKIN SOUP

(Zuppa di Zucca)

1 cup water
3 cups pumpkin, diced
1 tblsp. sugar
croutons (crostini)
2 tblsp. butter
3 cups milk
salt

Mix water, pumpkin, sugar and butter; cook slowly until very tender, adding more water if necessary. Remove from fire and press through a sieve. Bring milk to boiling point, add pumpkin and very little salt; reheat. Serve with croutons.

NOTE: This soup is used on fast days in Italy.

SOUP WITH RICE BALLS

(Zuppa con Polpettini di Riso)

3 oz. rice
1 oz. Parmesan cheese, grated
nutmeg
salt to taste
1 oz. butter
1 egg yolk
2 qts. soup stock
1 cup milk

Boil rice in milk until thickened, add butter and salt; when boiled, remove from fire and slowly mix in egg yolk, cheese, and nutmeg. Bring soup stock to a boil, and drop a spoonful of rice at a time into stock; cook 7 to 8 minutes. Serves 6.

SOUP WITH RICE AND PEAS

(Zuppa di Riso e Piselli)

1 cup rice
1 medium onion, chopped
1 cup peas
¼ lb. butter
½ lb. ham, chopped
1 cup celery, chopped
1 quart soup stock
salt and pepper to taste

Cook rice in butter to a golden color, add onion, celery and ham; stir in hot soup stock gradually, add peas, stir and simmer about 30 minutes or longer. The soup, when ready to eat, should have the consistency of porridge.

SOUP ROMAINE

(Zuppa alla Romana)

1 head Romaine lettuce
garlic oil
croutons
1½ cups salted water
salt and pepper to taste
Parmesan cheese, grated

Wash, cut up, and boil Romaine in salted water until tender; remove from fire, season with garlic oil, salt and pepper. Toss in a few croutons, sprinkle with cheese and serve. Serves 2.

SEMOLINA GARNISH FOR SOUP

(Minestra di Semolina per Zuppa)

1 cup milk
⅓ cup Parmesan cheese, grated
butter
2 eggs
pinch of salt
nutmeg, grated
2 qts. soup stock
semolina

Bring milk to a boil, and add as much semolina as it will absorb; stir, and simmer about 20 minutes, or until mixture is very thick. Remove from fire; add cheese, a little butter, salt, nutmeg, and eggs, working mixture to the consistency of a liquid cream. Pour into a plain, well-buttered mould, set in a pan of hot water, and bake in a slow oven (275°F.) until mixture is easily detached from mould. Unmold and cut into small, diced pieces or rounds; cook in boiling stock about 5 minutes. Serves 6.

SPINACH SOUP

(Zuppa di Spinacci)

No. I

2 lbs. spinach
½ cup stock
4 tblsp. butter
3 tblsp. cheese, grated
salt and pepper
dash of nutmeg
1 or 2 eggs
croutons

Boil spinach in salted water until tender; drain thoroughly. Combine with butter and stock in an earthenware casserole, stir well, and add eggs, seasoning, and cheese; simmer gently until soup thickens. Serve hot with croutons. Serves 4.

No. II

2 lbs. spinach
½ cup olive oil
2 egg yolks, beaten
1 qt. chicken broth
salt and pepper
2 tblsp. grated cheese

Cook spinach in olive oil, then put through sieve. Mix in the egg yolks, salt, pepper and cheese. Add this to 1 quart of chicken broth. In this soup the eggs are allowed to curdle, causing the soup to thicken.

SPINACH AND EGG SOUP or TWO-COLOR SOUP

(Minestra di Due Colori)

1 lb. spinach, boiled
⅓ cup flour
⅔ cup Parmesan cheese, grated
3 eggs
dash of nutmeg
1 pint milk, hot
4 tblsp. butter
pinch of salt
1 qt. soup stock

Blend flour with melted butter, stir in hot milk, salt, and nutmeg; work with a wooden spoon into a smooth paste over a low fire. Remove from fire and cool; stir in eggs and cheese. Drain spinach and rub through a sieve; combine with half the paste. Drop small lumps of the spinach paste and egg paste, alternately, into the boiling soup stock. Serves 4.

SPLIT PEA SOUP

(Zuppa di Piselli)

2 qts. water
2 cups green split peas
2 stalks celery, chopped
1 carrot, chopped
1 onion, chopped
½ tsp. oregano
½ tsp. basil
½ tsp. marjoram
1 bay leaf
salt and pepper

Combine ingredients, cover and cook 20 minutes; reduce heat and simmer 30 minutes. Force mixture through a sieve, reheat; and serve with chunks of Italian garlic bread and a tomato salad. Serves 6.

VERMICELLI IN SOUP

(Tagliatelli in Brodo)

4 cups flour
4 whole eggs
2 qts. soup stock
1 or 2 egg yolks
pinch of salt

Work eggs, flour and salt into a firm dough; roll out very thin, and let stand about 1 hour to dry thoroughly. Cut into strips just under ½-inch wide; add to soup stock and cook a few minutes. Serve hot. Serves 6.

VERMICELLI SOUP

(Minestrone con Vermicelli)

3 pints water
1 lb. green string beans
4 medium-size potatoes
3 tomatoes, peeled and chopped
salt and pepper
¼ lb. vermicelli
3 cloves garlic, mashed
2 tblsp. sweet basil
1 peeled tomato
grated cheese

Let water come to a boil, add beans cut into 1-inch pieces, the potatoes cubed, and tomatoes; season and let boil fairly quick. When vegetables are almost cooked, add vermicelli and finish cooking gently. Combine the garlic, basil and tomato and make a smooth paste. Add about 3 tablespoons of the soup liquid, then mix with rest of soup. Serve with grated cheese. Serves 4.

TURKEY SOUP

(Zuppa di Tacchino)

bones from a 12 to 14 lb. turkey
1 cup diced celery
½ lb. shell macaroni
salt and pepper to taste
1 clove garlic
½ cup diced carrots
¼ cup chopped parsley
Parmesan cheese, grated

Crack turkey bones, add water and vegetables, cover and simmer about 2 hours. Strain—you should have 2 quarts of clear soup. Let clear soup come to a boil, add macaroni shells, cook until done (about 8 minutes). Serve in bowls sprinkled with cheese. Serves 6.

WINE SOUP WITH CHERRIES

(Zuppa di Ciliege al Vino)

1 qt. cherries
1 qt. water
¼ cup sugar
1 cup red wine
1 cup boiling water
4 buds cassia (cinnamon sticks)
½ lemon, sliced fine
2 tblsp. sago
2 egg yolks, beaten

Cook sago in boiling water until tender, adding more hot water as needed. Combine remaining ingredients, except egg yolks, and cook about 15 minutes; add cooked sago and bring to boil. Pour soup gradually over beaten egg yolks. Serve cold. Serves 6.

CHAPTER FOUR

Salads

In Italy, the salad is not thought of as a side-dish, but as a separate course. It is invariably served directly after the main course.

Since olive oil is the staple of most Italian cookery, and since the main course is often heavy, salads are generally kept simple and pungent. Wine vinegar, highly acid, serves as a refreshing contrast to the generally oil-based main course. Two parts of olive oil to one of sharp wine vinegar is the normal basic dressing. Add salt and pepper to taste. And do not omit a liberal sprinkle of dried oregano. Fresh herbs such as oregano, basil, mint, etc. are also highly esteemed in Italian salads.

Romaine lettuce or escarole (more flavorful than iceberg) are generally preferred. Thick slices of tomato, green peppers, and onion are salad staples, but the Italian is ever fond of using wild greens from the fields. Dandelions and chicory are especially delicious. Make sure that salad dandelions are young and tender. Whatever the ingredients, the rule for the good Italian salad is simple—keep it sharp and keep it crisp.

ANCHOVY TOMATO SALAD

(Insalata d'Acciughe e Pomidoro)

2 large tomatoes, peeled
lettuce
½ green pepper
1 tblsp. lemon juice
salt, pepper and oregano
8 anchovies, rolled
4 tblsp. cooked tomatoes, cold
8 stuffed olives
½ tblsp. olive oil

Marinate cooked tomatoes in lemon juice, olive oil and seasonings. Cut peeled tomatoes in half, place each half on a crisp lettuce leaf with 2 anchovies for each serving; cover with a tablespoonful of marinated tomatoes, and garnish with a slice of green pepper, topped with an olive. Serves 4.

ANCHOVIES AND CAPERS

(Capperi in Galera)

This more modest salad is extremely tasty. It consists of a biscuit moistened with a little water to make it soft, dressed with chopped anchovies, olives, capers, and a simple dressing of oil.

ARTICHOKE SALAD

(Insalata di Carciofi)

No. I

2 artichokes, boiled
½ tsp. salt
½ tsp. paprika
2 tblsp. wine vinegar
1 tblsp. onion, grated
1 tsp. sugar
½ tsp. mustard
4 tblsp. olive oil

Combine sugar, salt, paprika, mustard, vinegar, and olive oil; mix thoroughly, then blend in onion. Quarter artichokes and place on nest of endive; cover with dressing and garnish with pimento. Serves 4.

No. II

1 tblsp. olive oil
6 artichokes
salt and pepper
juice of 1 lemon
1 tsp. oregano

Boil artichokes 40 minutes or until leaves pull out easily; chill. Make a dressing of olive oil, lemon juice, oregano, salt and pepper. Cut the chilled artichokes in half, remove choke from artichoke and add the dressing. Serves 6.

NOTE: The artichokes may be served whole with mayonnaise, if desired.

CHICKEN SALAD

(Insalata di Pollo)

2 cups cooked chicken, cubed
2 tblsp. chopped green olives
¾ cup chopped celery
½ cup toasted almonds
2 tblsp. chopped ripe olives
2 tblsp. chopped pickles
2 hard-boiled eggs
¾ cup mayonnaise

Toss ingredients lightly until well dressed with mayonnaise. Serve on lettuce leaf. Serves 4.

CHICORY SALAD

(Insalata di Cicoria)

This salad is made with fresh white uncooked chicory, with a dressing consisting of oil, a little crushed garlic, a few sprigs of mint and a little salt.

ENDIVE SALAD

(Insalata di Endivia)

1 head endive
1 pt. potatoes, boiled and sliced
juice of 2 lemons
4 eggs, hard-boiled
¼ cup olive oil
salt, pepper, oregano

Wash endive thoroughly, wipe dry and remove outer green leaves. Rub salad bowl with garlic, arrange light, feathery leaves of endive with potatoes. Cut eggs lengthwise and place around potatoes. Mix olive oil, lemon juice and seasonings; pour over salad. Serves 6.

See also Spinach and Endive Salad, page 45.

LIMA BEAN SALAD

(Insalata di Fave)

6 cups dried lima beans, cooked
1 clove garlic
½ tsp. salt
¼ tsp. pepper
⅔ cup bean liquid
2 tblsp. sugar
¼ cup red onions, minced
¼ cup parsley, chopped
⅓ cup wine vinegar

Drain hot beans and save liquid. Crush garlic with salt, add remaining ingredients, mix with the liquid, add to beans, toss and let stand in refrigerator several hours. Serves 8.

MIXED SALAD

(Insalata Mista)

No. I

This is another of those delightful mixed salads made with wild herbs, celery, tomatoes, fennel roots, and dandelion leaves, with a dressing of oil, crushed garlic and sprigs of sweet basil. Season to your taste.

No. II

4 firm tomatoes, sliced
1 pimiento, sliced
2 pickles, sliced
¼ cup celery, chopped
¼ cup chives or shallots, chopped
2 or 3 sprigs of fresh, sweet basil

DRESSING:

8 thin slices caviar
3 tblsp. olive oil
juice of 1 lemon
1 tblsp. parsley, chopped

Toss lightly and serve on lettuce leaves. Serves 6.

No. III

1 cup diced beets
1 cup cooked clusters of cauliflower
1 cup green beans, cooked whole
¼ cup carrot sticks, cooked
2 boiled potatoes, sliced
3 tblsp. olive oil
2 tblsp. vinegar
¼ tsp. oregano

DRESSING:

1 tblsp. capers
3 anchovies, crushed
1 tblsp. parsley, chopped
3 tblsp. olive oil
juice of 1 lemon
salt and pepper to taste

On a foundation of semolina or unsweetened biscuits well rubbed with garlic, erect an imposing structure of cooked vegetables and other ingredients in the shape of a pyramid. Use diced beets, clusters of cooked cauliflower, young string beans, cooked carrot sticks, potatoes; add dressing listed above. Garnish the pyramid of vegetables here and there with bits of cooked fish, and lobster coated with the above dressing. Finally, the pyramid is dotted with a few small skewers threaded with dainty pieces of crayfish, olives, anchovies and hard-boiled eggs. When well arranged in the proper color scheme, this makes a picturesque ensemble.

MOM'S SALAD

(Insalata alla Mama)

No. I

1 tblsp. olive oil
1 tblsp. wine vinegar
salt and pepper
2 anchovies
1 slice bread
6 strips of salami
6 strips of cheese
oregano
shredded lettuce
2 Italian sausages

Toss all ingredients together, except sausages; shape on a slice of bread to resemble a head of lettuce, and cover with a lemon or vinegar dressing. Serve with sausages browned in wine. Serves 1.

No. II

4 red peppers, chopped fine
4 green peppers, chopped fine
1 sweet onion, chopped fine
½ cup parsley, minced
6 tomatoes, quartered
½ cup olive oil
5 tblsp. wine vinegar
½ tsp. powdered sugar
1 tsp. salt
lettuce

Mix peppers, onion, parsley with olive oil, vinegar, sugar and salt; let stand 1 hour. Shake well before using. Serve on lettuce leaves with tomatoes. Serves 6.

OLIVE SALAD

(Insalata alla Marchesa)

green and ripe olives
1 cup carrots, cooked and sliced
1 bunch radishes, sliced thin
1 bunch scallions, sliced
1 cup celery, diced
chicory for garnish
1 cucumber, peeled and sliced
½ cup mayonnaise
¼ cup cream
salt and pepper

Mix all ingredients together, except chicory and olives; chill. Serve on cold plates, garnished with chicory and olives. Serves 4.

NOTE: The above salad serves as an excellent first course or appetizer.

ORANGE AND PINEAPPLE SALAD

(Insalata di Aranci ed Ananassi)

6 oranges, cut up in chunks
10 marshmallows, cubed
1 large can pineapple, cubed
1 pt. sour cream

Combine ingredients and let stand for several hours in refrigerator. Serve sprinkled with freshly grated coconut. Serves 4.

RED BEAN SALAD

(Insalata di Fagioli Rossi)

2½ cups red kidney beans
½ lb. Italian sausage, cut up
¼ cup parsley, chopped
lettuce
tomato, sliced
1 cup celery, diced
½ cup sweet pickles, coarsely chopped
¼ cup onion, chopped
hard-boiled egg, sliced

Rinse kidney beans in cold water; mix with celery, sausage, pickle, parsley and onion.

DRESSING:

1 tblsp. sugar
¼ cup olive oil
1 clove garlic
¼ cup wine vinegar
1 pinch of pepper
1 pinch of oregano

Blend above ingredients well; discard garlic, and pour dressing over beans; chill 1 hour. Serve heaped on lettuce leaf, topped with tomato and egg. Serves 4.

ROMAINE SALAD

(Insalata di Lettuga Romana)

No. I

3 heads Romaine, chilled and crisp (torn to bite size)
6 tblsp. garlic oil
1 tblsp. hot sauce
6 heaping tblsp. Romanello cheese (freshly grated)
salt to taste
1 cup croutons
1 tsp. black pepper
1 egg
juice of 3 lemons

Mix all ingredients, except egg and lemon juice, in a large wooden bowl; break the egg over salad, then add juice of lemons. Toss lightly from the bottom, and serve immediately. Serves 6.

No. II

1 head of lettuce
1 clove garlic
3 tblsp. cheese, grated
8 anchovy fillets
½ cup croutons
1 tomato

LEMON AND OIL DRESSING:

3 tblsp. olive oil
juice of 2 lemons
salt and pepper to taste

Tear crisp head of romaine lettuce; place in a wooden bowl that has been rubbed with garlic; add grated cheese, rolled anchovies with capers, croutons, wedges of tomato and toss together lightly. Cover with a lemon and olive oil dressing. Serve with garlic bread. This makes a complete lunch and all will like it. Just be sure to make enough. Serves 6.

SALMON SALAD

(Insalata di Salmone)

2 cups salmon, canned
½ cup celery, chopped fine
2 tblsp. capers
2 tblsp. onion, grated
lettuce
2 cups potato chips, crushed
¾ cup mayonnaise, thinned with
2 tblsp. lemon juice
tomatoes, quartered

Have all ingredients chilled; mix together lightly. Serve heaped on lettuce and garnished with tomatoes. Serves 6.

SPINACH SALAD

(Insalata di Spinacci)

4 tblsp. garlic oil
½ lb. strips of Italian ham
salt and pepper
2 tblsp. wine vinegar
tender leaves of spinach, approximately 2 lbs.

Wash spinach carefully and shake off water. Mix olive oil, vinegar, salt and pepper; pour over spinach and add ham strips. Serves 6.

SPINACH AND ENDIVE SALAD

(Insalata di Spinacci ed Endivia)

1 bunch endive, quartered
¼ cup olive oil
salt and pepper
½ lb. spinach
juice of 1 lemon
oregano

Crisp endive and spinach in ice water; drain and dry well. Blend olive oil, lemon juice, salt, pepper, and oregano; pour over greens and toss lightly to coat each leaf. Serves 6.

STRING BEAN SALAD

(Insalata di Fagiolini)

1 lb. green beans, cut lengthwise
2 tblsp. wine vinegar
pinch of pepper
lettuce
Parmesan cheese, grated
4 tblsp. olive oil
½ tsp. salt
1 onion, minced
1 egg, hard-boiled and chopped

Cook string beans in boiling, salted water 15 minutes; drain and cool. Combine olive oil, vinegar, onion, salt and pepper;

mix with beans lightly, cover and chill. To serve, heap on lettuce leaf and sprinkle with egg and cheese. Serves 4.

TOMATO SALAD

(Insalata di Pomidoro)

6 large tomatoes, cut up
¼ cup olive oil
salt and pepper
1 large onion, sliced
3 tblsp. wine vinegar
sprinkle of oregano

Combine tomatoes and onion with olive oil, vinegar and seasoning in a wooden salad bowl. Sprinkle with oregano and serve with chunks of hot bread.

NOTE: A bunch of scallions may be used in place of onion, and 2 lemons, peeled and diced, may be used in place of wine vinegar. If lemon is used, add to mixture last.

TOSSED GARDEN SALAD

(Insalata Giardinetto)

1 head lettuce, pulled apart
2 tomatoes, cut up
1 green pepper, sliced
½ bunch celery, cut up
1 head endive, pulled apart
4 green onions, sliced
6 radishes, cut up
olive oil dressing

Have lettuce and endive crisp; add tomatoes, onions, pepper, celery and radishes and toss together. Cover with Olive Oil Dressing (see page 227), toss lightly to coat each leaf well. Serves 6.

TOSSED GREEN SALAD

(Insalata Verde)

Use a good sized bowl, preferably a wooden one, big enough to toss the salad without mishap. Rub the inside of the bowl thoroughly with a cut clove of garlic. Tear, rather than cut, the well washed and drained greens into not too small pieces, dropping them into the bowl. Over the greens sprinkle olive oil, adding enough so that leaves will be well coated when they are tossed. Sprinkle lightly with salt, pepper and handful of chives. Sprinkle generously with oregano, and add enough wine vinegar just before ready to serve, and toss. Serve.

NOTE: Basil can be substituted for oregano, or you can use a little of both. If you have never used herbs in your salads, you have been missing something. You, too, can grow some in a window box. The use of minced parsley, chives, tarragon, and basil leaves, with a few tender tip leaves of marjoram chopped, and oregano, will make all the difference in the world in your salad. Just a touch is all that is needed and watch the results.

CHAPTER FIVE

Spaghetti

THE PHILOSOPHY OF SPAGHETTI

When we speak of "spaghetti" in English, we generally are using a collective term for all the varieties that the Italian calls **pasta asciuta** (that is "dry **pasta**," so called to distinguish it from **pasta in brodo** which is "**pasta** in broth." **Pasta asciuta** is not really dry; it is, however, considerably drier than **pasta in brodo**). A glance at the table labeled—in deference to the English usage—SPAGHETTIS AND MACARONIS will show most of the common forms, but there are many more variants than can be shown here.

The origins of pasta are not precisely known. Many legends ascribe to it a Chinese origin, and some claim that Marco Polo brought it back from his Eastern journey. All guesses are conjecture, however. The fundamental fact is that, whatever its origin, pasta has become peculiarly Italian because it fits so naturally into the kind of productivity and economy that has so long existed in Italy. Obviously, however, the various pasta dishes fit not only the Italian agriculture and pocketbook, but the taste as well. As an evidence that the Italian is not alone in this, it may be mentioned that over a billion pounds are consumed annually in the United States.

The best grades of pasta are made of selected durum wheat semolina (the Italian word is **semolino**), which is the coarsely ground and carefully purified middlings of durum wheat. It consists of grits of different sizes, similar to granulated sugar. The term **pasta** also includes noodles, which are similar in every respect except that noodles contain eggs. It further includes **gnocchi** and **polenta** which are made of corn meal.

Each part of Italy tends to its favorite type. **Gnocchi** are especially popular in Northern Italy. The Neapolitans tend to prefer the long strings and the Genoese incline to the short hollow lengths. The Bolognese seem to like the fancy stamped cuts. And so it goes.

WHY SO MANY SHAPES AND FORMS?

These many variations on the basic article are not simply a form of Italian caprice. Pasta is essentially a shape of dough which is meant to be cooked and served with a sauce. **To be served with a sauce** is the important thing to understand here. The great variety of forms arises from the fact that each different form has its own characteristic way of absorbing the sauce. Thus **spaghetti** and **spaghettini** have no bore and are best with a thick sauce since they absorb only from the outside. At the other end of the scale are **zitoni**, great macaroni lengths with a bore of about a quarter to three-eighths of an inch into which a thin sauce flows easily—and deliciously. Even larger are **rigatoni** which come in short arched lengths (see table) and which have a fluted outside as well, thereby offering more absorbent surface to the sauce. In between lie the various "seashells" (**assabesi, tufoli,** and **conchiglie**). These not only absorb sauce from both inside and out, but offer an inner pocket, the inside of the "seashell." You have only to bite into one and to taste the richness of that inner pocket of sauce to realize at once that these differences in shape are much more than academic. Many of these "seashells" and "large bore" shapes, moreover, are delicious when stuffed and baked. The various flat cuts (such as **lasagne**) are specially favored for casseroles.

COOKING PROCEDURES

Nothing is simpler than cooking the pasta, but a few fundamental principles must be clearly grasped.

1. **Do not overcook.** The idea is to cook the pasta till it is tender but still chewy. **Al dente** is the Italian term, "to the tooth's taste"—it must not dissolve in the mouth but must be bitable.

2. **Cooking time.** Cooking time will vary according to the thickness of the particular shape, to the kind of flour the manufacturer has used, and to the taste of the individual. Follow the instructions on the box. These will vary from four to fifteen minutes, depending on the size and shape of the pasta. The safe way is to wait the minimum amount of time and then to fish out a strand or two every minute, dip it into a little sauce, and taste it. Your own pleasure will best tell when it is ready.

No one can give the correct cooking time, because of the difference in palate, but here are a few general guides:

Regular spaghetti	8 to 12 minutes
Thin spaghetti or spaghettini	6 to 10 minutes
Long macaroni	10 to 12 minutes
Macaroni shells	8 to 12 minutes
Broad noodles	6 to 9 minutes

Medium noodles	4 to 6 minutes
Fine noodles	4 to 6 minutes
Alphabets	5 to 7 minutes
Short Gavatoni	10 to 15 minutes

3. **Use plenty of water and keep it boiling.** Bring to a full boil at least one gallon of water (to which a tablespoon of salt has been added) for each pound of spaghetti. More water will do no harm. Then put the pasta in slowly.

If the water is not at full boil, or if the pasta is dumped in too rapidly, the temperature will drop below the boiling point and the strands may stick together. Nothing is more disastrous than such a bundle of stuck-together spaghetti, the outsides mushy and the insides about as tasty as undercooked rubber.

Note well: Do not break the spaghetti when putting it into the pot. Let the long ends stick out for a few seconds; as soon as the submerged ends have been reached by the heat a gentle pressure will bend them down into the water. Remember: no matter how long it is, it will fit into the pot.

After a few minutes stir with a long-handled fork or spoon, loosening any ends that have stuck to the bottom of the pot. A gentle stirring from time to time will do no harm. Avoid boiling over by regulating the heat, **but keep it boiling.**

4. **Drain at once.** Have a colander ready in the sink and pour the contents of pot into it immediately. Then transfer to a bowl or platter, and add the sauce. There is no need to blanch if you have cooked your pasta properly.

RAVIOLI AND STUFFED PASTA

Note especially that ravioli and stuffed pasta must be taken from the pot without breaking. Here's a simple trick that will prove useful: place the cooking pot in the sink and run cold water into it; as the cold water buoys up the ravioli, carefully slide the colander into the pot and under them. When transferring to the serving platter slide the pasta into the dish or bowl.

If you are preparing a large deep bowl of ravioli handle with special care, placing a layer at a time in the bowl and covering each layer with sauce and a sprinkling of grated cheese. You will thus be assured that your sauce is well distributed, for ravioli and other stuffed pasta cannot have the sauce stirred or mangled in as can spaghetti, for instance. Remember that the sauce belongs not on top but in around, under, over and above all next to the absorbent surface of the pasta.

(For Sauces see Chapter XII)

TYPES OF SPAGHETTI AND MACARONI

(Actual Size)

Courtesy V. La Rosa & Sons, Inc.

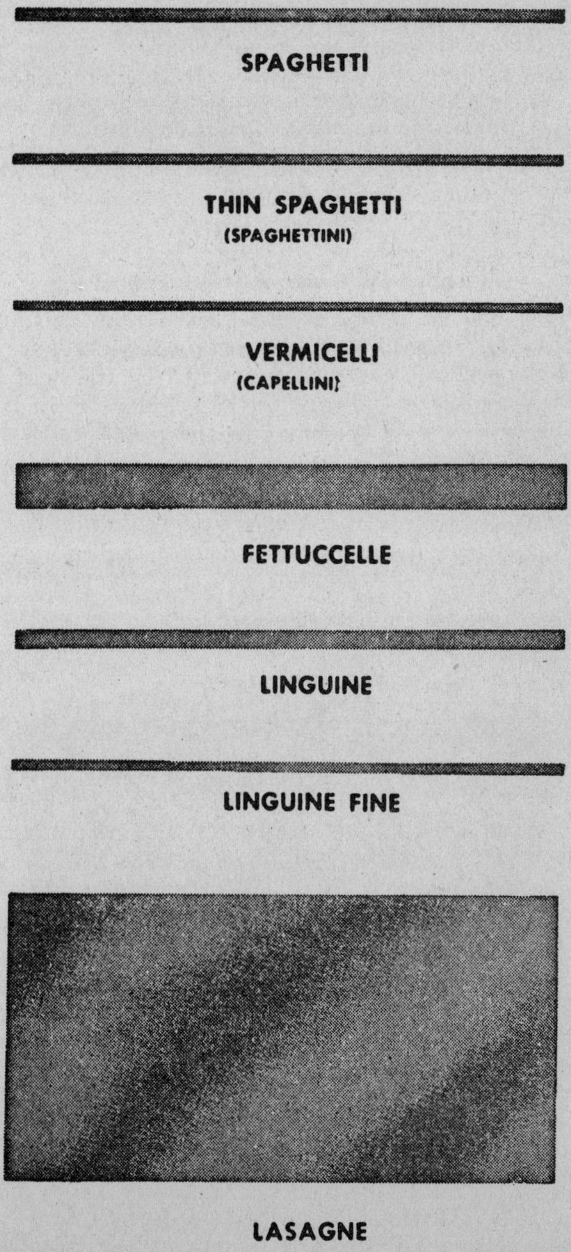

ZITI
(READY CUT TO COOKING LENGTH)

MEZZANI
(READY CUT TO COOKING LENGTH)

MACARONI (MACCARONCELLI)
(READY CUT TO COOKING LENGTH)

THIN MACARONI
(PERCIATELLI)

BUCATINI

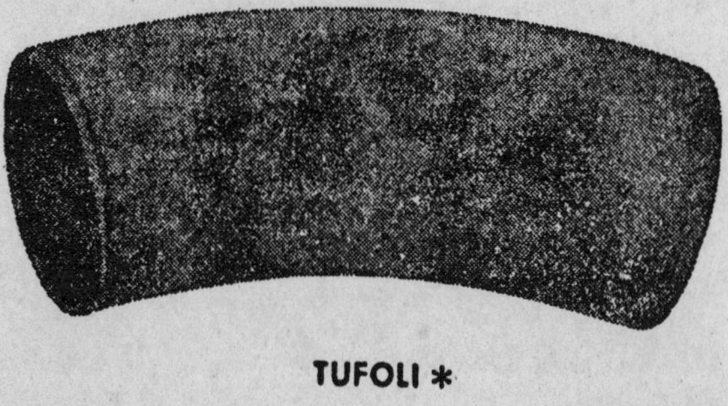

TUFOLI *

MOSTACCIOLI

MOSTACCIOLI RIGATI

RIGOLETTI

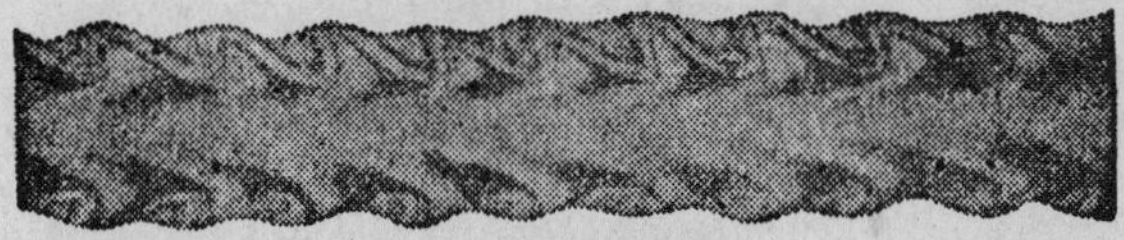

MAFALDE

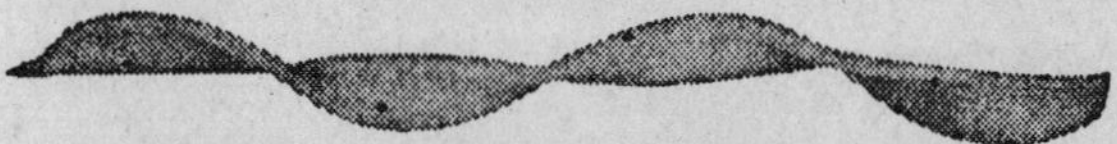

MARGHERITA

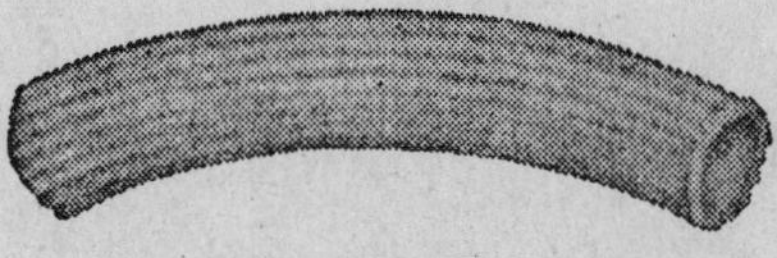

RIGATI

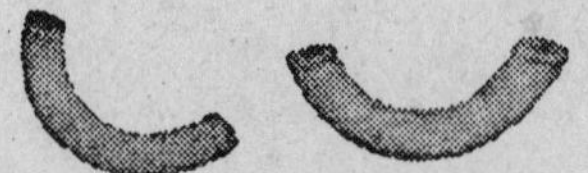

ELBOW MACARONI

DITALI

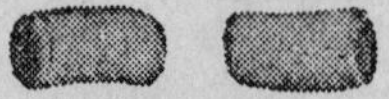

DITALINI

TUBETTI

TUBETTINI

ACINI DI PEPE

ORZO

STELLINI

SEME DI MELLONE

EGG BOWS
(FARFALLE)

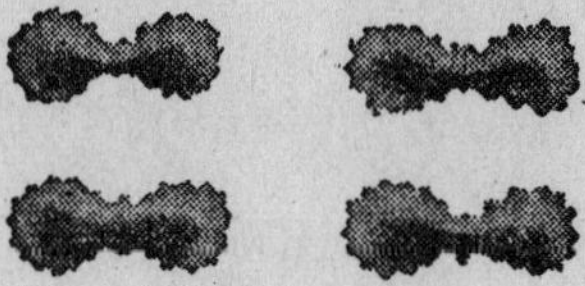

EGG BOWS
(TRIPOLINI)

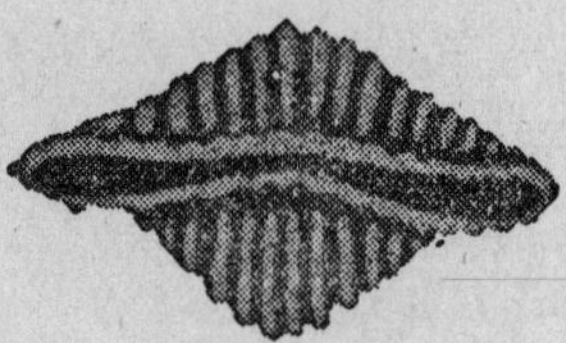

LARGE SHELLS
(MARUZZE)

SHELLS
(MARUZZELLE)

OCCHI DI LUPO

RIGATONI

FUSILLI

CAVATELLI

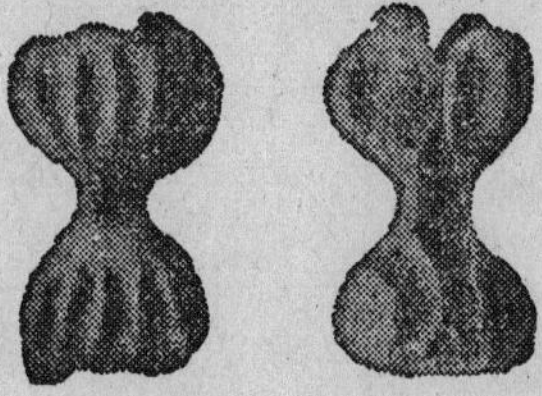

JUMBO MACARONI

SPIEDINI

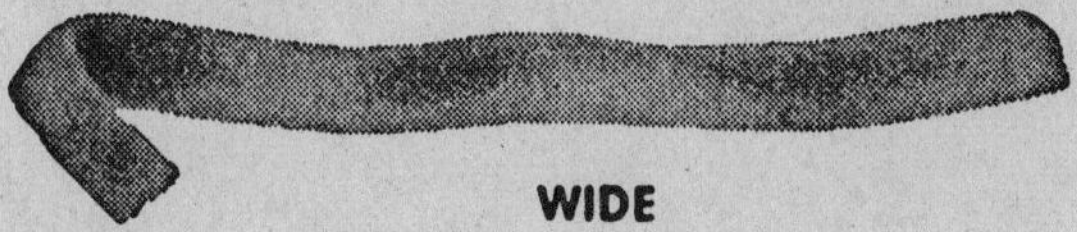

WIDE

MEDIUM

FINE—EXTRA FINE

MEDIUM-WIDE

FINE

(Last five illustrations are of noodles)

PLAIN SPAGHETTI
(Spaghetti Bolliti)

4 qts. boiling water
1 lb. spaghetti
2 tblsp. salt

Hold ends of spaghetti in rapidly boiling water, and as the spaghetti softens, let the ends slide in. Stir to prevent pasta sticking to bottom of pan. The boiling time is up to you—if you like it as most Italians do, you will test the spaghetti by pinching; if it pinches in two easily but still feels firm, the pasta is done al denti. Drain in a colander, and serve the way you like best. There are no limits to the way pasta can be served. The main thing is that you now have spaghetti cooked the real Italian way. Serves 6.

BAKED SPAGHETTI ELBOWS
(Spaghetti al Forno)

1 lb. elbow spaghetti
½ lb. mushrooms
1 tblsp. onion, minced
3 tblsp. olive oil
12 stuffed olives, sliced
3 tblsp. flour
1½ cups milk
salt and pepper
Parmesan cheese
buttered breadcrumbs

Cook spaghetti in boiling, salted water. Sauté onions in hot olive oil, add mushrooms and cook until brown; blend in flour, and add milk, stirring constantly; add olives and drained spaghetti elbows, mixing well. Season and turn into casserole; top with breadcrumbs, sprinkle with cheese, and bake in a moderate oven (350°F.) about 30 minutes. Serves 6.

SPAGHETTI WITH ANCHOVIES
(Spaghetti con Acciughe)

1 lb. spaghetti, cooked
2 tblsp. butter
½ lb. anchovy
(or 1 8-oz. can of prepared anchovy in olive oil)

If the anchovies are salted, soak 2 hours; remove skin, tails, heads and bones, shred meat. Mix cooked spaghetti with butter and add the anchovy meat. Serves 6.

BROCCOLI WITH SPAGHETTI

(Spaghetti con Broccoli)

1 bunch broccoli, cut up
2 tomatoes, quartered
1 clove garlic, chopped
salt and pepper
2 cups water
1 onion, chopped
1 lb. spaghetti

Boil broccoli in water until tender; add tomatoes, onion and garlic; cook until onion is almost tender. Cook spaghetti in boiling salted water until tender; drain, and combine with broccoli; heat through. Serves 6.

SPAGHETTI WITH BUTTER

(Spaghetti al Burro)

¼ cup sweet butter
2 tblsp. salt
1 lb. spaghetti
Parmesan cheese, grated

Cook spaghetti as described under Plain Spaghetti, on page 57. Turn cooked spaghetti into a hot dish, add butter and generous amounts of cheese; lift about with a fork or spoon until mixed to your liking. Serve sprinkled with more cheese. Serves 6.

SUPERIOR SPAGHETTI CASSEROLE

(Spaghetti "Extra" in Casserola)

½ lb. broken spaghetti
4 tblsp. olive oil
1 onion, chopped
1 green pepper, chopped
1 clove garlic, mashed
½ lb. beef, ground
1 qt. tomatoes, cut up
1 cup Parmesan cheese, grated
1 tsp. salt
½ lb. Italian sausage, cut up

Fry sausage lightly in hot olive oil; remove from pan and cook onion, green pepper, garlic, and seasoning until onion is soft; add ground beef and cook until brown. Combine sausage and tomatoes with meat mixture; cover and simmer 1 hour. Season to taste. Cook spaghetti in boiling salted water; drain, and mix with meat sauce and half the cheese. Bake in casserole in a slow oven (300°F.) about 1 hour. Uncover last 15 minutes of baking and let brown slightly. Serve sprinkled with cheese. Serves 6.

CURLED SPAGHETTI WITH CAULIFLOWER

(Spaghetti Arricciati con Cavolo Fiore)

1 lb. curled spaghetti, cut up
1 small cauliflower
1 onion, sliced
2 lbs. tomatoes, peeled
5 tblsp. olive oil
3 anchovy fillets
1 tblsp. pine nuts
salt and pepper
oregano
1 clove garlic

Cook cauliflower in boiling, salted water; drain. Cook spaghetti in boiling, salted water; drain. Brown onion and garlic in hot olive oil, stir in anchovy fillets; cook about 3 minutes, and add tomatoes; simmer about 20 minutes and add cauliflower, nuts, salt, pepper and oregano; heat through. Combine with spaghetti, mix well, and serve hot, sprinkled with grated Parmesan cheese. Serves 6.

CHICKEN-SPAGHETTI PLATTER

(Granpiatto di Pollo con Spaghetti)

1 3-lb. chicken, cut up
¼ cup olive oil
1 veal knuckle
2 tsp. salt
1 cup ripe olives, chopped
1 ½ cups Parmesan cheese, grated
1 tsp. paprika
¼ cup pimiento, chopped
1 lb. thin spaghetti
¼ tsp. pepper
¼ cup onion, minced
¼ cup green pepper, minced

Wash and dry chicken, then brown in hot olive oil; remove to deep kettle and add veal knuckle with enough boiling water to cover, add salt and pepper; cover and simmer until tender, about 2 hours. Remove meat from chicken and veal bones, and cut into small strips. Skim fat from broth, measure and add enough water to make 2 quarts. Cook onion and green pepper with paprika in skillet, in which chicken was browned, until lightly browned; add to broth with pimiento and cut-up meat, heat to boiling and add spaghetti; cook uncovered until spaghetti is tender. Do not drain. Add olives and 1 cup of cheese; heat. Serve on large, deep platter, sprinkled with remaining cheese. Serves 8.

CRAB AND SPAGHETTI

(Pranzo di Spaghetti e Granchi)

1 lb. crab meat, fresh or canned
1 lb. spaghetti
2 cups tomato sauce
1 tsp. parsley, chopped

¾ cup water
1 tsp. pepper
2 tsp. salt
¾ cup port wine
Parmesan cheese, grated
1 tsp. celery, chopped
1 clove garlic, chopped
½ cup onion, chopped
¼ cup olive oil

Sauté garlic, celery, onion, and parsley until brown; add tomato sauce (see recipe, Chapter XII), water and seasoning; simmer 1 hour. Add crab meat and simmer 10 minutes. Cook spaghetti in boiling, salted water; drain, and add part of the sauce. Pour spaghetti on hot platter, sprinkle with cheese and garnish with remaining sauce. Serve with garlic bread, romaine salad and wine—makes a very delicious meal. Serves 4 to 6.

SPAGHETTI DON ISADORO

3 tblsp. olive oil
1 onion, chopped
1 clove garlic, minced
¼ lb. mushrooms, peeled and sliced
1 6-oz. can tomato paste
dash of Worcestershire sauce
½ tsp. salt
dash of pepper
1 lb. spaghetti
Parmesan cheese, grated
4 cups water

Cook spaghetti in boiling, salted water; drain. Fry onion, garlic and mushrooms in hot olive oil until brown; add tomato paste, water, salt, pepper and Worcestershire sauce; simmer 30 minutes. To serve, pour sauce over spaghetti and sprinkle with cheese. Serves 6.

SPAGHETTI WITH EGGPLANT

(Spaghetti con Melanzana)

1 lb. spaghetti
1 eggplant, sliced lengthwise, ½-inch thick
1 large can tomatoes
1 onion, chopped
1 tblsp. parsley, chopped
½ cup Parmesan cheese, grated
½ cup olive oil
salt and pepper

Brown onion and garlic in 4 tblsp. olive oil; add parsley, tomatoes, salt and pepper; simmer about 1 hour. Sprinkle eggplant slices with salt, let drain in colander 30 minutes and squeeze dry; brown in hot olive oil until light brown. Cook spaghetti in salted, boiling water; drain and place on hot platter, cover with sauce and arrange eggplant on top. Serve sprinkled with cheese. Serves 6.

SPAGHETTI WITH ESCAROLE

(Spaghetti con Lattuga Arricciata)

½ lb. spaghetti
2 cups water
2 tblsp. olive oil
1 head escarole
salt and pepper
Parmesan cheese, grated

Cook spaghetti in boiling, salted water; drain. Boil escarole in water until tender; season, add olive oil and mix with spaghetti. Serve sprinkled with cheese. Serves 4.

FRESH FENNEL WITH SPAGHETTI

(Spaghetti alla Milanese)

1 bunch fresh fennel, chopped fine
2 6-oz. cans anchovies in oil
1 onion, chopped
1 clove garlic, chopped
½ tsp. parsley, minced
2 cups breadcrumbs
2 cans tomato paste
6 cups water
1 tsp. fennel seed
1 lb. spaghetti
½ cup olive oil
oregano and pepper

Sauté onion, garlic, and anchovies in hot olive oil until brown, add tomato paste, water, anise, fennel seeds, and other seasoning; simmer about 1½ hours. While sauce is simmering, brown bread crumbs in ¼ cup hot olive oil. Cook spaghetti in boiling, salted water; drain, and mix with half the sauce. Serve spaghetti on hot platter, sprinkle with browned bread crumbs and cover with remaining sauce. Serves 6.

SPAGHETTI WITH FENNEL SAUCE

(Spaghetti con Salsa di Finocchio all'Italiana)

1 lb. spaghetti
1 onion, chopped
½ cup raisins
1 gal. water
Parmesan cheese, grated
1 bunch fresh finocchio (fennel)
¼ cup olive oil
¼ cup pine nuts
salt and pepper

Cook a few stalks of the finocchio in the water, boiling and salted; remove finocchio and save water. Chop up remainder of finocchio; brown with onion in hot olive oil, add raisins, pine nuts, salt and pepper, and heat through. Cook spaghetti in boiling finocchio water; drain. To serve, cover spaghetti with finocchio sauce (see Chapter XII). Sprinkle with cheese. Serves 6.

SPAGHETTI FISHERMAN

(Linguine alla Marinara)

½ cup olive oil
1 No. 2 can tomatoes
½ tsp. thyme
2 tblsp. parsley, chopped
2 cloves garlic, chopped
salt and pepper
1 lb. linguine spaghetti

Fry garlic in hot olive oil, when brown add tomatoes and mash, stirring constantly with fork for 5 minutes; sprinkle in thyme and stir. Cook spaghetti in boiling, salted water; drain well. To serve, mix sauce and spaghetti together, and sprinkle with parsley. Serves 4 to 6.

SPAGHETTI FLORENTINE

1 lb. chicken livers, cooked
1 lb. spaghetti
Parmesan cheese, grated
1 green pepper, minced
tomato sauce
salt and pepper

Cook spaghetti in boiling, salted water; drain. Chop chicken livers and mix with green pepper, spaghetti and seasoning. Serve with a generous amount of tomato sauce (see recipe on page 234), sprinkled with cheese. Serves 6.

NOTE: Other meats and chopped mushrooms may be substituted for the chicken livers.

SPAGHETTI FRANCESCA

1 lb. spaghetti
4 eggs, beaten lightly
1 cup breadcrumbs, toasted
2 cups celery, diced
2 cups Ricotta cheese
1½ cups milk
1 green pepper, minced
2 tsp. salt
1 large onion, grated
toasted almonds, sliced

Boil spaghetti; drain, and mix with remaining ingredients. Bake in a greased loaf pan in a moderate oven (350°F.) about 45 minutes. Unmold on serving plate; garnish with sprigs of parsley and almonds. Serves 6.

SPAGHETTI WITH GARLIC AND OIL

(Spaghetti all'Aglio ed Olio)

1 lb. spaghetti
3 or 4 cloves garlic, chopped
parsley, minced
4 or 5 tblsp. olive oil
salt and pepper

Boil spaghetti in salted, boiling water, until nearly done; drain well. Sauté garlic in hot olive oil until slightly brown, add spaghetti and seasoning; cook and sprinkle with parsley, mix by turning frequently. Serves 6.

(Can also be mixed with fresh Ricotta just before eating.)

GREEN SPAGHETTI

(Lasagne Verdi)

1½ cups flour, sifted
2 eggs
½ tsp. salt
4 tblsp. boiled, drained, ground spinach
about 2 tblsp. water

Combine flour, salt, spinach and eggs, then add enough water to make the dough stiff enough to hold together. Roll into two balls and place on an uncovered dish in refrigerator for 20 minutes. Then remove dough, one ball at a time, to a floured board and roll as thin as possible, lifting from time to time and flouring board so it does not stick. Cut into 4-inch strips. Let dry about 1 hour before using. Have large saucepan of boiling salted water (1 tsp. salt to 1 qt. water) and slide lasagne into boiling water; boil about 7 minutes, drain. Spoon some tomato sauce (see page 234) into bottom of casserole, then place a layer of lasagne in it, then more sauce; sprinkle grated cheese over all, then another layer of lasagne, more cheese, more sauce, until all ingredients are used. Be sure there is a layer of grated cheese on top. Bake in moderate oven (325°) about 30 minutes. Serve at once. Serves 6.

BAKED SPAGHETTI WITH KIDNEY SAUCE

(Spaghetti al Forno con Salsa di Rognoni)

3 beef kidneys, ground
1 lb. spaghetti
¼ cup olive oil
1 pinch of cinnamon
1 can tomato paste mixed with 3 cups water

2 bay leaves
1 cup burgundy wine
paprika
¼ lb. Parmesan cheese, grated
salt and pepper

Heat olive oil in deep casserole, add beef kidneys, seasonings and wine; cover, and stew 1 hour. Remove cover and allow wine to simmer down, stir in tomato paste; simmer 30 minutes. Cook spaghetti in boiling, salted water; drain, place in casserole and cover with kidney sauce, sprinkle with cheese and paprika. Bake in a moderate oven (350°F.) about 10 minutes, or until the cheese is a golden brown. Serves 6.

SPAGHETTI WITH LIVER

(Spaghetti con Fegato)

1 ½-inch slice beef liver
1 onion, chopped
2 tblsp. olive oil
1 6-oz. can tomato paste
1 tsp. parsley, minced
3 cups hot water
salt and pepper
1 lb. spaghetti
Parmesan cheese, grated

Dice liver after removing skin and veins. Fry onion slowly in hot olive oil until slightly brown; add liver and cook 5 minutes. Add tomato paste, hot water, parsley, salt and pepper; simmer 30 minutes. Cook spaghetti in boiling, salted water until tender; drain. Mix spaghetti and liver sauce (page 237), sprinkle with cheese and serve. Serves 6.

SPAGHETTI MARGHERITA

1 lb. spaghetti, cooked
2 onions, chopped
1 med. can tomatoes, crushed to pulp
1 cup brown sauce
½ lb. mushrooms, sliced
½ lb. chicken livers, diced
8 artichoke hearts
5 tblsp. olive oil
1 pinch oregano
2 cloves garlic, chopped
salt and pepper
Parmesan cheese, grated

Brown onions in hot olive oil; add tomatoes and brown sauce (see recipe on page 237). Cook mushrooms and artichoke hearts in remaining olive oil about 10 minutes, add chicken livers and sauté 5 minutes; combine with sauce, add seasoning and garlic. Place spaghetti on a hot platter, cover with sauce and sprinkle with cheese. Serves 6.

SPAGHETTI WITH MEAT BALLS

(Spaghetti con Polpette)

1 lb. spaghetti, cooked
1 onion, chopped
1 6-oz. can tomato paste
2 eggs
¼ cup Parmesan cheese, grated
salt and oregano
1 large can tomatoes, peeled
1 clove garlic, chopped
1 ¼ lb. veal and pork, ground
1 cup breadcrumbs
1 dash red pepper
¼ cup water

Strain tomatoes to remove seeds; add water, onion, garlic and salt, and boil over slow fire. Brown about ¼ lb. meat mixture in hot olive oil, and add to tomatoes. Mix remaining meat with breadcrumbs, cheese, salt and eggs; shape into small balls about the size of golf balls. Brown meat balls in hot olive oil; add to tomato sauce and cook about 30 minutes. Dilute tomato paste with equal amount of water, season and add to sauce; cook at least an hour. Mix cooked spaghetti with part of sauce, sprinkle with cheese, and arrange meatballs on the side. Serves 6.

SPAGHETTI MEAT PIE

(Pasticcio di Carne con Spaghetti)

½ lb. spaghetti, cooked
2 eggs
1 lb. stew meat, cooked
3 tblsp. cheese, grated
1 onion, chopped
2 tblsp. parsley, minced
salt and pepper
butter

Grind meat with parsley and onion; add seasoning, cheese and eggs. Combine meat and spaghetti, place in a greased baking dish, dot with butter; bake in a moderate oven (350°F.) about 20 minutes. Serves 4.

SPAGHETTI WITH MEAT SAUCE

(Spaghetti con Salsa di Carne)

1 lb. spaghetti
1 clove garlic, chopped
1 tblsp. parsley, chopped
1 cup Parmesan cheese, grated
1 cup mushrooms, chopped
salt and pepper
1 large can tomatoes
1 onion, chopped
1 lb. beef, chopped
¼ cup olive oil
½ tsp. oregano
1 bay leaf

Sauté beef in hot olive oil until brown, add onion, garlic, parsley and mushrooms; cook 10 minutes and add salt, pepper, oregano, bay leaf, and tomatoes; simmer until thickness desired is obtained. Cook spaghetti in boiling, salted water; drain. To serve, place spaghetti on serving platter, cover with part of the sauce, sprinkle with cheese and remaining sauce. Serves 6.

See also page 231.

SPAGHETTI WITH MUSSELS

(Spaghetti con Mitilo)

3 qts. mussels
1 onion, chopped
1 clove garlic, minced
1 lb. spaghetti
½ cup pitted black olives
2 stalks celery, chopped
1 pt. water
1 glass white wine
grated Parmesan cheese
salt and pepper to taste

In large saucepan add water, wine, onion, garlic, celery, and mussels. Cover and cook 20 minutes, or until shells open. Strain the mussels, saving the liquid. Cook spaghetti, drain. Heat the mussels in the liquid, add the olives, salt and pepper to taste. Pour over spaghetti and serve sprinkled with chopped parsley and grated cheese. Serves 6.

SPAGHETTI NEAPOLITAN

(Spaghetti alla Napolitana)

1 onion, chopped
2 cloves garlic, chopped
2 tblsp. olive oil
3 tblsp. ham, minced
2 sausage, highly spiced
6 mushrooms, chopped
1 cup meat broth
½ cup tomato paste
½ cup water
salt and pepper
1 lb. spaghetti, cooked
Parmesan cheese, grated

Sauté onion and garlic until brown; add ham, sausage, and mushrooms, and continue frying. Mix tomato paste with water, add with broth and seasoning to sausage mixture; cover and simmer until ingredients are well blended. Pile cooked spaghetti on platter, cover with sauce and sprinkle generously with cheese. Serves 6.

SPAGHETTI OR MACARONI WITH PEAS

(Spaghetti o Maccheroni con Piselli)

1 lb. spaghetti or macaroni
¼ lb. butter
Parmesan cheese, grated
1 lb. fresh peas, cooked
salt and pepper
4 eggs, beaten

Cook spaghetti in salted, boiling water until tender; strain all but ½ cup of water. Stir in eggs and peas with seasoning. Serve sprinkled with cheese. Serves 6.

SPAGHETTI PIETRO

(Spaghetti alla Pietro)

2 lbs. spaghetti
¼ cup butter
1 clove garlic
1 cup onions, sliced
½ cup celery, chopped
1 med. can mushrooms
½ lb. pork, ground
½ lb. veal, ground
Parmesan cheese, grated
½ cup olive oil
1 large can tomatoes
1 6-oz. can tomato paste
1 tblsp. salt
½ tsp. pepper
1 tsp. oregano
½ lb. beef, ground
1 bay leaf
1 cup parsley, chopped

Heat olive oil and butter, and sauté garlic, onions, celery, mushrooms, and meat until golden brown; add tomatoes, tomato paste, and bay leaf; simmer 1 hour. Boil spaghetti (or other pasta) until tender; drain, and return to saucepan with a lump of butter, 2 tblsp. cheese and parsley; blend well. To serve, place spaghetti on a large platter, cover with part of the sauce, sprinkle with cheese and remaining sauce. Serves 10.

SPAGHETTI POLACK

(Spaghetti alla Polacca)

1 lb. spaghetti
2 eggs, hard-boiled, chopped
4 tblsp. Parmesan cheese, grated
2 tblsp. heavy cream
1 tblsp. breadcrumbs
2 tblsp. olive oil
2 tblsp. parsley
salt and pepper

Cook spaghetti in boiling, salted water; drain. Mix olive oil with spaghetti; add cream, salt and pepper, and mix well. Place spaghetti in casserole, garnish with mixture of parsley, cheese and eggs; bake about 20 minutes in a moderate oven (300°F.). Brown breadcrumbs in hot olive oil, pour over spaghetti and brown under broiler. Serves 6.

NOTE: For a variation, mix in slightly sautéd lamb kidneys.

SPAGHETTI SAMUEL

(Spaghetti alla Samuele)

¼ cup olive oil
1 lb. beef, finely ground
salt and pepper
¼ cup dried mushrooms
2 cups warm water
1 cup canned tomatoes, strained

1 med. onion, chopped
2 6-inch stalks celery, chopped
3 sage leaves
3 basil leaves
1 clove garlic, chopped fine
lemon rind
1 lb. spaghetti, cooked
1 6-oz. can tomato paste
¼ tsp. nutmeg
1 cup boiling water
¼ cup butter
Parmesan cheese, grated
1 tblsp. parsley, chopped fine

Brown beef in hot olive oil, add salt, pepper, onion and celery; cook gently until golden brown, and add sage, basil, parsley, garlic and a piece of lemon rind; stir well. Soak mushrooms in warm water until soft; remove from water and chop fine, add to beef sauce with water mushrooms were soaked in, together with tomatoes, tomato paste, and nutmeg; stir well and bring to a boil, add boiling water and lower heat; simmer slowly about 3 hours, stirring occasionally. When done, remove lemon rind, add butter and serve over hot spaghetti; sprinkle with cheese. Serves 6.

SPAGHETTI AND SAUSAGE OVEN DINNER

(Spaghetti con Salsiccia al Forno)

1 lb. bulk Italian sausage
⅓ cup onion, chopped
2 cups tomato sauce
1 lb. spaghetti
2 tblsp. olive oil
salt and pepper

Cook spaghetti in salted, boiling water; drain. Combine sausage and onion, shape into patties and brown in hot olive oil. Place spaghetti in baking dish, top with the patties and cover with tomato sauce (see recipe on page 234); bake in a medium hot oven (375°F.) about 30 minutes. Sprinkle with cheese. Serves 6.

SPAGHETTI WITH ZUCCHINI

(Spaghetti con Zucchini)

1 lb. small zucchini
4 tblsp. garlic olive oil
½ cup water
Parmesan cheese, grated
1 green pepper, cut up
2 tomatoes, quartered
1 lb. spaghetti
salt and pepper

Cut zucchini into 1-inch lengths and cook with green pepper in hot olive oil until brown; add tomatoes and water, cook a few minutes. Cook spaghetti in boiling water, drain and combine with zucchini sauce. Serve at once sprinkled generously with cheese. Serves 6.

SPAGHETTI WITH TOMATO SAUCE

(Spaghetti con Salsa di Pomidoro)

1 lb. spaghetti
1 onion, chopped
1 tblsp. olive oil
1 6-oz. can tomato paste
9 or 10 kernels fennel seed
½ cup Parmesan cheese, grated
3 cups water
1 clove garlic, chopped
½ tsp. parsley, minced
1 bay leaf
salt and pepper
pinch of oregano

Fry onion and garlic in hot olive oil until brown; add tomato paste, water, parsley, seasonings, and simmer about 45 minutes. Cook spaghetti in salted, boiling water until tender; drain, and mix with sauce. Serve hot, sprinkled with cheese. Serves 6.

SPAGHETTI WITH TOMATO-MEAT SAUCE

(Spaghetti con Sugo)

1 lb. spaghetti
1 small onion, chopped
1 clove garlic, chopped
1 bay leaf
1 No. 2 can tomatoes, strained
¼ cup olive oil
½ lb. lean beef, diced
3 tblsp. parsley, chopped
1 can mushrooms
salt, pepper and oregano
Parmesan cheese, grated

Brown onion, garlic and parsley in hot olive oil, add meat and cook, stirring to avoid sticking or burning; add tomatoes, bay leaf and seasoning; cook slowly about 1 hour. Cook spaghetti in boiling, salted water; drain, and place on hot platter. Pour part of the sauce over spaghetti, sprinkle generously with cheese, and add remaining sauce. Serves 6.

See also page 240.

SPAGHETTI VEAL DELUXE

(Spaghetti Vitello)

¼ cup olive oil
1 cup onions, sliced
½ tsp. oregano
1 tsp. salt
½ cup Parmesan cheese, grated
1½ lb. veal steak, 1-inch thick
¼ tsp. pepper
2 tblsp. flour
½ cup water
1 lb. spaghetti

Dip veal steak in flour mixed with salt, pepper, and oregano; brown in hot olive oil on both sides. Place in baking dish with onions and water, cover and bake in moderate oven (350°F.)

about 1 hour. Add cheese to sauce remaining from frying veal. Cook spaghetti in salted, boiling water until tender; drain. To serve, arrange veal in center of platter with spaghetti surrounding it; cover with cheese sauce, sprinkle with more cheese. Serves 5.

SEASHELL PASTA AND POTATOES

(Conchiglie e Patate)

1 lb. seashell pasta*	4 tblsp. olive oil
1 lb. potatoes, peeled and diced	salt and pepper
1 onion, sliced	parsley
2 lbs. tomatoes, peeled	1 cup Parmesan cheese, grated

Brown onions in hot olive oil; add potatoes and cook 10 minutes; add tomatoes, salt, pepper, and parsley, cover and cook slowly about 30 minutes. Cook seashell pasta in salted, boiling water until tender; drain, and mix with sauce and cheese. Sprinkle more cheese on top and serve. Serves 6.

* See table of spaghetti and macaroni, pages 51 to 56.

Macaroni Variations

Place alternate layers of cooked macaroni with layers of chopped meat in an oiled baking dish; cover with plenty of well seasoned gravy. Fowl, veal, beef, or ham may be used.

* * * * *

Chopped, stewed mushrooms is an excellent meat substitute; use a tasty sauce of their own liquor, thickened slightly.

* * * * *

Cauliflower buds, in plenty of thin cream sauce made yellow with butter and flavored with grated Parmesan cheese, may also be used instead of meat.

* * * * *

Creamed onions can be used in the same way, always remembering that the macaroni will absorb most of the liquid. The finished dish must be moist.

* * * * *

Slices of yellow cheese may alternate with macaroni layers. Cover with milk. Milk will be absorbed.

* * * * *

Vermicelli combines well with fish anchovies and other kinds of fish.

* * * * *

All of the above dishes should be sprinkled generously with grated cheese, or breadcrumbs dotted with butter.

BAKED MACARONI

(Maccheroni al Forno)

No. I

½ lb. large macaroni
1 lb. tomatoes, sliced
butter
Parmesan cheese, grated
olive oil
salt and pepper

Macaroni is cooked like spaghetti in plenty of boiling, salted water, except that it requires more cooking time. When tender, drain and place in a casserole with a little butter, olive oil and tomatoes; bake about 20 minutes. Serve sprinkled with cheese. Serves 4.

No. II

½ cup olive oil
1 clove garlic, chopped
1 basil leaf
⅛ tsp. pepper
1 lb. mezzani macaroni
1 med. eggplant
3 cups Italian style tomatoes, peeled
½ tsp. salt
Parmesan cheese, grated

Skin and slice eggplant; brown in hot olive oil, and remove from pan. Simmer tomatoes and seasonings in remaining olive oil about 15 minutes, stirring constantly with a fork. Cook macaroni in boiling, salted water; drain. Place 1/3 of the macaroni in a greased casserole, and cover with half the eggplant slices; sprinkle with cheese. Repeat layers ending with a layer of macaroni on top; cover with sauce, sprinkle with cheese and bake in a moderate oven (350°F.) 10 to 15 minutes. Serves 6.

CHICKEN AND MACARONI CASSEROLE

(Maccheroni e Pollo in Casseruola)

1 cup elbow macaroni
1½ tblsp. onion, grated
1 cup carrot, cooked and diced
1/16 tsp. pepper
2 eggs, beaten
⅔ cup green pepper, chopped
2 cups chicken, cooked and diced
¼ tsp. paprika
1½ tsp. salt
1½ cups milk

Cook macaroni in boiling, salted water until tender; drain. Combine onion, carrot, chicken, green pepper, paprika, salt and pepper; add to macaroni and place in a well oiled casserole. Mix eggs and milk, pour over macaroni, and set casserole in a pan of hot water. Bake in a moderate oven (350°F.) about 1 hour, or until firm. Serves 4.

ELBOW MACARONI WITH ALMOND SAUCE

(Maccheroni con Salsa di Mandorle)

1 lb. elbow macaroni
¼ lb. butter
Parmesan cheese, grated
1 pt. heavy cream, whipped
1 lb. almonds, ground

Cook macaroni in boiling, salted water; drain. Combine cream, butter and almonds with macaroni; sprinkle generously with cheese, heat and serve. Serves 6.

ELBOW MACARONI WITH CHICKEN LIVERS

(Maccheroni con Fegatini di Pollo)

1 lb. elbow macaroni
1 onion, chopped
4 strips salami, cut up
3 tblsp. butter
1 lb. chicken livers, chopped
1 tblsp. parsley, chopped
salt and pepper
Parmesan cheese, grated

Brown onion, parsley, chicken livers, and salami in melted butter; season. Cook macaroni in boiling, salted water until tender; drain. Combine macaroni with chicken liver mixture and serve hot, sprinkled with cheese. Serves 6.

BAKED ELBOW MACARONI

(Maccheroni al Forno)

1 lb. elbow macaroni
5 tblsp. flour
5 tblsp. butter
salt and pepper
1 qt. milk
2 cups tomatoes, chopped
1 cup Parmesan cheese, grated

Cook macaroni in boiling, salted water; drain. Melt butter, add flour, salt and milk; blend and add cheese. Combine macaroni and sauce; place in a baking dish a layer at a time with tomatoes between, ending with a layer of macaroni on top. Brown in oven about 30 minutes. Serves 6.

MACARONI AND EGGPLANT

(Maccheroni con Melanzana)

½ lb. macaroni
1 large eggplant, cubed
½ cup Parmesan cheese, grated
1 No. 2 can tomatoes, chopped
½ cup olive oil
1 ½ cups soup meat, cooked
2 onions, chopped
salt to taste

Cook macaroni in boiling, salted water; drain. Brown eggplant in hot olive oil and remove from pan; add tomatoes with seasoning, and simmer 15 minutes. Combine macaroni, eggplant, meat and tomatoes; place in a baking dish, sprinkle with cheese and bake in a moderate oven about 30 minutes. Serves 4.

MACARONI WITH LAMB

(Agnello con Maccheroni)

1 ½ lb. macaroni
3 tblsp. olive oil
1 tblsp. curry powder
salt and pepper
1 lb. lamb, cubed
2 tblsp. flour
3 cups milk, scalded
1 tsp. capers

Cook macaroni in boiling, salted water until tender; drain. Brown lamb in hot olive oil, add a little water and cook slowly until tender. Heat remaining olive oil, add flour, capers, curry powder and seasoning; stir in milk gradually until sauce thickens. Place a layer of macaroni in a greased baking dish, cover with a layer of lamb and sauce, and top with a layer of macaroni; cover, and bake in a moderate oven (350°F.) about 40 minutes. Serves 8.

MACARONI WITH OYSTERS

(Maccheroni con Ostriche)

1 lb. macaroni (short)
½ cup breadcrumbs
salt and pepper
Parmesan cheese, grated
3 doz. oysters (save liquid)
flour
oregano
olive oil

Cook macaroni in boiling, salted water until tender; drain and save water. Place layers of macaroni and oysters, alternately, in a greased casserole; cover with sauce made of oyster liquid, small amount of macaroni water, flour and seasoning. Brown breadcrumbs in hot olive oil, mix with cheese and oregano and spread over macaroni. Bake in moderate oven (350°F.) about 10 or 15 minutes. Serves 4.

BAKED MACARONI PISTACHIO

(Maccheroni al Forno con Pistacchi)

2 eggs and 2 additional yolks
½ cup olive oil
1 clove garlic, chopped
¼ cup red wine
1 tblsp. catsup
½ tsp. black pepper
1 tsp. fennel seed
½ cup and 1 additional tblsp. Parmesan cheese, grated
1 pt. milk, hot
½ tblsp. salt
1 large onion, sliced
2 lbs. beef, ground
½ cup canned tomatoes, crushed
½ cup pistachio nuts
½ tsp. cinnamon
1 lb. macaroni
⅛ lb. butter
1 ½ tblsp. flour

Sauté onion and garlic in hot olive oil; add meat and cook 20 minutes, breaking meat up with a fork. Add wine, tomatoes, catsup, nuts, pepper, cinnamon, fennel seed; stir until meat is nearly dry. Cook macaroni in boiling, salted water until tender; drain and return to pot. Beat eggs with ½ cup cheese and pour over macaroni; mix well, and place half the macaroni in a deep, greased baking dish, cover with meat mixture and the remaining macaroni. Melt butter, add flour gradually and hot milk; whip until smooth. Remove from fire; add additional egg yolks and 1 tblsp. cheese, mix and pour evenly over macaroni; bake in a moderate oven (350°F.) about 25 minutes. To serve, cut into 3-inch squares. Serves 6.

NOTE: This dish is enjoyable served cold, should any be left over.

MACARONI WITH RICOTTA

(Maccheroni con Ricotta)

1 lb. elbow macaroni
1 lb. Ricotta
salt
2 tblsp. butter
¼ cup parsley, chopped
Parmesan cheese, grated

Cook macaroni in salted, boiling water until tender, drain and return to pot. Mix Ricotta and parsley until smooth; add to macaroni with butter, cover and simmer 3 minutes. Serve hot sprinkled with grated cheese. Serves 6.

SHELLS WITH RICOTTA SAUCE

(Conchiglie con Salsa di Ricotta)

1 lb. shell macaroni
1 cup milk
salt and pepper
1 lb. Ricotta cheese
½ bunch parsley, minced

Cook macaroni shells in boiling, salted water until tender; drain. Place Ricotta in a double boiler with milk, parsley and seasoning; cook about 5 minutes, and mix with shells. Serve hot. Serves 6.

MACARONI WITH SHORT RIBS

(Costole con Maccheroni)

1½ lbs. short ribs of beef
2 tblsp. olive oil
3½ cups tomatoes, peeled
½ tsp. fennel seed
1 small onion, chopped
½ lb. macaroni elbows
2 tsp. salt
¼ tsp. pepper
1 bay leaf

Brown short ribs in hot olive oil, add tomatoes, onion, salt, pepper, fennel seed and bay leaf; cover and cook slowly 1 hour. Sprinkle macaroni elbows around ribs, cover and cook 15 minutes longer. Serve hot. Serves 4.

MACARONI WITH SPARERIBS

(Maccheroni con Costole)

½ lb. short macaroni
1 can crushed pineapple
2 apples, diced
1 cup prunes, pitted and soaked overnight
2 tblsp. flour
2 tblsp. brown sugar
4 lbs. spareribs
¼ tsp. cinnamon
½ tsp. pepper
1 tsp. salt

Cook macaroni in salted, boiling water about 9 minutes; drain, and mix with sugar, spice, and fruit. Cut spareribs into equal lengths, season, dredge with flour, and place half on the bottom of a roaster; cover with macaroni and top with remaining ribs; press together and bake 2 hours in a moderate oven (350°F.). Serves 4.

MACARONI WITH SPINACH

(Quadrettini con Spinacci)

½ cup butter
½ cup carrots, diced
3 stalks celery, chopped
1 lb. beef, ground
3 cups tomatoes, chopped
2 cups elbow macaroni (quadrettini)
Parmesan cheese, grated
¼ cup olive oil
⅓ cup onion, diced
3 cloves garlic, chopped
1 can (6 oz.) tomato paste
2 tsp. salt
1 lb. spinach, cooked, drained and chopped

Heat butter and olive oil in a heavy skillet, add carrots, celery and garlic; brown slightly and add beef, cook 10 minutes and add tomato paste, tomatoes and salt; simmer 1½ hours. Cook macaroni in boiling, salted water about 10 minutes before meat sauce is ready; drain. Combine macaroni, meat sauce and spinach, mixing lightly; pour into a greased casserole and sprinkle with grated cheese. Bake in a moderate oven (350°F.) until piping hot. Serves 6.

MACARONI WITH TOMATOES

(Maccheroni al Pomidoro)

½ lb. macaroni
1 onion, chopped
6 tblsp. butter
Parmesan cheese, grated
1 lb. tomatoes, chopped coarsely
1 sprig sweet basil
2 tbsp. olive oil
salt and pepper

Cook macaroni in boiling, salted water until tender; drain. Sauté onion in 2 tblsp. butter and 2 tblsp. hot olive oil until golden brown, crushing onion with a fork to flavor oil and butter; remove onion and add tomatoes, basil, salt and pepper; bring to a boil, simmer 1 hour or until tomatoes are pulpy. Rub sauce through a sieve; reheat and pour over macaroni with remaining butter, melted. To serve, sprinkle generously with cheese. Serves 4.

RING OF PLENTY

(Cerchio di Abbondanza)

½ lb. shell macaroni
2 cups breadcrumbs
1 small can pimentos
1 cup Caciocavallo cheese, diced
½ cup parsley, minced

2 tsp. salt
1 ½ cups milk, scalded
2 eggs, beaten
½ cup onion, minced
½ tsp. pepper
5 tblsp. olive oil

Cook macaroni shells in boiling, salted water until tender; drain. Combine shells with cheese, parsley, pimentos, onion, salt, pepper, milk and oil; blend in eggs, pour into an oiled ring mold, and set mold in a pan of hot water. Bake about 40 minutes in a moderate oven (350°F.). To serve, unmold on a serving dish and fill center with creamed vegetables. Serves 8.

PARMESAN RING

(Anelloni alla Parmigiana)

2 lbs. soup meat
2 tblsp. butter
½ onion, chopped
6 peppercorns
1 herb bouquet
⅛ lb. salt pork, chopped
2 qts. cold water
½ cup breadcrumbs, toasted
½ cup Parmesan cheese, grated
1 dash nutmeg
1 egg white, well beaten
1 recipe noodle dough (page 80)
1 cup light red wine
1 tsp. salt

Slowly fry onion in butter until golden brown; add peppercorns, herbs, soup meat and salt pork, cover with cold water, bring to a boil and add salt; skim and simmer 3 hours. Make a filling of breadcrumbs, cheese, nutmeg and egg white. Roll noodle dough very thin, and use doughnut cutter or glass to cut out disks about 2 inches in diameter. Place a teaspoonful of the filling in the center of each disk, fold over and seal edges securely, using a fork. Strain broth, bring to a fast boil, add wine and the stuffed pasta; cook 5 to 7 minutes. Serves 6.

EGG BOWS LEONARDO

(Farfalloni alla Leanardo)

1 lb. bow noodles (farfalloni)
2 lbs. Italian sausage meat
salt and pepper
1 6-oz. can tomato paste
¼ cup garlic olive oil
¼ cup white wine
1 No. 3 can plum tomatoes
1 tsp. oregano

Brown sausage meat in hot olive oil; add tomatoes, tomato paste, oregano, salt and pepper; simmer 2 hours. Cook egg bows in salted, boiling water; drain. To serve, arrange egg bow noodles on a platter, add wine to sauce and pour over noodles, sprinkle with grated cheese. Serves 6.

GNOCCHI

No. I

- ¾ cup corn meal
- 2 cups water
- 1 egg
- 1 cup Parmesan cheese, grated
- 1½ tsp. salt
- ⅜ tsp. pepper
- ½ cup olive oil
- 2 cloves garlic
- ½ cup onion, chopped
- 1 6-oz. can tomato paste
- 2½ cups canned tomatoes
- 1 tsp. salt

Place corn meal in saucepan, gradually add water and cook over low heat until mixture thickens and comes to a boil, stirring constantly; boil 3 minutes, remove from heat and add egg; beat well, and add half the cheese, salt, ¼ tsp. pepper and ¼ cup olive oil. Spread mixture about 1½ inches deep in pan, cool, cut into 2-inch squares and arrange in shallow baking dish. Heat remaining olive oil, add garlic and cook 3 minutes; remove from heat, discard garlic, add remaining ingredients and mix well. Pour sauce around corn meal squares, sprinkle with remaining cheese; bake in a hot oven (400°F.) about 30 minutes. Serves 6.

No. II

- 1 lb. potatoes
- ¾ cup flour
- 1 egg
- 1 egg yolk
- salt and pepper
- 3 or 4 tblsp. butter
- 2 cups Parmesan cheese, grated

Boil or steam potatoes and, while still hot, rub through a sieve; mix with flour, seasoning, egg and egg yolk, and roll into small balls the size of a walnut, then flatten out in the shape of small cylinders. Boil in salted water for 10 minutes; drain and serve with a little tomato sauce, sprinkled with Parmesan cheese. Serves 4.

No. III

- 3 potatoes, boiled, and strained through a sieve
- 1 breast of capon
- salt and nutmeg
- Parmesan cheese, grated
- 2 egg yolks
- ½ cup flour

Make a soup of the capon. Mix remaining ingredients on a board, beating until hard but flexible; roll into long rolls the thickness of a small finger; cut into 1-inch pieces and cook in boiling soup about 5 minutes. Serves 6.

No. IV

1 cup fine corn meal
pinch of salt
3 eggs, beaten
1 qt. water
1 cup Parmesan cheese, grated
⅛ lb. butter

Cook corn meal in boiling, salted water to a thick mush, free of lumps; remove from fire and gradually add eggs, cheese and butter, mix well. Spread corn meal paste about 1 inch thick on a bread board to cool; when cold, cut to desired shapes with cookie-cutter. (Dip cutter into cold water after each cut.) Place pasta in a shallow baking dish in layers dotted with butter and sprinkled with cheese, ending with butter on top. Bake in a hot oven until brown. Serves 4 to 6.

See also Egg Drop Dumplings, page 97.

STUFFED LASAGNE

(Lasagne Imbottite)

1½ lbs. fresh Ricotta cheese
3 eggs
salt and pepper
½ small Scamozza cheese, sliced
1½ lbs. Lasagne (broad noodles)
1 recipe tomato sauce
½ bunch parsley, chopped fine
2 tblsp. Parmesan cheese
½ lb. boiled ham, sliced
Parmesan cheese, grated

Slide Lasagne (full length) into salted, boiling water a few pieces at a time so as not to break; cook until almost tender, then let cold water run over it, while removing a few strips at a time from water. Place a little tomato sauce (see recipe on page 234) on bottom of a square baking pan, about 3 inches high; lay Lasagne a strip at a time across the pan with ends overhanging edge; repeat this process with strips running across so that ends hang from all sides of pan. Cover Lasagne with more tomato sauce. Mix Ricotta, eggs, seasoning, parsley and Parmesan cheese; place a layer of mixture over Lasagne, cover with tomato sauce and a layer of ham, a layer of Scamozza, more sauce and sprinkle with Parmesan cheese. Add a layer of short pieces of Lasagne the size of the pan, cover with Ricotta cheese mixture, ham, Scamozza, tomato sauce and Parmesan cheese. Carefully place hanging pieces of Lasagne over top of contents of pan; cover with tomato sauce, sprinkle with Parmesan cheese, and bake in a moderate oven (350°F.) about 30 to 40 minutes. When ready to serve—cut into serving pieces while still in baking dish; turn onto serving platter upside-down. Cover with more tomato sauce and garnish with freshly chopped parsley. Serves 8.

LITTLE COCKED HATS MARIA

(Cappelletti alla Maria)

½ lb. chicken or veal, cooked
1 lb. Ricotta cheese
3 tblsp. Parmesan cheese, grated
1 dash allspice
2 qts. chicken broth, seasoned
1 dash of nutmeg
1 egg, well beaten
1 egg yolk, well beaten
1 recipe noodle dough (below)
2 tblsp. olive oil

Lightly brown meat in hot olive oil; grind, and mix with cheeses, spices, and eggs. Roll noodle dough to ⅛-inch thickness, and cut into 2½-inch rounds. Place a small amount of meat mixture in center of each round, fold in half and seal edges with a fork. Heat chicken broth to boiling point, add Cocked Hats and cook from 5 to 7 minutes. Serve hot in soup plates. Serves 6.

NOTE: This is a special holiday or Christmas dish.

HOME MADE NOODLES

(Tagliatelli alla Casalinga)

2½ cups flour
pinch of salt
3 large eggs

Pile flour on a bread board and make a well in the middle. Break eggs into well and add salt; mix with hands until you have a stiff dough, using a little water if needed. Roll dough paper thin, flour and fold; cut into desired widths with a sharp knife, then loosen them apart, shake out flour and let dry before using. Cook in a generous amount of boiling, salted water about 10 minutes. Serve with any desired sauce and Parmesan cheese. Serves 6.

NOTE: A proper rolling pin to use in making noodles can be made from a broomstick, which has been sanded smooth. To make soup noodles, roll dough onto broomstick rolling pin, then cut dough the full length of rolling pin. Remove dough to bread board and cut into strips lengthwise; divide strips by cutting into smaller pieces. For long noodles, roll dough into long, thin sheets and fold crosswise several times; cut strips perpendicular to folds and shake out to full length. Suspend broomstick rolling pin between two chairs and hang noodles from it to dry.

HOME MADE NOODLES WITH ANCHOVIES

(Tagliatelli con Acciughe)

These are made in the same manner as the preceding recipe describes, but they are dressed with a rich tomato sauce to which 10 or 12 anchovies in oil, chopped garlic and parsley have been added. The anchovies should be chopped very fine or pounded in a mortar.

BAKED NOODLES

(Lasagne al Forno)

4 tblsp. olive oil
1 large onion, minced
1 6-oz. can tomato paste
3 cups water
½ tsp. sugar
salt and pepper
1 lb. broad noodles (Lasagne)
¾ lb. Mozzarella cheese
¾ cup Parmesan cheese, grated
½ tsp. cinnamon

Brown onion in hot olive oil, add tomato paste, water, cinnamon, sugar, salt and pepper; simmer 1 hour. Cook noodles in salted, boiling water about 9 minutes; drain. Place a layer of noodles in an oiled baking dish, cover with a layer of sauce, a layer of thinly sliced Mozzarella, and a sprinkle of Parmesan cheese. Repeat layers until ingredients are used up; bake in a moderate oven (350°F.) about 15 minutes. Serves 6.

BROAD NOODLES

(Lasagne Larghe)

½ cup olive oil
1 med. onion, sliced
3¼ cups hot water
1 6-oz. can tomato paste
½ lb. Lasagne
salt and pepper
1 clove garlic, mashed
1 tblsp. sugar
½ lb. Ricotta cheese
¾ cup Parmesan cheese, grated

Stir onion and ¼ cup hot water into 3 tblsp. hot olive oil; cook until onion is tender and liquid evaporated. Add remaining olive oil and cook until onions are a golden brown, stirring constantly. Dilute tomato paste in remaining hot water, add to onions with garlic, sugar, salt and pepper; simmer gently. Break Lasagne into small pieces and cook in 4 quarts of boiling, salted water about 18 minutes, or until tender; drain, saving 3 tblsp. of the cooking water. Rinse Lasagne with boiling water and drain again. Mix the 3 tblsp. cooking water with Ricotta cheese. Place a layer of Lasagne in a square baking dish, add a layer of sauce, a layer of Ricotta and a layer of Parmesan cheese; repeat layers until ingredients are used up; top with a sprinkle of Parmesan cheese. Place under broiler until top begins to bubble and turn a rich brown. Serve at once with a sprinkle of Parmesan cheese. Serves 6.

EGG NOODLES BOLOGNESE

(Tagliatelli alla Bolognese)

¼ lb. butter
1 tblsp. olive oil
1 med. can tomatoes
1 lb. egg noodles (¼" wide)
1 lb. beef, ground
1 tblsp. tomato paste
1 onion, chopped fine
Parmesan cheese, grated

Brown onion in hot olive oil; add beef, tomatoes, tomato paste; cook slowly for 1 hour. Boil noodles in salted water for 10 minutes; drain, cover with meat sauce, sprinkle with cheese and serve. Serves 6.

EGG NOODLES WITH CHICKEN LIVERS

(Tagliarellini con Fegatini di Pollo)

1 lb. tagliarellini (flat egg noodles, ⅛" wide)
4 tblsp. olive oil
1 cup mushrooms, sliced
4 chicken livers, chopped
1 pimiento, cut up
1 tblsp. flour
1 can tomato sauce
½ cup water
2 bouillon cubes
Parmesan cheese, grated

Cook tagliarellini in plenty of boiling, salted water until tender; drain. Fry mushrooms in hot olive oil 10 minutes; remove from oil to hot plate, and fry chicken livers, season and remove to hot plate. Stir in flour, adding more olive oil if needed, and brown; add tomato sauce, water, bouillon; stir until smooth and slightly thickened. Combine hot tagliarellini with chicken livers, mushrooms, pimiento and 1 heaping tablespoon of cheese. Heap tagliarellini on a platter, cover with sauce, and sprinkle with cheese. Serves 6.

EGG NOODLES WITH VEAL

(Lasagne con Vitello)

1 lb. Lasagne, cooked
2 lbs. veal steak
1 onion, sliced
½ cup olive oil
2 cups Parmesan cheese, grated
2 cans tomato soup
salt and pepper

Cut veal steak into strips and brown in hot olive oil with onion; add tomato soup and seasoning; cook slowly about 30 minutes and add a cup of cheese; simmer 10 minutes. Serve over cooked Lasagne, sprinkled with remaining cheese. Serves 6.

PANADA

(Panata)

⅓ cup stale bread, grated
6 tblsp. Parmesan cheese, grated
1 dash of nutmeg
4 eggs, beaten
2 cups hot meat broth
salt to taste

Mix breadcrumbs, cheese and nutmeg; stir in eggs, and add broth a little at a time, stirring constantly; season, and cook in a double boiler until very thick and mixture separates from side of pan. Heap on platter and serve very hot. Serves 6.

NOTE: Green peas or other vegetables are sometimes added to this dish. When this is done, vegetables should be cooked separately and added to the broth.

POLENTA

No. I

¼ lb. fine yellow corn meal
3 tblsp. butter
1 ⅓ cups Parmesan cheese, grated
2½ cups water
salt and pepper

Stir corn meal into salted, boiling water with a wooden spoon; stir constantly until thick, then simmer 30 minutes. Add remaining ingredients and mix thoroughly; serve hot. Serves 4.

No. II

1 cup fine yellow corn meal
1 qt. boiling water
2 tblsp. butter
2 cups rich hash or left-over fish
¼ cup Parmesan cheese, grated

Sprinkle corn meal into boiling, salted water, stirring constantly to prevent lumping; cook over low heat 30 minutes, adding butter while cooking. Pour corn meal onto platter in the form of a ring; fill center with hot hash or fish, and sprinkle generously with cheese. Serves 6.

No. III

Same as for POLENTA No. 1 recipe
Parmesan cheese, grated
tomato sauce

Cook corn meal as in POLENTA No. I recipe, and pour a thick layer into a buttered baking dish; cover with thick tomato sauce (see recipe on page 234), sprinkle with cheese; repeat process until ingredients are used up and there is a sprinkle of cheese on top. Brown in hot oven (400°F.). Serve with more sauce and cheese. Serves 6.

BAKED POLENTA

(Polenta al Forno)

No. I

Same as for POLENTA No. 1 recipe
Parmesan cheese, grated
Rich brown gravy with bits of chicken or meat

Cook corn meal as in POLENTA No. I recipe; let cook until stiff, and slice with a wet knife. Place a thin layer of Polenta in a buttered baking dish, cover with a layer of gravy and sprinkle with cheese; repeat process until mixture is used up and top is covered with gravy. Bake in a hot oven (400°F.) about 10 minutes. Serves 6.

No. II

½ cup onion, diced fine
1 clove garlic, minced
1 tsp. salt
rosemary, thyme and sage
½ cup canned mushrooms
3 cups tomatoes, cooked or canned
1¼ cups fine yellow corn meal
1 cup cold water
4 cups boiling water
½ lb. Parmesan cheese
¼ cup olive oil

Combine onion, garlic, seasoning and mushrooms with olive oil and cook slowly until onion is yellow; add tomatoes, cover and simmer gently about 1½ hours, or until thickened, stirring occasionally. Cook farina in cold water over direct heat for 5 minutes, stirring occasionally; place in double boiler top and cook until thick. Spread a ½-inch layer of mixture in a shallow baking dish, cover with ½ cup tomato mixture and a layer of cheese; repeat layers until mush and sauce are used, then sprinkle top with cheese. Bake at 325°F. about 30 minutes. Serve with extra sauce and grated cheese, if desired. Serves 6.

FRIED POLENTA

(Polenta Fritta)

1 small onion, chopped
½ clove garlic, minced
3 tblsp. olive oil
½ lb. ground beef
salt and pepper
1 stalk celery, sliced
1 green pepper, chopped
1 qt. boiling water
1 cup fine yellow corn meal
¾ cup flour

Fry onion and garlic in 1 tblsp. olive oil a few minutes; add meat and mash as it fries to prevent lumping. Turn into a saucepan with celery, pepper and boiling water; boil uncovered for 10 minutes, season and add corn meal a little at a time, stirring constantly. Finish cooking over steam, then pour into a mold to cool. Slice, dredge in flour and fry in remaining olive oil. Serves 6.

TOMATO POLENTA

(Polenta con Pomidoro)

1 cup boiling water
1 cup milk
½ cup fine yellow corn meal
⅛ tsp. pepper
2 cups Parmesan cheese, grated
½ tsp. salt
½ cup breadcrumbs, salted
¼ cup olive oil

Bring water and milk to a boil; add salt, stir in corn meal slowly, and cook 30 minutes in double-boiler; add pepper and cheese and pour into a shallow pan to cool. When cold, cut into serving pieces, roll in breadcrumbs, and brown in hot olive oil until golden brown on all sides. Serve with tomato sauce (see recipe on page 234), and cheese. Serves 4.

POTATO DUMPLINGS

(Gnocchi di Patate)

2 ½ cups potatoes, boiled and sieved
salt and pepper
1 cup flour
tomato sauce

Season flour and knead with potatoes; roll dough into strips. Break strips of dough into pieces the size of a dime, roll with thumb over back of a fork, and sprinkle with flour. Boil in salted water about 10 minutes; drain, and place on platter; cover with tomato sauce, sprinkle with Parmesan cheese, and more sauce. Serve with meat balls or Italian sausages. Serves 6.

RAVIOLI

1 ½ cups flour
1 egg, slightly beaten
tomato sauce (see page 234)
⅛ tsp. salt
1 tblsp. cold water
Parmesan cheese, grated

Heap flour on a bread board and form a well in center; drop in egg, salt and water, and work with a fork to a stiff dough; knead. Roll dough out very thin on a lightly floured board, and let rest before cutting in rounds the size of a drinking glass top.

FILLING:

1 cup cooked chicken, veal, turkey or any meat
2 tblsp. Parmesan cheese, grated
1 egg, beaten
1 tsp. parsley, minced
¼ tsp. lemon peel, grated
salt and pepper
1 tblsp. butter

Grind meat and mix thoroughly with remaining ingredients. Place a spoonful of meat mixture on each round of dough, fold in center and press together with a fork. If any filling remains, add to tomato sauce. Boil ravioli in salted water about 10 minutes; place on platter, cover with tomato sauce, sprinkle with cheese and more sauce. Serves 6.

CHICKEN RAVIOLI

(Ravioli di Pollo)

4 cups flour
2 eggs
1 egg yolk
Parmesan cheese, grated
2 tblsp. olive oil
pinch of salt
water
chicken stock

Mix flour, eggs and enough water to make a stiff dough; knead 20 minutes. Pour olive oil over dough and knead until smooth; let stand ½ hour. Roll dough out very thin on a floured board, and cut into rounds about 3 inches in diameter.

FILLING:

1 breast of chicken, boiled and cut up
½ lb. cooked veal, cut up
1 lb. spinach, chopped
garlic and celery salt
½ cup breadcrumbs
3 tblsp. Parmesan cheese, grated
salt and pepper
1 egg

Mix above ingredients together; place a spoonful of the mixture on each round of dough, fold dough in half and press edges together with a fork. Boil ravioli in stock about 20 minutes; remove from stock and place on a hot dish. Thicken a little of the stock with meat gravy, and pour over the ravioli. Serve sprinkled with cheese. Serves 12.

CREAM CHEESE RAVIOLI

(Ravioli con Ricotta)

1 cup parsley, chopped fine
¼ tsp. pepper
5 tblsp. Parmesan cheese, grated
2 cups flour
1 tsp. salt
5 eggs
1½ lbs. fresh Ricotta
meat sauce (see page 230)

Mix flour, ¼ tsp. salt and 2 eggs into a dough; roll thin and cut into rounds with a doughnut cutter. Put Ricotta through a sieve once, add parsley, Parmesan cheese, 3 beaten eggs and seasoning; mix thoroughly, and place a spoonful in the center of a round of dough; top with another round and pinch ends together to seal rounds. Cook ravioli in salted, boiling water about 10 minutes; strain. Serve with a meat sauce and sprinkle generously with Parmesan cheese. Serves 6.

RAVIOLI WITH SPINACH FILLING

(Ripieno di Spinacci per Ravioli)

1 cup spinach, cooked and chopped
1 cup Ricotta
3 tblsp. Parmesan cheese, grated
1 recipe noodle dough (see recipe on page 80)
1 egg, beaten
salt and pepper
1 tblsp. breadcrumbs

Drain and press spinach dry; mix with Ricotta, egg, seasoning, Parmesan cheese and breadcrumbs. Roll out dough thin and cut into 2-inch squares; place a spoonful of spinach filling on each square, top with another square and seal edges together with a fork. Cook ravioli in boiling, salted water about 10 minutes. Serve with butter sauce (recipe on page 243) or tomato sauce (recipes on page 234), generously sprinkled with Parmesan cheese.

NOTE: If spinach is too moist, use more breadcrumbs, but the addition may detract from the excellence of the dish.

RIGATONI

1½ lbs. rigatoni (see table of spaghetti and macaroni)
Parmesan cheese
Meat Sauce Eleanora (page 231)
4 qts. boiling water

Cook rigatoni in boiling, salted water about 20 minutes; drain. Serve on platter covered with Meat Sauce Eleanora, sprinkle with cheese and add more sauce. Serves 6.

RIGATONI WITH SAUSAGE

(Rigatoni con Salsiccia)

1 lb. rigatoni (see table of spaghetti and macaroni)
1 lb. Italian sausage
¼ cup garlic olive oil
1 onion, sliced thin
1 lb. fresh mushrooms, sliced
1 bay leaf
1 6-oz. can tomato paste
3 cups water
salt and pepper
pinch of oregano

Cut sausages in links of three, brown in hot olive oil; add onion, mushrooms, salt and pepper, and simmer 15 minutes; add tomato paste and water, cover and cook slowly about 1 hour. Cook rigatoni in boiling, salted water; drain, and place in a baking dish. Cover rigatoni with sausage sauce, sprinkle with grated cheese; bake in a moderate oven (350°F.) about 10 minutes. Serves 6.

ROMAN SEMOLINA DUMPLINGS

(Gnocchi alla Romana)

¼ lb. semolina
4 tblsp. butter
1⅓ cups Parmesan cheese, grated
2 eggs
1 cup milk
1 tsp. salt

Cook semolina in boiling milk until thick and smooth; add 2 tblsp. butter and 1/3 cup cheese; remove from fire, add eggs and mix thoroughly. Pour mixture to about ½-inch thickness into a dish, and let stand until cold. Cut semolina into small pieces and roll the size and shape of almonds; place in a baking dish with remaining cheese, salt and butter, melted. Bake in a moderate oven (350°F.) about 30 to 35 minutes. Serves 6.

TOPHATS WITH COTTAGE CHEESE

(Cappelletti con Ricotta)

CHEESE FILLING:

1 lb. Ricotta
½ lb. ground beef, browned
1 egg
⅛ tsp. nutmeg
½ tsp. cinnamon
salt and pepper to taste

Mix above ingredients together and set aside.

TOPHATS:

1 cup flour
1 tsp. salt
1 egg
grated cheese
water
2 quarts soup stock

Place flour and salt on bread board, make a well in center, add egg and a few drops of water, mix well, adding more water a few drops at a time as needed. When dough is pliable, roll paper-thin and cut into 2-inch disks. Place a teaspoon of cheese mixture in center of each disk, fold over and seal edges with prongs of fork.

Drop tophats into boiling soup stock about 9 or 10 minutes. Serve hot with grated cheese. Serves 6.

TORTELLINI BOLOGNESE

(Tortellini al Bolognese)

6 strips bacon
½ lb. Mortadella sausage
3 tblsp. beef marrow
ravioli pasta (see recipe on page 86)
2 eggs
2 qts. soup, clear
dash of nutmeg

Grind bacon and sausage together very fine. Cream the beef marrow and mix with meat; work to a paste, add egg and nutmeg and mix well. Roll ravioli dough thin; cut into 1½-inch rounds, and spread rounds with meat mixture; top with another round and seal edges together with a fork. Let filled ravioli stand about 15 minutes before cooking in clear, boiling soup for 8 minutes. Serve at once. Serves 6 to 8.

TORTELLINI WITH CREAM CHEESE

(Tortellini con Ricotta)

1 lb. Ricotta
2 tblsp. parsley, chopped
1 egg yolk
pinch of salt
nutmeg and/or other spices
ravioli pasta (see recipe on page 86)
6 oz. Parmesan cheese, grated
1 egg
butter

Roll ravioli pasta thin and cut into 2-inch disks. Mix remaining ingredients; place a mound on disks, top with another disk and pinch ends together. Cook filled ravioli in salted, boiling water; drain. Place on serving dish, dot with butter and sprinkle with cheese. Serves 6.

BAKED STUFFED TUFALI

(Tufali Ripieni al Forno)

Cook 1 lb. tufali (see table of macaroni, pages 51 to 56) in rapidly boiling, salted water 5 minutes; rinse with cold water and drain.

SAUCE:

5 tblsp. olive oil
½ tsp. salt
1 tsp. parsley, chopped
1 qt. hot water
1 med. onion, diced
1/16 tsp. pepper
1 6-oz. can tomato paste

Sauté onion in hot olive oil until golden brown; add salt, pepper, parsley, tomato paste, and pour in hot water, slowly, stirring until tomato paste is completely dissolved; cover and simmer 20 minutes.

See also Spaghetti Sauce Maria, page 230.

FILLING:

½ lb. beef, chopped
2 tblsp. olive oil
1 oz. Parmesan cheese, grated
1/6 tsp. pepper
½ lb. veal, chopped
1 tblsp. parsley, chopped
½ tsp. salt
2 eggs, beaten

Stuff cooked tufali with above ingredients, thoroughly mixed. Pour half the sauce in a casserole; fill with stuffed tufali and cover with remaining sauce; sprinkle with cheese, cover and bake in a moderate oven (350°F.) about 45 minutes. Serves 6.

VERMICELLI AND ANCHOVIES

(Vermicelii con Acciughe)

Same basic recipe as for macaroni with tomatoes (page 76)
1 tblsp. parsley, chopped
5 or 6 anchovies, mashed
Parmesan cheese, grated

This delicious dish is similar to macaroni with tomatoes, but the vermicelli-type macaroni is used, and the onion is not removed. When making the sauce, add the parsley and anchovies; pour over vermicelli and sprinkle generously with cheese. Serves 6.

CHAPTER SIX

Meats

MEAT ROASTING CHART

Thermometer Readings	
Beef	
Rare	140°
Medium	160°
Well Done	170°
Fresh Pork	185°
Smoked Pork	170°
Lamb	180°
Veal	170°

BEEF	Constant Oven Temperature	Minutes Per Pound		
		Rare	Medium	Well Done
Standing ribs (2 or 3 ribs)	300°	18-20	22-25	27-30
Standing ribs (1 rib)	350°	33	45	50
Rolled ribs	300°	32	38	48
Chuck ribs	300°	—	—	25-30
Rump	300°	—	—	25-30
Whole Tenderloin	300°	25	30	35

PORK — Fresh (Always cook well done)	Constant Oven Temperature	Minutes Per Pound
Loin — Center	350°	35-40
Loin — Whole	350°	15-20
Loin — Ends	350°	50-55
Shoulder — Whole	350°	30-35
Shoulder — Boned and rolled	350°	40-45
Shoulder — Cushion	350°	35-40
Spareribs	350°	40-45
Pork Butt	350°	45-50
Ham	350°	30-35

PORK — Smoked	Constant Oven Temperature	Minutes Per Pound
Ham — Whole	300°	25
Ham — Whole — Tenderized	300°	15
Ham — Half	300°	30
Ham — Half — Tenderized	300°	20
Ham — Shank end	300°	40
Ham — Butt end	300°	45
Cottage butt	300°	35
Picnic	300°	35

LAMB	Constant Oven Temperature	Minutes Per Pound
Leg	300°	30-35
Shoulder — Rolled	300°	40-45
Shoulder	300°	30-35
Cushion	300°	30-35
Rack of Ribs (6-7 ribs)	300°	45-50
Crown (12-15 ribs)	300°	30-35

VEAL	Constant Oven Temperature	Minutes Per Pound
Leg Roast	300°	25
Loin	300°	30-35
Rack (4-6 ribs)	300°	30-35
Shoulder	300°	25
Shoulder — Rolled	300°	40-45

Beef

BEEF BROCHETTE

(Bue allo Spiedo)

1 lb. beef, cut in thin slices about 4" square
3 tblsp. olive oil
1 cup breadcrumbs
⅓ cup Romano cheese, grated
1 tsp. parsley, minced
2 tomatoes, quartered
1 onion, chopped
4 or 5 bay leaves
¼ tsp. pepper

Flatten beef and dip in olive oil. Mix breadcrumbs, cheese, pepper and parsley and spread on one side of each piece of beef, with a covering of onion and pieces of tomato; roll and fix on long skewers with a bay leaf between each piece of rolled meat. Dip the whole in olive oil, then in breadcrumb mixture; place in broiler and, when they start to brown, turn and brown gently until tender. Serves 4.

NOTE: Place a pan containing a cup of water under the broiler to catch drippings, season and use for gravy.

ROAST BEEF GIACOMO

(Arrosto di Bue al Giacomo)

3 to 4 lbs. ribbed sirloin of beef
2 tsp. tart cheese, melted
½ cup dry Vermouth
salt and pepper
6 thin slices Spanish onion
½ cup parsley, chopped
2 tblsp. olive oil

Season beef, and top with 3 slices of onion and 1 tsp. melted cheese; cook in a moderate oven (350°F.), allowing 15 minutes to the pound. Baste every 10 minutes. Turn roast over and top with remaining onion and cheese; cook and baste to degree of rareness desired. Mix parsley, olive oil, dry vermouth and seasoning to taste; pour over roast so as to mix with the gravy. Serves 6 to 8.

HAMBURGER

See PIZZA HAMBURGERS (page 104).

BEEF A LA MODICA

(Carne di Bue alla Modica)

3 lbs. top round beef
1 large carrot, chopped
1 large onion, sliced
1 thick slice bread
¾ cup tomato purée
1 clove garlic
4 stalks celery, chopped
1½ tsp. salt
½ tsp. pepper
2 tblsp. olive oil

Rub meat well with cut clove of garlic. Cook onion slightly in hot olive oil, using dutch oven or any kettle with close-fitting cover, add meat and brown thoroughly on both sides. Add carrot, celery and seasoning; cover tightly, cook slowly about 2½ hours. Tear bread into small pieces and add to meat with tomato purée; cover and cook until meat is quite tender. Serves 6.

BEEF POT ROAST

(Bue Arrosto in Marmitta)

4 lbs. pot roast of beef
1 tsp. salt
1 onion, chopped
3 stalks celery, cut up
6 cloves
2 cups red wine
1 tsp. peppercorns
1 clove garlic
¼ tsp. marjoram
¼ cup olive oil

Lard beef all over and insert cloves; marinate overnight in wine, salt, peppercorns, onion, garlic, celery and marjoram. Dry beef with a clean cloth, rub with flour and sear in hot olive oil; cover with marinating mixture and cook very slowly in a covered saucepan until tender. Serves 8.

BEEF AND RICE BALLS

(Polpette di Riso)

1 lb. beef, ground
1 tblsp. onion, grated
2 tblsp. green pepper, chopped
1 tsp. salt
1 clove garlic, minced
1 tsp. celery salt
½ cup rice, washed, drained
2 cups tomato sauce
4 cloves
½ tsp. cinnamon
2 tblsp. sugar

Combine beef, onion, green pepper, salt, celery salt, garlic and rice; form into balls about 1½ to 2 inches in diameter. Heat tomato sauce (see recipe on page 234), cloves, cinnamon and sugar in a heavy skillet; drop in meat balls, cover tightly, and simmer 50 minutes. Serves 4.

BEEF ROLLS

No. I

(Polpette di Bue)

2 lbs. top round steak, cut into 6 pieces
1 can mushrooms
1 clove garlic, chopped
1 No. 3 can tomatoes, strained
2 or 3 rosemary leaves
salt and pepper
4 tblsp. olive oil
1 onion, chopped
3 tblsp. parsley, chopped
½ lb. Italian ham, chopped
½ cup Parmesan cheese, grated

Pound meat to flatten. Mix ham, cheese, salt and pepper and half the parsley; place some of this mixture on each piece of meat, roll tightly and secure with toothpicks. Brown rolls of meat on all sides in hot olive oil; add rosemary, mushrooms, onions, garlic and remaining parsley and brown; add tomatoes and cook slowly about 2 hours. Serves 6.

NOTE: The sauce may be used with spaghetti.

No. II

(Braccioline Composte)

1 lb. beef, ground
1 cup breadcrumbs
1 egg, beaten
salt and pepper
½ cup milk
½ cup Parmesan cheese, diced
¼ cup olive oil
3 eggs, hard-boiled, sliced
½ cup celery, boiled
4 thick slices salami, diced
1 small onion, sliced

Combine beef, breadcrumbs, beaten egg, salt and pepper with milk; mix and flatten into a large patty. Place sliced eggs, celery, salami, cheese and onion on meat patty, and mold into a roll; fry in hot olive oil, browning well on all sides. Place meat roll in a casserole with a little water; bake in a moderate oven (350°F.) for 1 hour. Serves 4.

NOTE: Sliced carrots, potatoes and onions may be placed around the meat roll and baked with it.

BEEF SCALOPPINE

(Scaloppine di Bue)

1½ lbs. beef, sliced very thin
juice of lemon
salt and pepper
olive oil
oregano
flour

Cut beef into six serving pieces, season, flour lightly and fry in hot olive oil. Serve with its own juice, a little lemon juice and oregano. Serves 6.

BROILED STEAK

(Bistecca Arrosto)

To broil any thick beef steak, such as T-bone, top sirloin. etc., marinate steak in garlic olive oil at least 1 hour. To cook, dip in breadcrumbs mixed with grated cheese, salt, pepper, rosemary and plenty of oregano; broil to your taste. You will discover a superb flavor and have a steak that will "melt in your mouth."

See also page 98.

BEEF STEW

No. I

(Stufato di Bue)

3½ lbs. beef
½ onion, chopped
¼ turnip, cut up
¼ cup carrots, cut up
egg drop dumplings (see recipe that follows)
2 tblsp. olive oil
2 potatoes, cut up
salt, pepper, oregano, rosemary
¼ cup flour

Remove all small pieces of bone from meat, cut meat into small pieces. Place the larger bones and tough pieces of meat into a kettle, cover with cold water and cook. Dredge the rest of the meat with flour, season and brown in hot olive oil with onions. Pour into kettle with bones and simmer 2 or 3 hours until meat is tender. Half an hour before serving, add vegetables; cook 15 minutes, then add plain dumplings and take out the pieces of bone and fat; thicken gravy with flour, if necessary, then pour stew into serving dish and replace dumplings on top. Serves 6.

NOTE: If tomatoes are desired, add ½ cup strained tomatoes.

EGG DROP DUMPLINGS:

1 ¼ cups flour	½ cup milk
3 tsp. baking powder	1 egg, slightly beaten
½ tsp. salt	

Sift flour, mix with baking powder and salt, mix milk and egg and pour all at once over flour mixture. Mix lightly with a fork until ingredients are just dampened, but not smooth. Drop by tablespoons into boiling stew. Cover and let boil for 12 minutes. Make 12 dumplings.

No. II

(Stufato di Bue al Garofani)

2 or 3 lbs. top round of beef	6 cloves
suet	¼ cup olive oil
1 lb. tomatoes, quartered	mixed spices
½ cup red wine	parsley, chopped
3 or 4 cloves garlic	salt and pepper

Brown beef, thickly larded with suet, in hot olive oil; add tomatoes, wine, garlic, parsley, spices, and seasoning; bring to a boil, then simmer gently for 2 hours, or until meat is tender Serves 6.

TOMATO HERB STEW

(Stufato di Legumi con Pomidoro)

2 lbs. stew beef	flour
salt and pepper to taste	½ clove garlic, chopped
½ tsp. oregano	½ tsp. marjoram
1 cup tomato paste	3 cups water
4 carrots, sliced	4 small onions

Dredge meat in seasoned flour, and brown in hot olive oil; add water, tomato paste, herbs and garlic and bring to a boil. Turn into a casserole and bake, covered, about 2 hours in a moderate oven (350°F.). Add carrots, onions, and seasoning if needed, and bake another 25 minutes. If a thicker stew is desired, thicken with a paste of the left-over seasoned flour and a little water. Serves 6.

NOTE: This stew is good served with rice or plain buttered spaghetti.

SWEET-SOUR CHOPPED BEEF

(Polpettini di Bue Agro-dolce)

1 lb. chopped beef
1 onion, grated
1 egg, beaten
salt, pepper and oregano
2 tblsp. cheese, grated
1 tblsp. breadcrumbs
1½ cups hot water
¼ cup raisins
¼ cup sugar
1 lemon, sliced
1 tblsp. olive oil
1 tblsp. potato flour

Combine beef, onion, egg seasoning, cheese and breadcrumbs, mix well and form into small balls. Pour hot water over the raisins, sugar and lemon, add the meat balls, cover and cook slowly for 30 minutes; add olive oil, blend in flour and let simmer a few minutes before serving. Serves 6.

BROILED BEEF TENDERLOIN

(Filetto di Vaccina Arrosto)

3 lbs. beef tenderloin, sliced thick
¾ cup olive oil
1 tblsp. oregano
salt and pepper
juice of 2 lemons

Flatten beef slices a little by pounding, season with salt and pepper and dip in olive oil; broil. To remaining olive oil add lemon with oregano, and baste meat while broiling. Serves 6.

BEEF TONGUE

(Lingua di Bue)

3 lbs. beef tongue
6 button onions
salt and pepper to taste
2 cups mixed vegetables
3 small tomatoes
flour

Boil tongue for about 2 hours, then skin. Mix vegetables, onions and tomatoes with seasoning, and spread on bottom of roaster; place tongue over vegetables with some of the water in which tongue was boiled, cover and cook slowly for 2 hours or until tongue is tender. Remove tongue and vegetables to a hot platter. Brown the flour and stir into gravy to thicken; pour a little over the tongue, and place the remainder in a gravyboat. Serves 6.

NOTE: The liquid remaining from boiling the tongue is an excellent base for soup stock.

BEEF IN WINE

(Bue con Vino)

3 lbs. pot roast of beef
salt and pepper
¼ cup olive oil
4 cloves
flour
1 cup white wine

Insert cloves in roast, season with salt and pepper, roll in flour, and brown in hot olive oil. Place in a roaster, cover with wine; cook slowly, covered tightly, until tender, about 3 hours in a moderate oven (325°F.). Serve with boiled rice. Serves 6 to 8.

MARROW BONES

(Osso Bucco)

8 3-inch marrow bones
5 tblsp. olive oil
1 small onion, minced
1 small carrot, grated
parsley
salt and pepper to taste
1 cup tomatoes, strained
1 tsp. sugar
½ tblsp. flour
crostini (croutons)

Select bones of young beef, not too thick or too heavy. Cook bones with onions, carrots and seasoning in hot olive oil, covered, basting and turning frequently. When bones and onions begin to color, add tomato, sugar and flour with remaining olive oil; cook until marrow is heated through. Remove bones and lay on a hot dish; skim fat from sauce and strain over bones. Serve with a plate of crostini on which marrow is to be spread individually. Garnish bones with parsley. Serves 4.

MEAT BALLS

No. I

(Polpettoni di Bue)

1 lb. beef, ground
6 slices salami, cut into strips
2 eggs, scrambled
½ cup white wine
¼ cup olive oil
2 cups tomato sauce
salt, pepper, oregano seed
3 slices Mozzarella cheese, cut into strips
flour

Spread beef on a lightly floured board to about ½-inch thickness; place strips of salami and cheese over the meat, then the eggs and seasonings. Roll meat into a loaf, brush lightly with olive oil and flour; brown in hot olive oil on all sides, then simmer, covered for about 30 minutes. Add wine and cook until wine has evaporated; add tomato sauce (see recipe in Chapter XII) and cook about 30 minutes, or until done. Cool and slice. Serve hot or cold with sauce as a garnish, if desired. Serves 4.

No. II

(Polpette)

2 lbs. beef, ground
1 egg
⅓ cup Parmesan cheese
½ cup breadcrumbs
½ tsp. pepper
1 tsp. oregano
2 drops garlic oil
1 onion, chopped fine
2 tsp. salt

Mix the ingredients together and form into balls; brown in hot olive oil. Serves 6.

No. III

½ lb. round steak, chopped
2 tblsp. parsley, chopped
1 egg, beaten
salt and pepper
tomato sauce
¼ cup breadcrumbs
⅛ cup milk
3 tblsp. Parmesan cheese, grated
oregano and marjoram

Mix all ingredients, except tomato sauce, thoroughly; shape into tiny meat balls. Brown meat balls in hot olive oil, and add to tomato sauce (see recipe in Chapter XII); simmer 30 minutes. Serves 4.

MEAT BALLS WITH HAM

(Polpettine con Prosciutto)

1 lb. beef and pork, ground
1 onion, chopped
2 tblsp. Parmesan cheese, grated
1 cup breadcrumbs
3 slices salami, chopped
1 egg, beaten
1 cup olive oil
4 tblsp. milk
salt and pepper

Heat part of the olive oil and sauté onions until light brown. Combine meat, onions, egg, cheese, breadcrumbs, milk, salami, salt and pepper; mix thoroughly and form into balls about 2 inches in diameter. Heat remaining olive oil and fry meat balls, browning on all sides. Serves 4.

NOTE: Can be served plain or with tomato sauce (see recipe in Chapter XII).

SWEET SOUR MEAT BALLS

(Polpette all'Agro-Dolce)

1 lb. beef, ground
salt and pepper
1 cup bread, cubed
½ cup milk
1 egg
2 tblsp. olive oil

Mix ingredients, shape into balls and fry in hot olive oil until brown all over.

Make a sauce of:

2 onions, chopped
1 cup water
½ cup vinegar
2 tblsp. sugar
1 cup peas
salt and pepper

Brown onion in olive oil remaining from frying meat, add water, vinegar, peas and sugar with salt and pepper to taste and mix well. Add meat balls and simmer 1 hour. Serves 4.

MEAT LOAF

(Formato di Carne)

No. I

4 tblsp. olive oil
2 medium onions, chopped
2 tblsp. Parmesan cheese, grated
1 cup breadcrumbs
1 cup green beans, cut fine
1 egg, beaten
1 tblsp. salt
⅛ tsp. pepper
1½ lbs. beef, chopped
½ tsp. oregano

Brown onions in hot olive oil; add green beans, cover and cook for 10 minutes. Add remaining ingredients, mix well, then turn into a small baking pan and bake in a moderate oven (350°F.) for 30 to 40 minutes. Serves 6.

No. II

½ lb. veal, ground
1 lb. beef, ground
1 tsp. salt
1 or 2 eggs, well beaten

small piece of suet, ground
¼ loaf bread, soaked in water
¼ cup almonds, sliced thin
1 tsp. oregano
onion or celery salt
½ cup canned tomatoes
bacon
1 tblsp. olive oil

Squeeze bread dry and combine with meat, suet, egg, almonds, tomato and seasoning; mix thoroughly and form into a loaf. Lay strips of bacon over top of meat loaf in a roasting pan, add olive oil; bake in a moderate oven (350°F.) about 1 hour, basting frequently. Add water only if necessary. Serves 6.

MEAT LOAF PIETRO

(Formato di Carne alla Pietro)

1 lb. round steak, ground
salt and pepper
3 strips bacon
2 cups stuffing (see recipe on page 250)
1 pork chop, ground
1 small onion, minced
milk
tomato sauce

Season meat with salt, pepper and onion, adding as much milk as meat will absorb. Alternate layers of meat and stuffing in a baking dish until ingredients are used up, ending with a top layer of meat; place strips of bacon over meat, cover with tomato sauce (see recipe in Chapter XII), and bake in a moderate oven (350°F.) for 1 hour. Serves 6.

NOTE: If desired, meat can be rolled to ½-inch thickness, stuffing placed in center, and meat rolled as in a jelly roll.

STUFFED MEAT LOAF

(Formato di Carne Ripieno)

¾ lb. beef, ground
1 large potato, grated
1 tsp. salt
1 small onion, sliced thin
salt and pepper
¼ tsp. pepper
2 tblsp. tomato juice
½ green pepper, sliced thin
1 cup whole tomatoes, canned

Combine meat, potato, seasoning and tomato juice. Spread half the meat mixture in a greased loaf baking dish, covering the bottom and sides. Add layers of pepper, onion and tomatoes; season with salt and pepper, cover with remaining meat mixture; bake in a moderate oven (350°F.) for 1 hour. Serves 4.

MEAT ROLL

(Involto di Carne)

1½ lbs. round steak, cut ½" thick
½ lb. sliced ham
suet
¼ lb. veal and pork, ground
6 eggs, hard-boiled
salt and pepper
¼ cup olive oil
tomato sauce

Cover steak with strips of suet and slices of ham; spread well seasoned veal and pork over prosciutto, then arrange whole eggs in the center and roll steak around them, tying with string to keep together. Brown steak roll in hot olive oil on all sides, and place in simmering tomato sauce; cook slowly until tender. To serve, remove string and slice. Serve hot or cold. Serves 6.

INDIVIDUAL MEAT ROLLS

(Involtini di Carne)

¾ lb. beef, ground
¼ lb. pork, ground
1½ cups breadcrumbs
¼ tsp. pepper
½ tsp. oregano
1 tblsp. wine
2 tblsp. olive oil
2 tblsp. green pepper, minced
½ cup onion, minced
1¼ tsp. salt
1 8-oz. can tomato sauce
½ cup water
3 tblsp. cheese, grated

Combine breadcrumbs, olive oil, ½ tsp. salt, ⅛ tsp. pepper, oregano, cheese and wine. Mix meat, green pepper, onion, remaining salt and pepper; divide into 4 portions. Flatten each portion on wax paper to ¼-inch thickness, place ¼ of the breadcrumb mixture in center of each portion of meat, fold meat in half and press edges together. Place meat rolls in a shallow pan, pour diluted tomato sauce over them and bake in a moderately hot oven (375°F.) for 45 minutes. Serves 4.

MEAT ROLL WITH TOMATO

(Involto di Carne con Pomidoro)

1 can large plum tomatoes
2 lbs. round steak
½ cup Parmesan cheese, grated
1 clove garlic, minced
2 tblsp. tomato paste
¼ cup olive oil
2 tblsp. parsley, minced
1 onion, minced

salt and pepper
salami cut into strips
wine vinegar
1 cup water

Cut steak into individual servings, and on each piece spread a teaspoonful of cheese, a dash each of garlic, parsley, salt and pepper, and a few strips of salami. Roll and tie with heavy thread; place rolls in a saucepan containing olive oil, onion and water; cook slowly until brown, then add vinegar and cook 2 minutes. Combine tomato paste with tomatoes, cook and strain; add to meat rolls and cook 30 minutes. This sauce over 1 lb. cooked spaghetti will serve 4.

MOCK CHICKEN LEGS

(Gambe di Pollo)

1 lb. beaf steak, cut ⅜" thick
1 lb. veal (or pork), cut ⅜" thick
2 tsp. salt
½ tsp. white pepper
½ tsp. dry sweet basil
¼ cup olive oil
¾ cup cracker crumbs mixed with ¼ cup cheese, grated
½ tsp. oregano
6 or 8 wooden skewers

Cut veal and well-pounded steak into 1- or 1½-inch squares. On each skewer, arrange 6 pieces of meat, alternating the beef and veal with smaller pieces top and bottom to represent a drumstick; roll in olive oil and crumbs, season with salt, basil, pepper and oregano, and brown on all sides in left-over olive oil. When well browned, cover pan tightly and cook slowly for 1½ hours, or until meat is tender. Add more water, if necessary. Serves 6 or 8.

NOTE: If a milk gravy is desired, brown a sliced onion in hot olive oil with flour, add milk gradually to make a smooth paste, slightly thickened; pour over meat in casserole, cover and bake.

PIZZA HAMBURGERS

(Pizza alla "Hamburghese")

1 lb. beef, ground
½ tsp. pepper
½ cup Scamozza cheese, cut into strips
½ tsp. basil
1 ½ tsp. salt
1 cup tomatoes, drained
2 tblsp. parsley, minced
2 tblsp. onion, chopped

Season beef with salt and pepper, and flatten; spread with tomatoes and sprinkle with remaining ingredients. Bake in a moderate oven (350°F.) for 20 minutes. To serve, cut in wedges. Serves 6.

Kid

ROAST KID

(Capretto Arrosto)

The Italian, who likes his veal as young as he can get it, particularly enjoys tender kid. The cavorting kid is as juicily gelatinous as suckling pig, while veal is often tough and hard to digest. The Italian chef overcomes this toughness by flaying the veal for about 15 minutes before he dips it into egg and breadcrumbs to fry. In Naples, on the dot of 11:30 in the morning and for about 15 minutes, the city resounds with the pounding of veal cutlets (scallopini), resembling trick drummers practicing intricate beats and trying out their traps.

If you have a mind to try Roast Kid as the Italians prefer it, try the following:

1 young kid
salt and pepper
3 cloves garlic, crushed
2 onions, minced
2 bay leaves
2 sprigs Italian thyme
1 blade mace
1 clove
1 cup olive oil
1 cup white wine
1 cup Marsala wine
1 lb. dates, stoned
thin slices of salt pork
¼ cup flour

Mix the seasonings, onions and garlic with olive oil and white wine. Rub mixture over inside and outside of a well cleaned kid, then set the whole in a crock for a day, turning kid occasionally. Drain and dry the kid, and strain the marinating liquid. Chop the dates and pour warmed marsala wine over them and let stand about 30 minutes until wine is absorbed. Stuff the kid with dates, sew up; cut ligaments at the joints, fold legs close to the body and tie securely. Lay strips of salt pork over breast and back and wrap with twine. Place kid in an oiled paper bag, lay in roasting pan and bake for 1 hour, turning every 15 minutes. Remove paper, add heated marinating liquid and bake until tender, basting often. Remove pork and twine the last 15 minutes of baking. To make gravy, remove kid and add flour gradually, while stirring. If a more delicate flavor is desired, discard marinating liquid and finish last basting with ½ cup melted butter.

Lamb

BROILED KIDNEYS

(Rognoni Arrosto)

4 lamb kidneys
1 tsp. oregano
2 tblsp. olive oil
parsley, chopped
toast
¼ lb. bacon
juice of 1 lemon
salt, paprika
melted butter
skewers

Wash and split kidneys lengthwise; remove skins, white tubes and fat. Slice in thin strips and soak in salted water for 1 hour; drain and dry, then rub with lemon juice and brush with olive oil. Arrange alternate layers of kidney and bacon on skewers and broil on both sides for 6 minutes. Serve on toast with melted butter to which a little salt, lemon juice and paprika have been added; garnish with parsley. Serves 6.

ROLLED BREAST OF LAMB

(Petto di Agnello Involto)

4 lbs. breast of lamb, boned
4 tblsp. olive oil
few rosemary leaves
1 lb. bulk Italian sausage
salt and pepper
½ cup water

Spread lamb with sausage and seasonings; roll and tie into shape. Brown meat in hot olive oil on all sides; add water, cover tightly, and bake in a moderate oven (350°F.) until tender, approximately 2 to 2½ hours. Serves 6.

LAMB CHOPS IN CHEESE JACKETS

(Cotolette di Agnello con Formaggio)

4 thin lamb chops
¼ cup grated cheese
½ tsp. oregano
8 slices Scammoza cheese

1 egg beaten
salt and pepper to taste
¾ cup breadcrumbs
4 tblsp. tomato sauce
5 tblsp. olive oil

Sprinkle chops with salt and pepper. Dip in crumbs mixed with cheese and oregano, then in beaten egg, then in crumb mixture again. Heat oil and brown chops. On a cookie sheet place the slices of cheese, then the chops, spreading each chop with a tablespoon of tomato sauce, then cover the chops with another slice of cheese. Place in a preheated 350° oven until cheese melts and runs over sides. Lift out with a pancake turner and serve at once. Serves 4.

LAMB CUTLETS MILANESE

(Cotolette di Agnello alla Milanese)

4 lamb cutlets
½ cup breadcrumbs, sifted
salt and pepper
½ cup cheese, grated
1 egg, well beaten
¼ cup olive oil

Trim fat from cutlets; season and dip alternately in egg, mixture of breadcrumbs and cheese, and again in egg. Sprinkle with olive oil and grill until tender. Serves 4.

ROAST LEG OF LAMB

(Coscia di Agnello Arrosto)

5 lb. leg of lamb, boned
2 tblsp. olive oil
½ tsp. red pepper
¼ cup mint jelly
1 tsp. rosemary, crushed
1 tsp. basil
1 clove garlic, minced
salt

Mix pepper, rosemary, basil, and garlic with olive oil; rub leg of lamb all over with the mixture and sprinkle with salt. Let penetrate about 2 hours before baking. Bake in a slow oven (325°F.) for 2½ hours. About 20 minutes before lamb is done, top with mint jelly; baste thoroughly with the sauce during remaining cooking period. Serves 8.

LEG OF LAMB WITH WINE

(Coscia di Agnello con Vino)

2 or 3 cloves garlic
salt and pepper
1 tsp. capers
1 leg of lamb
rosemary
1 cup white wine

Insert 2 or 3 slices of garlic between meat and bone at each end; sprinkle with salt, pepper, rosemary and capers. Place lamb fat side up in a roasting pan and roast in a slow oven (250°F.) allowing 40 minutes per pound. Baste frequently with white wine and drippings.

LAMB WITH PEAS

(Agnello con Piselli)

2 cloves garlic
8 sprigs rosemary or mint
3 lb. leg of lamb
⅛ lb. salt pork, chopped
3 cups green peas, cooked
1 tblsp. olive oil
salt and pepper
2 tblsp. butter
3 tblsp. tomato paste
heated meat broth

Cut garlic into tiny slivers; remove leaves from rosemary, and cut stems into short lengths. Make small cuts all over lamb and insert slivers of garlic and stems of rosemary protruding for easy removal later. Heat salt pork with olive oil in casserole slowly; add seasoned leg of lamb and cook until meat is slightly colored all over; add butter and tomato paste with a little broth, cover and simmer in a moderate oven (350°F.) about 2½ hours, or until tender. Turn lamb to prevent scorching, and add more broth as needed. When meat is tender, add peas and heat; remove rosemary. To serve, place lamb on a hot platter surrounded with peas, and covered with strained sauce. Sprinkle sparingly with finely minced mint. Serves 6.

LAMB STEW

(Stufato di Agnello)

2 lbs. lamb shoulder, lean
2 cloves garlic
4 tblsp. olive oil
3 cups water
2 onions, sliced
flour, salt and pepper
1½ cups white wine
2 cups mixed vegetables (carrots, potatoes, celery, lima beans or peas)

Cut lamb into 2-inch cubes and marinate with onions, garlic and wine about 3 hours; discard garlic. Remove meat, roll in seasoned flour and brown in hot olive oil; add water, onions, and wine used for marinating; cover and simmer until tender, approximately 1½ hours. Add vegetables, season to taste, and cook until vegetables are tender. Serves 6.

LAMB STEW WITH BROCCOLI

(Stufato di Agnello con Broccoli)

2 tblsp. pastina
4 tblsp. cooked lamb, chopped fine
salt to taste
2 cups lamb broth
½ cup broccoli, cooked and diced

Cook pastina in hot lamb broth until tender; stir in lamb, broccoli and seasoning; heat thoroughly. Serves 4.

Liver

CALVES LIVER WITH PARMESAN

(Fegatini di Vitello alla Parmigiana)

1 lb. calves' liver
salt and pepper to taste
1 tsp. parsley, minced
2 tblsp. green onions, minced
2 tblsp. olive oil
4 tblsp. cheese, grated
2 tblsp. breadcrumbs
½ clove garlic

Remove skin and veins from liver; sprinkle with mixture of onion, garlic, parsley, and seasoning, and brown quickly on both sides in hot olive oil, taking care not to overcook. Place liver in an ovenproof dish sprinkled with breadcrumbs and cheese mixed, dot with olive oil, and broil until breadcrumbs are brown. Serves 4.

FRIED LIVER

(Frittura di Fegato)

1½ lbs. liver
1 large onion, sliced
¼ cup olive oil
½ cup flour
salt, pepper and oregano
3 tblsp. parsley, chopped

Have liver sliced thin, dredge with flour that has been seasoned with the salt, pepper and oregano. Fry in olive oil, remove to warm serving plate, brown onions and pour over liver, sprinkle with chopped parsley. Serves 6.

LIVER LOAF

(Formato di Fegato)

½ cup pastina
1 pt. boiling water
2 tblsp. olive oil
1 tsp. salt
2 eggs, beaten
1½ lbs. beef liver, in one piece
½ cup onion, diced
2 tblsp. flour
1 cup milk
parsley

Cook pastina 8 minutes; drain. Wipe liver with damp cloth and remove skin, place in saucepan with boiling water; simmer covered for 45 minutes or until tender. Remove veins and grind liver in a food chopper. Sauté onions in olive oil, stir in flour and salt, add milk gradually, stirring constantly; bring to a boil and cook until thickened, then cool to lukewarm. Stir eggs into sauce, and combine with pastina and liver, mixing well. Place liver in a greased loaf pan, and bake until firm. Serve sprinkled with parsley. Serves 6 to 8.

NOTE: Liver loaf can be served with a white sauce (see page 247) or tomato sauce (see page 234).

Pork

PIG'S HEAD

(Testa di Maiale)

1 pig's head
1 cup Marsala wine
2 bay leaves
¼ tsp. oregano
1 cup carrots, onions, celery diced
6 peppercorns

I'll grant you this does not sound very interesting, but it is a tasty dish and considered quite a delicacy by the Italians.

Just get a pig's head and boil it in salted water with carrots, onions, celery, mixed herbs and peppercorns. When quite tender, remove the head from the stock and bone it. Mix a little vinegar with about a cup of Marsala wine and mixed spices and add to the stock. Place boned pig's head in a deep bowl and cover with the stock; set in a cool place until stock has set into a firm jelly. Serve the jellied stock as a cold consomme and the pig's head, sliced, as a meat course.

BARBECUED PORK CHOPS

(Braciole di Maiale all'Americana)

6 pork chops
1 cup onion, diced
1 cup tomatoes, drained and chopped
¾ cup celery, diced
½ tblsp. dry mustard
1 tsp. salt
⅓ cup olive oil
2 tblsp. brown sugar
¾ cup green pepper, diced
1 cup catsup
2 cups meat stock
½ tsp. marjoram

Brown onion in 2 tblsp. hot olive oil; add all ingredients except pork chops and remaining olive oil; cook slowly for 1 hour or until liquid has reduced to about 2 cups. Heat remaining olive oil and brown chops well on both sides; add barbecue sauce, cover and cook until chops are tender. Serves 6.

PORK CHOPS GIACOMO

(Braciole di Maiale alla Giacomo)

6 pork chops
1 tsp. salt
1 small green pepper, chopped
1 cup corn, creamed
2 cups breadcrumbs
1 egg, beaten
1 small onion, chopped
2 tblsp. olive oil

Brown chops in hot olive oil; arrange in a covered baking dish. Mix remaining ingredients and sprinkle over chops, adding a little milk or water if mixture seems too thick. Bake chops in a moderate oven (350°F.) about 1½ hours. Serves 6.

PORK CHOPS MILANESE

(Braciole di Maiale alla Milanese)

6 loin pork chops
salt and pepper
½ cup olive oil
½ cup breadcrumbs, sifted
½ clove garlic, minced
1 tblsp. green onion, minced
2 cups tomato sauce, heated
½ cup cheese, grated

Trim chops, season and dip in olive oil, and then in breadcrumb and cheese mixture. Brown onion and garlic lightly in olive oil, add chops and brown on both sides. Place chops in a baking dish, cover and bake for 15 minutes in a moderate oven (350°F.). Add tomato sauce (see recipe in Chapter XII) and continue baking until very tender. Serves 6.

NOTE: Chops baked in this manner are a grand accompaniment to macaroni with additional tomato sauce.

TIPSY PORK

(Maiale Ubriacato)

4 lbs. loin of pork
salt and pepper
¼ cup olive oil
1½ cups red Chianti wine
2 tblsp. parsley, chopped
2 cloves garlic, minced

Season pork with salt and pepper, and brown in hot olive oil with garlic and parsley; add wine and simmer until meat is well done. To serve, place meat on a hot platter and cover with wine sauce (see page 249). Serves 6.

PORK LIVER WITH FENNEL SEED

(Fegato di Maiale con Fiori di Finocchio)

1½ lbs. pork liver
salt and pepper
butter
fennel seed
bread

Cut liver into 2-inch squares, season and roll in fennel seed, covering liver completely. String liver squares on skewers and roast in oven until tender. Melt butter in a skillet and brown slices of bread; serve with liver. Serves 6.

SAUSAGE CASSEROLE

(Salsiccia al Forno)

1 lb. Italian sausage
¼ cup green pepper, chopped
1 or 1¼ cups condensed tomato soup
½ cup water
¼ cup onion, chopped
1 lb. elbow macaroni, cooked

Cook sausage with water in covered frying pan until tender, approximately 20 minutes; remove sausage and cook green pepper and onion for 5 minutes, then add the condensed tomato soup and heat through. Combine sauce with spaghetti and mix well; place in casserole with sausage arranged on top. Bake in a moderate oven (350°F.) for approximately 30 minutes. Serves 4

SPARERIBS

(Costole)

3 lbs. spareribs
½ green pepper, chopped
1 large can mushrooms, sliced
½ tsp. salt
3 tblsp. olive oil
1 onion, chopped
1 can tomatoes
¼ tsp. pepper
½ tsp. chili pepper

Brown onion, green pepper, mushrooms in hot olive oil; add tomatoes and seasonings; simmer 5 minutes. Pour over spareribs and bake in a moderate oven (350°F.) about 1½ hours, basting frequently. Serves 6.

STUFFED BARBECUED SPARERIBS

(Costole all'Americana Ripiene)

2 or 3 lbs. spareribs
salt and pepper to taste
3 cups breadcrumbs, soft
3 tblsp. onion, finely chopped
1 tsp. green pepper, chopped
1 egg, beaten
3 tblsp. olive oil
3 tblsp. celery, finely chopped

Place two sides of uncooked spareribs together forming a pocket; season inside and out with salt and pepper. Combine remaining ingredients and stuff pocket.

BARBECUE SAUCE:

½ cup onion, finely chopped
3 tblsp. vinegar
¼ cup lemon juice
1 cup water
3 tblsp. olive oil
3 tblsp. brown sugar
1 cup catsup

Combine above ingredients and simmer for 15 minutes. Dot stuffing with 1 or 2 tablespoons of sauce, then place ribs on a rack in a shallow pan and cover with remaining sauce. Bake in a moderate oven (350°F.) for about 2 hours. Serves 6.

See also page 236.

SWEET-SOUR SPARERIBS

(Costole di Maiale all'Agro-dolce)

2 lbs. spareribs, cut in 2-inch lengths
1 tblsp. olive oil
¾ cup green pepper, diced
1 cup pineapple juice
1 tblsp. soy sauce

2 tblsp. brown sugar
2 tblsp. cornstarch
½ tsp. salt
¼ cup vinegar
¼ cup cold water
1 bouillon cube
¼ cup boiling water
¼ cup onions, diced
¾ cup pineapple, diced
¾ cup carrots, diced

Separate ribs, cover with boiling salted water and simmer, covered, for 1 hour; drain. Brown ribs slowly in hot olive oil. Combine sugar, cornstarch, salt; stir in vinegar, cold water, pineapple juice, soy sauce and bouillon cube dissolved in boiling water. Add this mixture to ribs and cook until sauce is transparent; add onion, pineapple, carrots and green pepper, and cook until vegetables are tender but crisp. Serves 4.

NOTE: Try this dish with fried noodles.
See also Veal Birds, page 117.

Tripe

BAKED TRIPE

(Trippa al Forno)

1 onion, chopped fine
3 lbs. tripe
1 green pepper, chopped
1 lb. mushrooms, chopped
¼ cup olive oil
salt and pepper
1 can tomato paste
3 stalks celery, chopped
Parmesan cheese, grated
3 cups water

Wash tripe several times in cold water, cut into 2-inch strips, and cook in salted water about 2 hours. Fry onion, pepper and celery in hot olive oil until brown; add mushrooms, tomato paste and water with seasoning; simmer 1 hour. When tripe is tender, drain. Place alternate layers of tripe, sauce and cheese in a casserole until ingredients are used up; cover, and bake in a moderate oven (350°F.) about 30 minutes. Serves 6.

TRIPE WITH MUSHROOMS

(Trippa con Funghi)

3 lbs. tripe
1 lb. fresh mushrooms
1 green pepper, sliced
plain tomato sauce (see recipe on page 234)
salt and pepper
Parmesan cheese, grated

Cut tripe into 2-inch strips; cook in salted, boiling water about 2 hours. To the plain tomato sauce add mushrooms, green pepper and seasoning if needed; simmer 1 hour. Drain tripe and combine with sauce; heat and arrange on serving platter. Serve covered with sauce and sprinkled with cheese. Serves 6.

TRIPE WITH OYSTERS

(Trippa con Ostriche)

1 lb. tripe, cooked and diced
2 cups white wine sauce
¼ cup parsley, minced
1 pt. stewing oysters
1 small onion, grated
salt and paprika

Combine above ingredients; bring to a boil and cook 5 minutes; season to taste. Serves 6. (See recipe on page 249 for white wine sauce.)

TRIPE PATTIES

(Focaccia di Trippa)

3 tblsp. olive oil
1 egg
1 tsp. onion, chopped
dash of pepper
1 lb. tripe, ground
½ cup breadcrumbs
1 tsp. salt
3 tblsp. Parmesan cheese, grated

Combine all ingredients; shape into patties and fry in hot olive oil until browned. Serves 4.

STEWED TRIPE

(Trippa Stufata)

1 lb. tripe
1 pt. water
1 tblsp. flour
¼ tsp. salt
¼ tsp. sugar
¼ tsp. prepared mustard

Wash tripe carefully, and cut into 1-inch squares. Place in saucepan with salt, sugar, mustard and sufficient water to cover; boil, then simmer 2 hours, skimming carefully. Be sure tripe does not stick to bottom of pan. Mix flour with a little cold water, and stir into tripe; simmer 30 minutes. Use additional seasoning, if necessary. Serves 6.

NOTE: If vegetables are used, add them for the last 30 minutes of cooking.

TRIPE STEW WITH ONIONS

(Stufato di Trippa)

2 lbs. tripe
4 onions
salt and pepper
1 cup hot milk
3 tblsp. olive oil

Cover tripe and onions with warm water; simmer about 2 hours. Remove onions, chop fine and add to hot milk with seasoning and olive oil; pour over tripe and serve at once. Serves 6.

STEWED TRIPE WITH TOMATO SAUCE

(Trippa con Salsa Pomidoro)

2 lbs. tripe
1 tblsp. butter
salt and pepper
2 onions, halved
2 tblsp. flour
2 cups tomatoes, chopped

Cover tripe with warm water, add onion; simmer about 1 hour, covered. Cook tomatoes, strain through sieve; add with seasoning to melted butter and flour; cook until thick. Drain tripe and cut into strips; add to tomato sauce and heat through. Serves 6.

See also page 234.

Veal

VEAL CASSEROLE

(Vitello Spincione)

8 slices veal cutlet
½ cup celery, diced
1 No. 2 can tomatoes
1 tsp. sugar
¼ cup olive oil
2 cups breadcrumbs
¼ cup parsley, chopped
salt and pepper to taste
¼ cup Romano cheese, grated

Dip meat in the breadcrumbs and place in casserole containing the olive oil; cover with celery, parsley, seasonings, cheese and remaining breadcrumbs; add tomatoes and bake in a moderate oven (350°F.) for 45 minutes. Serves 4.

VEAL ANCHOVY

(Vitello all'Acciughe)

1 lb. veal, cut very thin
¼ lb. butter
4 slices Italian ham
1 egg
¼ cup olive oil
6 anchovy
1 tblsp. parsley, minced
2 tblsp. cheese, grated
2 tblsp. flour

Mash anchovy and blend with butter and parsley. Spread veal with anchovy butter and slices of ham, sprinkle with cheese and cover with another slice of veal; dip into egg and flour and brown in hot olive oil until tender. Serve hot. Serves 4.

VEAL BIRDS

(Vitello all'Uccelletto)

No. I

2 slices veal steak, ½" thick
½ lb. Italian bulk sausage
3 tblsp. cheese, grated
salt, pepper and oregano
2 slices salt pork, chopped
1 ½ cups breadcrumbs
1 small onion, minced
¼ cup olive oil

Cut veal steak into individual servings. Brown sausage and salt pork in hot olive oil; add breadcrumbs, cheese and seasonings. Place a spoonful of sausage mixture on each piece of meat, roll and tie with string. Brown meat rolls in hot olive oil, add ½ cup water and simmer about 1 hour. Serves 6.

No. II

2 lbs. veal steak, ½" thick
1 cup breadcrumbs
1 tsp. mint leaves
salt and pepper to taste
2 onions, sliced thick
1 cup water
3 eggs, beaten
3 tblsp. cheese, grated
pinch of allspice
4 eggs, hard-boiled
4 strips of bacon, cut in small pieces

Cut veal into 3-inch squares. Combine breadcrumbs, salt, pepper, cheese, allspice and mint leaves; dip meat in eggs, then in breadcrumb mixture. Place a slice of hard-boiled egg on each piece of meat with a piece of bacon; roll like a jelly-roll and hold together with toothpicks. Alternate rolls of the meat with onion on skewers; brown in hot olive oil, then place in roaster with 1 cup water, cover. Bake for 1 hour in a moderate oven (350°F.). Serves 6.

STUFFED BREAST OF VEAL

(Petto di Vitello Ripieno)

3 lbs. breast of veal
2 cups breadcrumbs
½ cup parsley, chopped
salt and pepper
4 tblsp. garlic olive oil
4 tblsp. cheese, grated
1 small onion, chopped
3 eggs, slightly beaten
rosemary

Have a pocket made in the breast of veal. Mix together cheese, breadcrumbs, onion, celery, seasoning and eggs; pack in veal pocket and sew edges together. Brush meat with garlic oil and rosemary and place in a roasting pan; bake in a moderate oven (350°F.), allowing 30 minutes to a pound. Baste frequently with garlic oil. Serves 6.

VEAL WITH CARROTS

(Vitello con Carote)

¾ lb. veal cutlet, cut ¼" thick
½ tsp. salt
½ tsp. oregano
1 clove garlic
½ cup white wine
2 tblsp. flour
⅛ tsp. pepper
2 tblsp. olive oil
3 carrots, halved

Season flour with salt, pepper and oregano. Cut meat into 2-inch squares; roll in flour and brown in hot olive oil with garlic. Discard garlic, add carrots and wine; cover and simmer about 30 minutes. Serve meat and vegetables on a hot platter covered with gravy. Serves 2.

VEAL CHOPS WITH MUSHROOMS

(Braciole di Vitello con Funghi)

4 veal chops
4 carrots, sliced
1 cup mushrooms, sliced
2 tomatoes, peeled and chopped
salt and pepper
3 tblsp. olive oil
1 onion, chopped
⅓ cup white wine

Season chops with salt and pepper, and sear in hot olive oil until brown; add tomatoes, carrots, onion and wine; cover, and simmer about 1 hour. Add mushrooms that have been sautéed in hot olive oil a few minutes. Serves 4.

VEAL CHOPS IN WINE

(Braciole di Vitello con Vino)

4 thick veal chops with kidney
salt and pepper to taste
3 tblsp. flour
4 tblsp. olive oil
1 cup fresh mushrooms, sliced
1 onion, sliced
1 cup white wine

Season chops, roll in flour, and brown lightly in hot olive oil; remove to a casserole. Brown onion in remaining olive oil, add mushrooms, and cook 5 minutes, then add to the chops. Heat wine in the same pan with olive oil, and pour over chops. Bake in a moderate oven (350°F.) for 45 minutes. Serves 4.

VEAL CUTLETS

(Cotolette di Vitello con Salsiccia)

No. I

1 lb. veal cutlet, cut thin
3 Italian sausages
3 tblsp. green pepper, chopped
salt and pepper
2 cups tomato sauce
3 tblsp. parsley, minced
2 tblsp. cheese, grated
¼ cup olive oil

Cut meat into serving sizes, rub with garlic and sprinkle with salt and pepper. Remove skin from sausages and mix meat with parsley, cheese, green pepper; place a mound of this on each piece of meat, roll and fasten with toothpicks. Brown meat rolls in hot olive oil, add tomato sauce (see recipe in Chapter XII), and cook for about an hour or until tender. Serves 4.

No. II

2 lbs. veal cutlet
5 tblsp. olive oil
3 tblsp. tomato paste
½ cup wine
2 onions, chopped
1 clove garlic, chopped
1 cup tomato pulp
1 tsp. salt
½ tsp. pepper
1 cup mushrooms, sliced
butter

Brown cutlet on both sides in 3 tblsp. hot olive oil; add tomato paste with wine and simmer. Sauté onions and garlic in 2 tblsp. olive oil; add tomato pulp, salt and pepper, heat through, and pour over simmering cutlet; cover, and simmer about 1½ hours. Just before serving, add mushrooms that have been sautéd in butter a few minutes. Serves 6.

No. III

6 slices veal, cut ½" thick
1 or 2 eggs, beaten
¼ cup olive oil
cheese, grated
salt and pepper
breadcrumbs
mint leaves, chopped

Season veal and dip in a mixture of breadcrumbs, cheese and mint leaves; let stand 15 minutes. Dip in egg and again in breadcrumb mixture and let stand 15 minutes. Fry on both sides in hot olive oil until well browned, cover and cook slowly about 30 minutes. Serves 6.

CUTLETS MILANESE

(Cotolette di Vitello alla Milanese)

1 lb. veal cutlets
2 eggs, slightly beaten
½ cup flour
1 cup breadcrumbs
4 tblsp. parsley, minced
2 cloves garlic, minced
½ cup olive oil
1 lemon, sliced
salt and pepper

Season cutlets with salt and pepper; dredge in flour and dip into eggs, then into breadcrumbs mixed with garlic and parsley. Fry cutlets in hot olive oil over a medium fire until a golden color, and tender. Serve with lemon slices. Serves 4.

POUNDED VEAL CUTLETS

(Cotolette di Vitello Pestate)

1½ lbs. veal cutlets
¼ cup olive oil
salt and pepper
¾ cup breadcrumbs
5 tblsp. Parmesan cheese, grated
flour

Pound veal quite thin and cut into 2 x 4-inch pieces; brush one side of each piece with olive oil, sprinkle with a mixture of breadcrumbs, cheese, salt and pepper, then roll and tie with string. Place meat rolls in a shallow pan, sprinkle with olive oil and flour, and bake in a hot oven (400°F.) for 30 minutes or until brown. Serves 6.

VEAL AND HAM

(Cotolette di Vitello al Prosciutto)

1 lb. veal, sliced thin
1 lb. ham, cut ½-inch thick
salt, pepper and basil
1 lb. Scamozza cheese, sliced
¼ cup olive oil
2 eggs, beaten
1 cup breadcrumbs

Cut meat into 3-inch squares; place a slice of ham on a slice of veal and hold together with toothpicks. Dip meat squares in egg, then in seasoned breadcrumbs, and brown in hot olive oil with ham side down. Remove from skillet and place a slice of cheese on each square; broil until cheese melts. Serve with lemon, a meat gravy, or tomato sauce. Serves 6.

VEAL AND HAM WITH WINE

(Prosciutto e Vitello con Vino)

2 lbs. veal and ham, ground
1 green pepper, minced
pepper to taste
⅓ cup Marsala wine
1 onion, grated
2 tsp. salt
1 egg, beaten

Mix the meat with onion, green pepper, salt and pepper to taste; add the egg and wine and shape into a loaf. Bake in a hot oven (400°F.) for 45 minutes. Serves 6.

VEAL KIDNEY WITH PARMESAN

(Arnione di Vitello alla Parmigiana)

1 veal kidney, cut in ½" slices
¼ cup white wine
salt and pepper
½ bay leaf
1 small sprig thyme
1 sprig parsley
3 tblsp. olive oil
¼ cup Parmesan cheese, grated
½ tsp. sugar
⅛ tsp. cinnamon

Combine meat with wine, seasonings, herbs and 1 tblsp. olive oil; toss and cook for 8 minutes or until most of liquid has been absorbed. Remove to baking dish and cover with a mixture of cheese, sugar and cinnamon; sprinkle with remaining olive oil and brown under broiler. Serves 4.

VEAL KIDNEYS WITH MUSHROOMS

(Rognoni di Vitello con Funghi)

2 veal kidneys, cubed
2 tblsp. olive oil
½ lb. mushrooms, sliced and parboiled
salt and pepper to taste
1 small onion, chopped
1 cup water
1 tblsp. flour

Sear the cubed kidneys in a hot, dry skillet for about 10 minutes, turning them when browned. In a separate pan, sauté the mushrooms in hot olive oil; add kidneys, onions, seasoning, and water; cover and simmer about 45 minutes or until tender. Mix flour with cold water into a thick paste, and add to meat; cook until thickened, stirring constantly. Serves 4.

VEAL KNUCKLE STEW

(Garretto di Vitello Stufato)

2 or 3 lbs. knuckle of veal
3 or 4 carrots, chopped fine
1 or 2 stalks celery, chopped
1 cup tomato pulp
½ cup white wine
flour
2 tblsp. olive oil
veal stock or water
strip of lemon peel, chopped fine
sprig of thyme
parsley, chopped
1 bay leaf
salt and pepper

Have knuckle of veal sawed (not chopped, as marrow must remain inside bone) into 2-inch lengths. Combine vegetables, meat and seasoning with olive oil and cook until meat and vegetables are well browned; add a paste of about 1 tblsp. of flour and about 1 tblsp. olive oil, stir and cook until flour begins to brown. Add tomato pulp, wine, and sufficient stock or water to barely cover the meat, add herbs and simmer very gently for 1 to 1½ hours. Ten minutes before serving, remove meat and strain sauce; combine and serve hot, garnished with lemon peel and parsley. Serves 6.

VEAL WITH OLIVES

(Vitello con Olive)

6 thin slices veal, cut from lean fillet
12 anchovies
12 green olives

12 capers
1 egg, beaten
2 tblsp. olive oil
wedges of lemon
flour
salt and pepper
parsley

Make a paste of anchovies and capers pounded together; spread on veal slices and roll; secure with toothpicks. Fry in hot olive oil until tender; season. Mix flour, egg, and seasoning to a thick batter; dip each olive in the batter before frying in hot olive oil until a golden color. Serve veal rolls with fried olives and wedges of lemon, garnished with sprigs of parsley. Serves 6.

VEAL PARMESAN

(Vitello alla Parmigiana)

2 lbs. veal cutlets, cut ½-inch thick
½ tsp. pepper
5 tblsp. Parmesan cheese, grated
2 tsp. salt
1 tsp. oregano
¼ cup olive oil

Remove white fibres from veal cutlets, divide into serving sizes, and flatten to about ⅛-inch thickness by pounding with back of knife. Season with salt, pepper and oregano; coat evenly with cheese and brown in hot olive oil about 3 minutes on each side. Serves 6.

VEAL PATTIES

(Focaccia di Vitello)

2 cups veal, cooked
¼ cup white wine
1 tsp. salt
1 egg, beaten
¼ tsp. celery salt
1 cup breadcrumbs
3 tblsp. Parmesan cheese, grated
1 tsp. onion, chopped
¼ tsp. pepper
¼ cup olive oil

Chop meat very fine, add seasoning, cheese, breadcrumbs and egg; mix well and form into small patties. Place patties in a shallow baking pan, cover with olive oil, and bake in a moderate (350°F.) oven about 30 minutes, or until a delicate brown. Serve with tomato sauce (see page 234). Serves 6.

ROAST VEAL

(Vitello Arrosto)

No. I

roast of veal
salt and pepper
salt pork

Season veal with salt and pepper; place on a rack in an open pan, cover with strips of salt pork to prevent drying; bake in a slow oven (about 300°F.) until tender. Allow 30 minutes to the pound, and do not add water.

No. II

2 lbs. veal
garlic, slivered
salt, pepper, flour
2 tblsp. olive oil

Dredge veal with seasoned flour; insert pieces of garlic in little pockets made in veal. Brown veal in hot olive oil in a hot oven (500°F.) until brown all over, baste with oil; cover and reduce heat to 300°F. and cook until tender, basting frequently. Add water, if necessary. Serves 4.

TIPSY VEAL ROAST

(Arrosto di Vitello Ubriacato)

6 lbs. rump roast of veal
8 large onions, sliced thin
3 tblsp. flour
¼ tsp. rosemary
1 cup white wine
3 tblsp. olive oil
suet
salt and pepper
1 cup boiling water

Heat olive oil in an iron pot and brown roast; remove roast and brown onions lightly. Make a paste of flour and water, add to olive oil and brown; add boiling water and stir to a smooth sauce, add wine and meat, cover tightly and roast in a moderate oven (350°F.) for 2½ hours. Add more wine as needed to replace evaporated liquid. Stir frequently to prevent sticking. Serves 8.

NOTE: If the onions are cut very thin, they will vanish in the sauce, and you will have a brown wine sauce to smack your lips over.

VEAL ROLLS

No. I

(Braccioline di Vitello Composte)

2 slices veal
2 eggs, hard-boiled, sliced
2 cloves garlic
2 slices salami, cut into strips
1 can mushroom caps
5 tblsp. olive oil
4 cups water
salt and pepper
¼ cup cheese, grated
few sprigs parsley
2 bay leaves
butter
1 small can tomato paste

Salt the veal slices, dot with butter and spread with slices of hard-boiled egg, salami; sprinkle with parsley and cheese. Roll slices very tight and wrap thread around them; brown in hot olive oil with garlic, then remove garlic. Add tomato paste, water and bay leaf and bring to a boil; simmer for 1 hour then add mushroom caps and cook until meat is tender. Add more water if sauce becomes too thick. When meat is done, remove thread and slice. Serve hot or cold. Serves 4.

No. II

(Involto di Vitello)

3 lbs. veal steak, boned
3 anchovies
1 onion, sliced
1 carrot
2 bay leaves
4 strips suet
1 qt. water, salted
2 stalks celery
2 sprigs parsley
4 whole cloves

Place suet and anchovies on steak; roll, and tie to retain shape. Mix remaining ingredients in saucepan; add meat-roll and bring to a boil; simmer 1½ hours and drain. Cool and cut into thin slices.

SAUCE:

1 small can tuna, shredded
3 tblsp. olive oil
1 tsp. capers
3 anchovy fillets
juice of 2 lemons

Heat olive oil and add remaining ingredients; add the slices of veal and heat through. Remove veal slices to a hot platter, cover with the sauce, sprinkle with chopped parsley and serve. Serves 6.

NOTE: Sauce prepared 2 days in advance is preferable.

VEAL SCALOPPINE

(Scaloppine di Vitello)

2 lbs. veal steak, cut thin
olive oil
1½ cups white wine
flour
1 cup mushrooms
salt and pepper

Flour meat lightly and brown in hot olive oil; cover with wine, add seasoning and simmer over low fire. Sauté mushrooms in olive oil and add to meat; cover and simmer slowly about 20 minutes. Serves 6.

BAKED VEAL SCALOPPINE

(Scaloppine di Vitello Arrosto)

1 lb. veal steak, sliced thin
3 tomatoes, sliced thick
½ cup wine
¼ cup olive oil
1 clove garlic
1 cup mushrooms
½ cup cheese, grated
salt and pepper

Cut meat into four pieces and brown with garlic in hot olive oil; add tomatoes, mushrooms, and stir in cheese and wine mixed. Bake in a hot oven (400°F.) for 25 minutes or until mixture is bubbling hot and cheese tinged with brown. Serves 4.

SCALOPPINE IN GRAVY

(Scaloppine al Sugo)

1 lb. veal steak, sliced thin
2 tblsp. olive oil
½ cup veal or beef gravy
¼ cup white wine or Marsala
salt and pepper
⅛ tsp. nutmeg
1 tblsp. lemon juice

Cut veal into 3-inch squares and pound each piece well with flat side of cleaver. Brown veal slowly on both sides, add heated gravy and simmer for 5 minutes; add wine, salt, pepper and nutmeg, cover closely and simmer until very tender. To serve, sprinkle with lemon juice. Serves 4.

NOTE: The gravy from the above recipe may be used with spaghetti or tagliatini.

VEAL SCALOPPINE WITH MARSALA

(Scaloppine di Vitello al Marsala)

1 ½ lbs. veal cutlets, cut 2 ½" thick
½ cup Parmesan cheese, grated
1 cup mushrooms, sliced
1 tsp. beef extract
5 tblsp. Marsala wine
cayenne
1 cup breadcrumbs
salt, oregano, pepper
2 tblsp. olive oil
2 tblsp. hot water
olive oil

Mix breadcrumbs, cheese, and seasonings. Dip cutlets in olive oil, then in breadcrumbs, and brown in hot olive oil. In a separate pan, cook mushrooms in 2 tblsp. hot olive oil seasoned with salt and cayenne; add beaf extract, water and wine, and cook about 1 minute more. Arrange cutlets on a platter and cover with mushroom sauce. Serve with fresh green peas or other vegetable. Serves 6.

SCALOPPINE WITH MUSHROOMS

(Scaloppine con Funghi)

Use recipe for Scaloppine in Gravy. While veal is browning, add 6 mushrooms, sliced. (Italians prefer dried mushrooms soaked overnight.) The nutmeg may be omitted. Serves 4.

SCALOPPINE WITH VEGETABLES

(Scaloppine con Verdura)

1 lb. veal steak, sliced thin
2 tblsp. olive oil
½ cup celery, chopped
1 cup lima beans
2 green peppers, sliced
3 cups tomatoes, quartered
1 cup peas
1 cup carrots, chopped
2 or 3 onions, chopped

Cut veal into 3-inch squares and pound well. Brown veal slowly on both sides in hot olive oil, add vegetables and seasoning; simmer until very tender. Serves 4.

SCALOPPINE WITH ZUCCHINI

(Scaloppine con Zucchini)

Partly sauté zucchini and add to recipe for Scaloppine in Gravy 5 minutes before scaloppine is done. Serves 4.

SKILLET VEAL SLICES

(Fette di Vitello in Padella)

- ¾ lb. veal shoulder, sliced ¼" thick
- ¼ cup flour
- 1 tsp. salt
- ⅛ tsp. pepper
- ¼ tsp. celery salt
- 1 tblsp. cold water
- ⅔ cup dry breadcrumbs
- ¼ cup olive oil
- 1 ¼ cups hot water
- 1 tsp. lemon juice
- 1 egg, slightly beaten

Mix flour with seasoning and coat veal slices well; dip in egg combined with cold water, then dip in breadcrumbs. Sauté a few slices at a time in hot olive oil until golden-brown on both sides. Arrange all slices in skillet, add hot water and lemon juice, cover and simmer 30 minutes or until tender. Remove meat to hot platter. Thicken gravy to desired consistency with left-over flour mixed to a smooth paste with equal amount of water. Pour gravy over veal slices and serve. Serves 4.

POTTED VEAL STEAK

(Vitello Invasato)

- 3 lbs. veal steak, cut 1 ½" thick
- 3 tblsp. olive oil
- salt, pepper, and paprika
- milk
- flour
- ginger
- mustard

Score steaks with large knife; pound in flour, ginger, mustard, salt, pepper, and paprika. Place in hot olive oil and brown all over; cover with milk and cook slowly for about an hour, covered tightly. Serve hot. Serves 6.

POTTED VEAL STEAK WITH VEGETABLES

(Vitello Invasato con Legume)

- 3 lbs. veal steak, cut thick
- 3 tblsp. olive oil
- 3 stalks celery, cut up
- salt, pepper and paprika
- mustard
- milk
- 3 onions, cut up
- 3 carrots, cut up
- 1 cup fresh lima beans
- flour
- ginger

Mix flour, ginger, mustard, salt, pepper, and paprika; and pound into well scored steaks, then brown in hot olive oil.

Place vegetables in oiled casserole, with meat on top, and cover with milk. Bake in a moderate oven until tender (350°F.), approximately 1 hour. Serves 6.

YOUNG VEAL STEW

(Stufato di Vitellino)

1½ to 2 lbs. leg of young veal
1 cup tomato pulp
6 tblsp. white wine
2 or 3 cloves garlic
2 sprigs rosemary
4 tblsp. olive oil
salt and pepper to taste

Slice meat into 2-inch chunks. Brown garlic slightly in hot olive oil; add meat with seasoning, and brown slightly, then add tomato pulp, wine and rosemary, bring to a boil and simmer for 1½ hours or until meat is very tender. Serves 4.

STUFFED VEAL

(Vitello Ripieno)

3 tblsp. olive oil
1 lb. veal steak
¼ lb. prosciutto, sliced
juice and peel of ½ lemon
fresh tomato sauce
salt and pepper
3 or 4 fresh sage leaves

The veal must be cut very thin. On each slice of veal squeeze a little lemon juice, place a slice of prosciutto the same size as meat and 1 sage leaf on each slice. Roll and tie with thread. Roll in flour and brown in olive oil. Then finish cooking in well seasoned tomato sauce about 20 minutes. Remove string before serving. Serves 4.

VEAL TARRAGON

(Vitello alla Tarragonese)

4 veal cutlets
2 tblsp. olive oil
2 tblsp. butter
flour
½ cup white wine
2 tblsp. tarragon leaves
salt and pepper
parsley or watercress

Pound veal cutlets to paper thinness with a mallet; season and dust with flour. Sauté in hot olive oil and butter until a golden brown; spread with tarragon leaves and wine, cover and simmer about 20 minutes. Serve garnished with parsley or watercress. Serves 4.

VEAL WITH TUNA FISH AND ANCHOVIES

(Vitello con Tonno ed Acciughe)

2 lbs. filet of young veal
4 large anchovies in brine
1 6-oz. can tuna fish in oil
1 onion
2 carrots, sliced
1 stalk celery, chopped
1 bay leaf
2 cloves
juice of 1 large lemon
2 tblsp. capers
1 tblsp. salt
⅛ tsp. pepper
2 tblsp. olive oil

Remove all fat and gristle from meat. Split anchovies in half and remove bones; cut into strips, lay strips of anchovies on filet of veal, roll and tie with string. Push cloves into a whole peeled onion and place in saucepan with carrots, celery, bay leaf and salt, together with sufficient water to cover veal; bring to a boil and reduce heat. Simmer for 1½ hours. Remove meat, drain liquid and reserve. Carve meat into thin slices and place in casserole.

Bone remaining anchovies and mix thoroughly with tuna fish; add olive oil gradually, lemon juice and capers; add to meat liquid. Marinate for 1 hour; then pour over meat, then heat through in moderate oven (325°) about 30 minutes. Garnish with lemon slices. Serves 6.

See also Veal Rolls No. II, page 125.

MIXED GRILL

(Tritato Misto)

4 slices calf's liver
4 slices sweetbreads
4 slices calf's brains
4 slices kid's kidneys
4 lamb chops
salt and pepper
⅔ cup milk
4 artichoke hearts, cooked
4 slices yellow cheese
4 slices eggplant, blanched
4 flowerettes cauliflower, cooked
4 slices zucchini
1 cup flour
2 eggs, beaten
deep olive oil for frying

Cook sweetbread and brain in cold water for 1 hour; blanch, skin and remove large veins. Skin kidney. Make a batter of the flour, milk, eggs and seasoning; dip remaining items separately in the batter and fry in deep hot olive oil; drain on absorbent paper. Arrange all together on a large hot platter. Serves 6.

CHAPTER SEVEN

Poultry and Game

CAPON WITH PINENUTS

(Cappone con Pignoli)

1 capon
salt and pepper
vinegar
1 clove garlic, crushed
1 tsp. parsley, minced
2 cloves, crushed
1 tblsp. green onion, minced
½ lb. ham, chopped
½ lb. lamb, chopped
3 eggs, hard-boiled
1 egg, raw
1 pt. pinenuts (roasted 5 min.)

Salt and pepper capon inside and out, and wrap in a cloth dipped in vinegar. Mix garlic, parsley, cloves and onion; spread mixture over cloth covering capon, and let stand during day, removing cloth just before baking. Make a stuffing of chopped capon liver, ham, lamb, hard-boiled and raw eggs, mix well and stuff bird. Wrap bird in two thicknesses of oiled paper and bake 5 minutes in a hot oven (400°F.), then reduce heat to moderate (325°F.) and bake until tender. Remove top layer of paper when it begins to scorch. To serve, garnish capon with pinenuts. Make a gravy of the pan contents, if desired. Serves 6.

Pinenuts can be roasted on cookie sheet in oven a few minutes. Roasting develops the flavor of these mild nuts.

BOILED CHICKEN

(Pollo Lesso)

1 5-6 lb. chicken
3 or 4 stalks celery
1 tsp. salt
2 small onions

Cover chicken with boiling water, add salt, celery and onions; simmer gently until tender, approximately 2½ hours. Serves 6 to 8. Use soup stock, with rice, or egg pastina.

NOTE: Rice or noodles may be added, if desired, to make a wonderful soup. If chicken is to be used in making Chicken Supreme (see recipe on page 139), let chicken cool in broth, discard skin and bones, and cut meat of chicken into 1-inch pieces.

CREAMY CHICKEN BALLS

(Polpette di Pollo in Crema)

4 tblsp. flour
1 tblsp. salt
⅛ tsp. pepper
1 tsp. Worcestershire sauce
breadcrumbs
1 cup milk
1 tblsp. olive oil
2 eggs, beaten
2 cups cooked chicken, chopped

Combine dry ingredients with milk; add olive oil and cook until thick and creamy, stirring occasionally. Stir in chicken, and cool; mold into balls, roll in breadcrumbs, dip in eggs, and roll in breadcrumbs again. Fry in hot olive oil until a golden brown. Serves 4.

DEVILED CHICKEN

(Pollo al Diavolo)

1 young chicken (2-3 lbs.)
salt and pepper
1 small onion, chopped
3 tblsp. olive oil
½ tsp. ginger
2 tblsp. parsley, chopped

Crush chicken to flatten; skewer for grilling, brush well with olive oil, season highly with salt, pepper and ginger, sprinkle with chopped onion and parsley; grill over a clear charcoal or wood fire. Serve very hot. Serves 4.

CHICKEN FRANCESCA

(Pollo alla Francesca)

4 broiling chickens, split to serve ½ chicken to each person
1 cup brandy
2 large cans mushrooms
1 tsp. curry powder
1 pint heavy cream
1 onion
salt and pepper
butter

Gently sauté chicken in plenty of butter to which has been added a finely sliced onion. When chicken is a delicate, even brown, place in a self-basting roasting pan and dot with butter, cover with cream and mushroom caps; replace top of pan and allow to steam in a slow oven (300° to 350°) for 1 hour, basting every 15 minutes. About 15 minutes before chicken is done, add brandy and baste well with the sauce. Remove chicken to a serving platter. Add curry powder to the cream sauce and blend in well; season and pour sauce over the chicken. Serves 8.

NOTE: This dish is delicious served on a bed of wild rice, equally as good when warmed over the next day. If larger chickens are used, have them quartered.

FRIED SPRING CHICKEN

(Pollo Fritto)

1 young fryer, disjointed
¼ cup flour
2 tblsp. lemon juice
¼ cup olive oil
butter
¾ tsp. salt
¼ tsp. pepper
1 bay leaf, dried and rubbed to powder
grated cheese

Roll pieces of chicken in flour and lay in a bowl. Mix lemon juice with olive oil, salt, pepper, and bay leaf, and pour over chicken; let stand 1 hour then drain off liquid. Roll chicken in cheese and fry in butter until a golden brown and tender. Serves 2.

FRIED CHICKEN HOME STYLE

(Pollo Fritto alla Casalinga)

1 frying chicken
1 cup flour
salt and pepper
1 cup olive oil
3 cups milk

Cut chicken into serving pieces, wash and drain. Mix flour, salt, and pepper in a paper sack with pieces of chicken and shake bag in order to coat all parts of the chicken with flour. Heat olive oil in a heavy skillet and brown chicken on all sides slowly until tender; remove chicken and drain on brown paper. Remove ⅓ cup olive oil from skillet and add ¼ cup of the flour used to coat chicken, blending well. Add milk slowly, stirring constantly with a wooden spoon. Place chicken on a serving platter, pour the gravy over it and serve. Serves 5.

HUNTER STYLE CHICKEN

(Pollo alla Cacciatore)

No. I

1 3-lb. chicken
1 cup onion, minced
½ cup olive oil
2 green peppers, chopped

2 cloves garlic, minced
3 cups tomatoes, fresh or canned
½ tsp. salt
½ tsp. oregano
dash sharp pepper (optional)
1 6-oz. can tomato paste
½ cup wine
½ tsp. allspice
3 bay leaves
salt to taste

In large saucepan, heat oil and cook chicken until evenly browned. Add onions, green peppers and garlic; brown lightly, add rest of ingredients and simmer 40 minutes or until chicken is tender. Serves 6.

No. II

1 fryer
4 small onions
¼ cup olive oil
½ cup flour
1 tblsp. parsley, chopped
salt and pepper
1 clove garlic, chopped
2 cups tomatoes
1 cup mushroom caps
1 green pepper, sliced
1 carrot, sliced
½ cup sherry

Clean and cut chicken into serving pieces; brown in hot olive oil, then add vegetables, salt and pepper to taste, and simmer about 15 minutes. Add sherry and tomatoes, cover and simmer until chicken is tender. If liquid evaporates, add a little water. Serves 4.

CHICKEN MILANESE

(Pollo alla Milanese)

1 cup chicken, cooked and diced fine
1 cup tongue, cooked and diced fine
½ cup truffles, minced
½ cup macaroni, cooked
salt and pepper to taste
3 tblsp. cheese, grated
thick cream sauce
2 eggs, well beaten
1 tblsp. olive oil
breadcrumbs, sifted
sprigs of parsley
deep oil for frying

Mix meats, truffles, macaroni, salt, pepper and cheese with enough cream sauce to hold all together. Form into croquettes, dip in egg and olive oil covering completely, then dip in crumbs. Fry in hot olive oil; drain on brown paper. Drop sprigs of parsley in hot fat and fry until crisp. Serve croquettes with fried parsley in cream sauce. Serves 4.

CHICKEN WITH MUSHROOMS

(Pollo con Funghi)

No. I

1 3-lb. chicken
1 onion, sliced
salt and pepper
¼ cup olive oil
1 lb. fresh mushrooms

Cut chicken into serving pieces, sprinkle with salt and pepper. Brown onion in hot olive oil; add chicken and brown on both sides to a golden brown; cover, and cook gently until tender, approximately 45 minutes. Cook mushrooms in salted, boiling water about 5 minutes; drain, and add to chicken, cook about 15 minutes. Serve hot. Serves 4.

No. II

1 cold roast chicken
1 cup carrots, sliced
6 mushrooms, sliced
1 tblsp. flour
large croutons
1 cup onions, sliced
1 cup white wine
½ cup olive oil
salt and pepper

Brown vegetables and flour in hot olive oil; season, add wine and simmer 15 minutes; add chicken and heat through. Serve on a hot platter covered with the wine sauce, and garnished with croutons. Serves 4.

No. III

3 cups chicken, diced
½ cup Italian sausage
1 large onion
1 cup celery, chopped
4 tblsp. olive oil
1 green pepper, chopped
3½ cups tomatoes, chopped
2 tsp. chili powder
3 cups spaghetti, broken
1 cup Parmesan cheese, grated
1 cup mushrooms, sliced
season to taste

Fry onion in hot olive oil with sausage, celery, green pepper, mushrooms, and chicken a few minutes; add tomatoes, chili powder, and salt and pepper to taste; cover, and simmer about 30 minutes. Cook spaghetti in salted, boiling water until almost done; drain. Spread a layer of spaghetti in a buttered casserole, with a layer of chicken mixture, and cover; bake in a slow oven (300°F.) about 1½ hours. Serve sprinkled with cheese. Serves 8.

CHICKEN WITH OLIVES

(Pollo con Olive)

1 young chicken, disjointed
1 onion, chopped
1 small tomato, chopped
15 large olives
3 tblsp. tomato paste
3 tblsp. butter
3 tblsp. olive oil
1 carrot, minced
broth of chicken
salt and pepper

Slowly brown chicken, onion, and carrot in hot olive oil with butter; add tomato and continue cooking for 15 minutes. Cover with broth. Cut up 4 olives, combine with pounded pulp of 4 others and the remaining whole olives; add to chicken with seasoning, but use salt sparingly as the olives are salted. Cook slowly until chicken is tender, add tomato paste, and cook 10 minutes. Thicken gravy, if desired. Serves 4.

CHICKEN PIETRO

(Pollo alla Pietro)

2 young fryers
2 tblsp. butter
3 tblsp. olive oil
salt and pepper
⅛ tsp. nutmeg
2 tblsp. flour
½ cup white wine
1½ cups meat broth, heated
1 tomato, chopped
juice of 1 lemon

Cut each chicken into 6 pieces; fry slowly in heated butter and olive oil until lightly browned. Sprinkle with seasoning, nutmeg, and flour; continue frying until a golden brown. Add wine and broth, cover tightly and simmer, turning occasionally, until tender. Add tomato and simmer 5 minutes, then add lemon juice and serve. Serves 4.

CHICKEN WITH POLENTA

(Pollo con Polenta)

1 4-lb. stewing chicken, cut up
1 cup onion, minced
1 clove garlic, minced
½ cup parsley, minced
1 6-oz. can tomato paste
1 No. 2 can tomatoes
½ cup olive oil
¼ tsp. rosemary
¼ tsp. oregano
salt and pepper to taste
2½ quarts water
1 tblsp. salt
3 cups yellow corn meal

In large saucepan heat olive oil. Sprinkle chicken with salt and pepper and arrange in saucepan and brown evenly on all sides, removing pieces as they brown. In remaining oil cook to a golden brown the onion and garlic. Add the chicken and remainder of ingredients except the corn meal. Cover and simmer 3 hours. Sauce should be thin, add hot water if necessary.

One hour before chicken is done prepare polenta. Bring salted water to a rapid boil, gradually add corn meal, stirring constantly to prevent lumps, cook 10 minutes; place over pan of hot water, cover and cook 30 minutes. Turn out onto large platter, pour chicken over all. Serve with grated cheese. Serves 8.

CHICKEN AND RICE CASSEROLE

(Pollo con Riso in Casseruola)

- 1 cup rice, steamed
- 2 cups chicken, cooked
- ½ tsp. salt
- ¼ tsp. celery salt
- 1 egg, beaten
- ⅛ tsp. pepper
- 1 tsp. onion, chopped
- 2 tblsp. breadcrumbs
- 1 tsp. cheese, grated
- 1 cup hot water or stock

Chop chicken very fine, add seasoning, egg, breadcrumbs, and water enough to moisten. Line bottom and sides of a greased mold ½-inch thick with rice, pack in the meat and then the remaining rice. Cover with wax paper and steam 45 minutes. To serve, loosen around the edge of the mold and turn out upon a hot platter. Pour tomato sauce (see recipe on page 234) over it and garnish with parsley. Serves 4.

ROAST STUFFED CHICKEN

(Pollo Ripieno Arrosto)

- ½ cup breadcrumbs
- 3 slices salami, cut in strips
- ¼ tsp. marjoram
- 1 stalk celery, chopped
- ¼ cup cheese, grated
- 1 cup potatoes, boiled and mashed
- 1 tblsp. parsley, chopped
- salt and pepper to taste

Mix above ingredients well, adding a very little water to hold stuffing together.

- 1 chicken
- 4 tblsp. water
- 3 tblsp. olive oil

Clean, salt, and rub chicken inside and out with butter, then insert stuffing. Heat olive oil in roasting pan and brown chicken on both sides; add water, cover and roast for 1 hour, basting occasionally. Serves 4.

CHICKEN SALVATORE

(Pollo alla Salvatore)

- 4-lb. chicken
- garlic salt
- 1 cup celery, diced
- 1 small onion, minced
- ¼ cup red wine
- salt and pepper
- ½ cup olive oil
- 1 cup carrots, diced
- 1 cup thin cream

Cut chicken into serving pieces, sprinkle with salt, pepper, and garlic salt, and brown in hot olive oil, turning frequently. Arrange pieces of chicken in a casserole. Place vegetables in skillet used to fry chicken, and cook a few minutes, then pour over the chicken in casserole. Add wine, and cream; cover, and bake in a moderate oven (350°F.) for about 45 minutes. Serves 6.

CHICKEN SAUTE

(Pollo alla Griglia)

- 2 or 3 very young chickens, disjointed
- 2 or 3 onions, chopped
- 1 cup stock
- salt and pepper
- ½ cup white wine
- ½ pt. shelled peas
- 1 cup rice
- olive oil

Brown chicken in hot olive oil with chopped onions, salt and pepper; add stock, wine, rice, and peas, and stew gently until the rice and peas are quite tender. Serves 6.

CHICKEN STEW

(Stufato di Pollo)

No. I

- 1 4-lb. chicken
- 1 onion, sliced
- ¼ cup chicken fat
- 1 can tomatoes
- ½ cup carrots, diced
- ¼ cup celery, sliced
- 1 green pepper, sliced
- 1 can mushroom buttons
- 1 can peas, drained
- seasoning to taste

Clean and cut chicken into serving pieces; season with salt, pepper and paprika. Brown onion in hot chicken fat; add chicken and brown lightly on both sides; cover and simmer gently 1 hour. Add tomatoes, carrots, celery, and green pepper; cover and cook until tender; add mushrooms and peas, and heat through. Season to taste, and serve. Serves 6.

No. II

- 1 chicken, disjointed
- salt and pepper
- 1 or 2 egg yolks
- 3 or 4 onions, chopped fine
- 1 tsp. lemon juice
- olive oil

Brown onions in hot olive oil; add chicken, salt and pepper; cover, and cook very slowly for 1½ hours. Before serving, stir egg yolks and lemon juice into sauce. Serves 4.

CHICKEN SUPREME

(Pollo Supremo)

- 6 cups chicken, cooked
- 6 cups rice, cooked
- 4 tblsp. butter
- 1 tblsp. salt
- 1 cup almonds, blanched and sliced
- 1 cup cornflakes, crushed
- 4 cups chicken broth
- 3 cups milk
- ¾ cup flour
- ⅛ tsp. pepper
- 2 cups mushrooms, sliced
- 2 pimentos, cut fine

Pour 1 cup chicken broth over cooked rice. Make a rich gravy by adding milk to remaining broth, thicken with melted butter and blend in flour with salt and pepper. Fry almonds, mushrooms and pimento in a little olive oil until brown. Cover the bottom of a buttered casserole with rice, then a layer of chicken and a generous amount of gravy, and dot with almond, pimento, mushroom mixture. Repeat layer of rice, chicken, gravy and almond mixture, then sprinkle buttered cornflakes over top, and paprika. Bake in a moderate (350°F.) oven for 45 minutes. Serves 12 to 16.

NOTE: This dish can be prepared the day before and re heated. See recipe on page 131 for boiled chicken with broth.

CHICKEN TETRAZZINI

(Pollo alla Tetrazzini)

- diced
- 1 cup chicken, cooked and
- ½ tsp. pepper
- 1 cup macaroni shells, cooked

½ tsp. celery salt
½ cup mushroom caps
1 tblsp. flour
½ tsp. salt
3 tblsp. olive oil
1 cup milk
⅓ cup Parmesan cheese, grated

Sauté mushrooms in hot olive oil until light brown, add flour, stir until smooth, and add seasonings and milk; cook until thickened, stirring constantly, and remove from heat. Blend half the sauce with chicken and remaining half with macaroni shells. Bank shells around edge of baking dish, pour chicken mixture into center, sprinkle with cheese; brown under broiler. Serve garnished with parsley. Serves 4.

See also Turkey Tetrazzini.

THRICE-COOKED CHICKEN

(Pollo tre volte Cucinato)

2 fat broilers
salt and pepper
milk, heated
½ cup flour
½ cup olive oil
2 cups boiled rice

Rub chicken with salt and pepper, dredge with flour and brown in hot olive oil until a light brown; lay in roasting pan which contains about 1-inch of milk. Cover and bake in a hot oven (400°F.) for 10 minutes; turn off heat, leave in oven until milk is absorbed. Uncover and brown in broiler. Add 1 cup of milk to contents of frying pan tu make gravy, adding more flour if necessary. Serve this gravy separately. Remove chicken to a hot serving platter and serve with Italian rice to which has been added the chopped chicken giblets. Serves 4.

TIPSY CHICKEN

(Pollo Ubriacato)

1½ cups boiled chicken, diced
2 eggs, hard boiled, chopped fine
3 tblsp. red wine
1 cup white sauce
¼ tsp. salt
dash of cayenne pepper

Mix chicken with sauce, chopped eggs and seasonings; cook 2 minutes, add wine and serve. Serves 4.

WHITE SAUCE: (Salsa Bianci)

2 tblsp. butter
2 tblsp. flour
½ tsp. salt
1 cup milk

See also page 247.

Melt butter in saucepan, add flour and salt, blend until smooth. Stir in cold milk gradually and cook over direct heat, stirring constantly until sauce becomes thick and smooth.

CHICKEN WITH WHITE WINE

(Pollo al Vino Bianco)

1 young chicken, disjointed
1 cup white wine
2 tblsp. olive oil
salt and pepper
¼ tsp. nutmeg
1 tblsp. tomato paste
1 tsp. parsley, minced
1 tsp. basil
¼ cup butter
1 tblsp. flour
2 tblsp. water

Combine wine, olive oil, salt, pepper, nutmeg, and parsley, and marinate chicken in this mixture for 4 hours. Pour into a buttered casserole, cover and simmer until tender. Make a thin paste of the flour and water and sprinkle over chicken, then add tomato paste. Shake casserole to mix; simmer until flour thickens. Serve from casserole. Serves 4.

BREAST OF DUCK

(Petto di Anitra)

3 ducks, average size
1 cup breadcrumbs
1 tsp. salt
2 bay leaves
2 cloves, garlic, minced
½ cup catsup
½ cup red wine
3 eggs, beaten
bacon drippings
1 tsp. pepper
4 whole cloves
¼ cup wine vinegar
1 tblsp. kitchen bouquet
1 jar currant jelly

Use only breasts and legs of the ducks, filleting the breasts and cutting them lengthwise; dip in beaten eggs, then breadcrumbs, and brown on both sides in bacon drippings to which salt, pepper, bay leaf, cloves and garlic have been added. Mix vinegar, catsup, and kitchen bouquet, and pour over meat; let simmer for 1 hour. Add wine and currant jelly 10 minutes before cooking is finished. Serves 8.

NOTE: Use the remaining parts of the duck to make a soup.

DUCK WITH WIDE FLAT MACARONI

(Anitra con Pappardelle)

1 young duck, disjointed
1 lb. tomatoes, chopped
½ cup red wine
mixed herbs
salt and pepper
butter and olive oil
1 lb. pappardelle macaroni, boiled

Cook tomatoes in hot butter and olive oil until soft; add duck, wine, herbs, salt and pepper to taste. Chop duck liver very fine, add to sauce; simmer about 1½ hours. Mix macaroni with sauce and serve with pieces of duck on top. Serves 6.

NOTE: Pappardelle and tagliatelle are made of the same ingredients, with the exception that pappardelle is cut into wider strips, about 1½" to 2" wide.

DUCK WITH OLIVES

(Anitra con Olive)

1 young duck, disjointed
strong beef stock
salt and pepper
2 onions
2 or 3 doz. olives

SAUCE:

Chop the onions, duck liver, gizzard, and heart with about 12 stoned olives, and mix with sufficient hot beef stock to cover duck; add seasoning and stir well until sauce is thick.

Place pieces of duck in the sauce and simmer gently for 1 to 1½ hours. To serve, place duck on a hot dish, pour sauce over it and garnish with olives. If duck has been cooked in a casserole, just add olives for garnish and serve. Serves 6.

ROAST DUCK

(Anitra Arrosto)

1 4- or 5-lb. duck
½ cup olive oil
duck sauce
2½ cups macaroni shells (conchiglie)
salt and pepper

Quarter duck and sauté in hot olive oil until brown all over. Place in a roasting pan, cover with duck sauce (see recipe above), and bake in a moderate oven (350°F.) about 1 hour or until tender. Just before duck is done, boil macaroni shells in boiling, salted water; drain. Place macaroni in a serving dish, cover with sauce from duck and toss lightly; arrange duck on top and serve. Serves 6.

ROAST WILD DUCK

(Anitra di Montagna Arrostita)

1 wild duck 2 to 3 lbs.
1 tsp. salt
⅛ tsp. pepper
⅛ tsp. marjoram, crushed
4 strips of bacon
3 tblsp. olive oil
1 tblsp. butter

Remove pin feathers and singe. Soak in 3 quarts of cold water and 1 cup of vinegar overnight. Drain thoroughly, sprinkle inside and out with salt, pepper and marjoram, lay strips of bacon across the breast. Place in roasting pan breast side up. Add oil to bottom of pan and butter in the cavity of duck. Cover roaster tightly and place in hot oven (500°). After 10 minutes, turn duck, cover and roast 10 minutes more. Remove cover and continue to roast 10 minutes more, in 500° oven until brown on back side, or until bird is an appetizing brown. Serve with jelly sauce (page 256). Serves 3.

ROAST PARTRIDGE

(Pernice Arrosto)

1 dressed partridge
(2½ to 3 lbs.)
½ lb. day old bread
¼ cup chopped celery
2 tblsp. parsley
2 tblsp. olive oil
¾ cup wine (or water)
¾ tsp. salt
ground giblets
1 egg, slightly beaten
1 tsp. oregano
3 tblsp. chives, chopped
¼ lb. bacon
2 or 3 tblsp. flour
1 cup milk

Remove pin feathers and singe partridge. Rinse inside and out with warm water. Drain and dry with cloth. Tear bread into small cubes (about 1 quart loosely packed). Sauté celery, giblets in olive oil 5 minutes. Remove from heat, add water, cool and pour over cubes, add seasonings, egg, chives and oregano, toss lightly to mix. Pack in salted cavity of partridge and sew it up. Lay bacon slices over breast and tops of legs and place breast up on rack in roaster. Cover and bake in a moderate slow oven (325°) for about 2 hours. Remove cover and roast ½ hour longer to brown partridge. Turn off heat, place partridge in the cover of roaster, cover and set back in oven to keep hot. Skim off all but 3 tablespoons of bacon fat. Make gravy from drippings, flour and milk. Serves 4.

GRAVY:

In roaster where partridge was cooked skim off all but 3 tablespoons of bacon fat. Allow all drippings from meat to remain in pan. Blend in 2 or 3 tablespoons of flour thoroughly and brown slightly. Stir constantly and scrape bottom of pan to loosen all the residue. Gradually add 1 cup of milk, stirring constantly until mixture boils and thickens. Add more milk to obtain consistency desired. Season to taste.

PHEASANT

(Fagiano)

1 pheasant
2 cups water
¼ cup butter
1 cup sour cream

Remove feathers from pheasant, clean and singe. Wash thoroughly, cut off wings and legs, leave breast whole, but cut back into pieces. Salt slightly, then brown in butter. Add water and cover; cook over medium heat for about 1 hour. To make a gravy, add sour cream to liquid in pan.

QUAIL

(Quaglie)

Follow recipe for Broiled Squab, allowing 10 to 20 minutes for cooking. Serve on toast with mint jelly. Allow 1 quail to a serving.

RABBIT AUGUSTINO

(Coniglio alla Agostino)

1 rabbit, disjointed
1 tblsp. raisins
dash of nutmeg
red wine
butter
2 tblsp. pinenuts
few strips of lemon peel
salt and pepper
sugar
beef stock

Chop the heart, liver, gizzard of the rabbit fine and place in a deep dish; cover with red wine and add raisins, pinenuts, nutmeg, a pinch of sugar, and let stand for several hours. Heat a little olive oil and butter with salt and pepper and brown the rabbit; cover with stock, bring to a boil then add the wine, liver, etc. Simmer gently for 1½ to 2 hours. Serves 4.

RABBIT DON ISADORO

(Coniglio alla Don Isadoro)

1 rabbit, disjointed
1 tsp. salt
½ tsp. oregano
1 bouillon cube
1 cup sour cream
¼ cup olive oil
½ cup flour
½ tsp. pepper
½ cup wine
2 tblsp. parsley, chopped
grape jelly

Soak rabbit 2 hours in one part vinegar and one part water before cooking; dredge in seasoned flour. Brown in hot olive oil, and place in roaster. Combine wine, bouillon cube, and parsley, and add to oil in which rabbit was browned; pour sauce over rabbit. Bake rabbit in a slow oven (250°F.) 1 hour, covered; remove cover, add sour cream, and bake until rabbit is tender. Remove rabbit to serving dish; thicken gravy with grape jelly, and serve with rabbit. Serves 4.

FRIED RABBIT

(Coniglio Fritto)

1 rabbit, disjointed
6 slices bacon
2 tblsp. olive oil
1 bay leaf
1 cup vinegar
2 tblsp. salt
pinch of sage
lemon slices

Cover rabbit with cold water, add vinegar, salt and bay leaf; let stand over night, then rinse and dry. Fry bacon; remove from pan and add olive oil, sage, and rabbit slightly salted. Cook rabbit until a golden brown and tender. Serve with lemon slices. Serves 4.

RABBIT HUNTER STYLE

(Coniglio alla Cacciatora)

1 rabbit
¼ cup garlic oil
1 lb. tomatoes, peeled
salt and pepper
2 cups red wine
1 onion, chopped
pinch of rosemary

Cut rabbit into serving pieces, cover with cold, salted water and let stand overnight. Brown onion in garlic oil; add tomatoes, salt, pepper and rabbit, cover and cook slowly 30 minutes. Add rosemary and wine, and cook until rabbit is tender. Serves 4.

RABBIT IN WINE

(Coniglio in Vino)

2 young frying rabbits
1 cup red wine
salt and pepper
1 onion, chopped
1 tsp. cloves and your favorite herbs
olive oil

Disjoint rabbits, cover completely with wine combined with onion, herbs and seasoning and soak for 24 hours. Remove rabbit from wine and brown in hot olive oil; add wine in which rabbit was soaked and simmer slowly until tender. Serves 6.

ROAST RABBIT

(Coniglio Arrostito)

1 rabbit
2 carrots, sliced
½ cup water
1 tblsp. salt
1 tsp. thyme
1 large onion, sliced
6 slices salt pork
½ cup red wine
salt and pepper to taste
½ cup hot water

Place rabbit in cold water with 1 tblsp. salt, and let soak overnight, then rinse and dry. Sprinkle inside of rabbit with thyme, salt and pepper, insert 2 slices of salt pork and lay the other 4 slices over the rabbit. Roast in a hot oven (400°F.) until brown on both sides, or approximately 30 minutes. Add wine and hot water mixture and roast for 30 minutes more. Serves 4.

RABBIT WITH SWEET-SOUR SAUCE

(Coniglio al Agro-dolce)

1 rabbit, disjointed
½ cup tomato pulp
chopped olives
3 or 4 tblsp. sugar
1 cup wine vinegar
2 or 3 stalks celery, chopped
capers
dash of salt

SAUCE:

Mix vinegar, tomato pulp, celery, olives, capers, sugar and salt.

NOTE: Sweet-sour sauces are very typical of Sicilian cooking.

Stew rabbit in this sauce for about 1½ hours or until quite tender. Serves 4.

BROILED SQUAB
(Piccionetto Arrostito)

6 squabs
salt and pepper
crostoni croutons
3 tblsp. olive oil
½ tsp. oregano
juice of 1 lemon

Wash squab under running water, split down the back and flatten; season to taste and broil. Baste squab while broiling with lemon juice, oregano and olive oil mixed. Serve on crostoni covered with drippings. Serves 6.

SQUAB MARIA
(Piccionetto alla Maria)

6 squabs
½ cup vinegar
2 or 3 cloves garlic
few dried olives
¼ cup olive oil
5 or 6 anchovies
1 cup tomato sauce
fried bread

Pound garlic, anchovies and dried olives together in a mortar; mix with vinegar and tomato sauce. Brown squab in hot olive oil, add to anchovy sauce and cook about 45 minutes. To serve, place each squab on a piece of fried bread, and cover with sauce. Serves 6.

ROAST SQUAB
(Piccionetto Arrosto)

To prepare squab for stuffing, cut off head close to neck, clean and draw, removing crop carefully. Loosen skin from breast with fingers to form a pocket for the stuffing from wishbone almost down to bottom of breastbone. Prepare stuffing (see recipe on page 253) and drop it from a teaspoon down through opening at top of neck, fill pocket and neck and tie at top. Fasten legs to the back, place squab close together in a pan and dot with butter. Bake in a hot oven (400°F.) for 5 minutes, then reduce heat and bake for 45 minutes or until tender, basting frequently.

SQUAB SMOTHERED IN RICE

(Piccionetto con Riso)

6 squabs, quartered
½ cup butter
1 tblsp. flour
2 onions, minced
½ clove garlic, minced
1 grating of nutmeg
1 cup white wine
salt and pepper
1½ cups stock
1½ cups cooked rice
1 cup Parmesan cheese, grated

Sauté flour and onions in ¼ cup melted butter until yellow; add squab, chopped giblets and seasoning; heat and add stock and wine a little at a time. Heat remainder of butter, mix with ½ cup cheese and nutmeg and add to rice. Arrange squab in a baking dish, cover with rice and strained gravy, and sprinkle with cheese; cover, and set in a pan of hot water. Bake in a slow oven (325°) about 45 minutes. Serve with duck sauce. (See recipe on page 142.) Serves 6.

ROAST STUFFED TURKEY

(Tacchino Ripieno)

1 10 to 14-lb. turkey
liver and gizzard
¼ lb. salami, cut into strips
1 lb. Italian sausages
1 bunch shallots
1 cup prunes, pitted
¼ lb. veal
¼ cup grated cheese
1½ tsp. salt
½ tsp. pepper
¼ cup olive oil
1 lb. chestnuts, roasted
2 eggs
white wine

Grind the liver, gizzard, sausage, shallots, prunes and chestnuts through a food chopper, add seasonings, cheese, salami and moisten with wine and brown in hot olive oil. When cool, use your hands to knead in the eggs. Stuff the turkey, sew up the opening, bind the legs tight to the body of the bird, then bake in a medium hot oven (350°F.) until tender, allowing about 25 minutes to the pound.

NOTE: The mixture used in making this stuffing may seem a little unusual, but the result is excellent.

ROAST TURKEY WITH CHESTNUT DRESSING

(Tacchino Arrosto Ripieno con Castagne)

1 15-lb. turkey
salt and pepper
chestnut dressing
1 lb. butter, melted
2 cups red wine, heated

Stuff turkey with chestnut dressing (see recipe on page 251), including neck; sew up, tie wings and drum sticks in snuggly; place bird in roasting pan with butter, and bake in a slow oven (300°F.), allowing 30 minutes per pound. When turkey is half done, season with salt and pepper, add wine and baste with pan drippings. Continue baking until bird is tender and golden brown. Serves 8.

TURKEY TETRAZZINI

(Tacchino alla Tetrazzini)

2 cups spaghetti, broken
1½ cups left-over turkey, diced
½ cup mushrooms, sliced
3 tblsp. flour
1 cup broth, made from turkey bones
¾ cup white wine
½ cup cream
celery salt
salt and pepper
3 tblsp. olive oil
½ cup breadcrumbs
¼ cup Parmesan cheese, grated

Cook spaghetti in boiling, salted water until barely done; drain and rinse with hot water. Fry mushrooms in hot olive oil about 5 minutes; blend in flour, broth and wine, and cook until smooth; add cream and seasoning. Place a layer of spaghetti in a buttered casserole, add a layer of turkey and a layer of mushroom sauce; repeat layers until ingredients are used up and end with a layer of spaghetti on top. Mix breadcrumbs and cheese, sprinkle over spaghetti and dot with olive oil; bake in a hot oven (450°F.) about 25 minutes. Serves 5.

NOTE: Chicken can be used in this manner, too.

VENISON

(Selvaggina)

4 lbs. venison
2 cups vinegar
1 clove
3 tblsp. parsley, chopped

4 cups water
1 cup sherry
4 strips salt pork
salt and pepper to taste
½ can peas
1 clove garlic
2 large onions, sliced
3 tblsp. flour
1 tsp. oregano
1 cup carrots, diced

Combine vinegar and water and bring to boil, add garlic, parsley, clove, onion, oregano and cool. Place venison in this mixture and let stand, covered, overnight. When ready to cook, dry venison and place in a casserole with salt pork and sliced onion covering; brown on both sides for about ½ hour. Add vegetables with a little of their juice, and bake in a moderate oven (350°F.) for about 1½ hours. Before serving, add sherry and simmer 10 minutes. Serves 6.

CHAPTER EIGHT

Fish and Seafood

BASS SICILIAN STYLE

(Pesce Lupo alla Siciliana)

1½ lbs. filet of bass
¼ cup white wine
¾ cup fish broth made by boiling fish bones
1 scallion, minced
½ cup lobster meat, diced
¼ cup butter
3 mushrooms, chopped
1 tblsp. flour
1 doz. clams or oysters, poached
salt and pepper

Place bass in oiled casserole, add wine and broth, sprinkle with scallion, salt and pepper, dot with 2 tblsp. butter; cover tightly and bake in a moderate oven (350°F.) until tender. Brown mushrooms in remaining butter, stir in flour until well mixed, add a little clam liquid to thin, season and boil 5 minutes; add lobster and bring to a boil, then add clams or oysters and pour over fish. Serve in casserole. Serves 6.

BAKED BLUEFISH

(Bluefish al Forno)

1 4-lb. fish
2 tblsp. olive oil
1 cup Italian fish sauce
salt and pepper
½ cup white wine

Clean, wash, trim fins and tail of fish, season and lay it in a baking dish with olive oil. Cover with wine and bake in a moderate oven (350°F.) for 20 minutes, basting occasionally. Remove from oven, pour the fish sauce over the fish and return to oven to bake another 20 minutes. Serves 6. (For Italian fish sauce, see recipe on page 244.)

CONNELLONI CLAMS

(Connelloni e Vongoli)

1 can clams, minced
3 tblsp. onions, minced
3 tblsp. parsley, minced
12 mushrooms, minced

¼ cup breadcrumbs
½ cup Mozzarella cheese, sliced thin
pepper to taste
2 tblsp. cream
1½ cups flour
¼ cup Parmesan cheese, grated
¼ cup Ricotta cheese
2 eggs, beaten
1 tsp. salt
semolina

To make Connelloni, mix eggs, cream, salt and flour gradually until stiff; knead on a floured board, adding remaining flour until dough is stiff but pliable. Cover dough and let stand 1 hour; divide in half, roll paper thin on a well floured board, and let stand 5 minutes before cutting into 3-inch squares. Cook squares in boiling, salted water about 10 minutes; let cold water run through and drain. Arrange Connelloni separately on a board that has been sprinkled with semolina. Mix remaining ingredients, spread on squares, and roll like a jelly-roll; place close together in a greased, shallow baking pan, and heat in a moderate oven (350°F.). Serve 4 Connelloni per person.

NOTE: If desired, tomato sauce may be poured over Connelloni before heating, and they may be served sprinkled with cheese.

CLAM AND EGGPLANT CASSEROLE

(Ostrichette con Melenzane in Casserola)

2 small eggplants
1 onion, minced
3 tblsp. olive oil
3 tblsp. cheese
2 cans clams, minced
2 cups breadcrumbs
salt and pepper

Cook diced eggplant in salted, boiling water for 10 minutes; drain. Sauté onion in hot olive oil until soft, then add clams drained of liquid. Place a thin layer of breadcrumbs in an oiled casserole, then a layer of eggplant and a layer of clams, season and repeat layers until ingredients are used up, then top with a layer of breadcrumbs. Pour in the clam liquid, sprinkle with olive oil and bake in a moderate oven (350°F.) for 45 minutes. Serves 6.

BAKED COD WITH WINE SAUCE

(Merluzzo al Forno con Vino)

1 lb. codfish
2 tblsp. onion, chopped
1 tblsp. parsley, chopped
2 tblsp. olive oil

2 tblsp. flour
½ tsp. garlic salt
½ cup red wine
1 tsp. salt
½ cup milk
½ tsp. pepper

SAUCE:

Brown onion in hot olive oil, stir in flour, ½ tsp. salt, pepper and milk; cook until thickened.

Stir wine in gradually. Cut fish into serving pieces, sprinkle with rest of salt, garlic salt, and cover with the sauce; bake in a moderate oven for 30 minutes. To serve, sprinkle with parsley. Serves 4.

CODFISH BOLOGNESE

(Merluzzo alla Bolognese)

1 lb. codfish, cut in one piece
2 tblsp. olive oil
salt and pepper
2 tblsp. lemon juice
1 clove garlic, minced
1 tomato, well chopped
2 tblsp. butter
1 tsp. parsley, minced

Heat olive oil slowly in an earthenware casserole. Salt and pepper codfish and place in casserole, sprinkle with garlic, spread with chopped tomato, dot with butter and cover; simmer. Turn fish before it is too tender or it will break. Serve in casserole sprinkled with lemon juice and parsley. Serves 4.

NOTE: This recipe serves for a cut of any large fish.

CODFISH CAKES

(Pasticci di Merluzzo)

1 4-oz. pkg. shredded codfish
1 tblsp. butter
½ tsp. savory salt
1 egg
3 med. potatoes, diced
dash of pepper
4 tblsp. olive oil

Cover codfish with water and let stand about 1 hour or more to extract part of the salt; drain and squeeze out remaining water with hands. Combine fish and potatoes in cold water and boil 15 minutes; drain thoroughly, stir in butter and seasoning, and beat vigorously with a fork to a light fluffiness; beat in egg and chill 30 minutes. Since codfish, like pastry, thrives on little handling, drop mixture from a fork into hot olive oil; fry until a golden brown on both sides. Serves 4.

FRIED CODFISH

(Merluzzo Fritto)

2 lbs. dried salt cod
2 or 3 onions, chopped
4 or 5 anchovies, chopped
milk
3 tblsp. olive oil
plain tomato sauce
1 tblsp. butter

Fry onion in hot olive oil and butter until a golden brown, add the fish, which has been soaked overnight and drained; cook for about 15 minutes without browning fish. Stir in a little milk, add anchovies to tomato sauce (see recipe on page 234) and pour over fish; cover tightly and simmer very gently for about 1 hour. Serves 6.

SALT CODFISH

(Merluzzo Salato alla Parmigiana)

2 cups salt codfish
1 cup tomato sauce
buttered breadcrumbs or grated cheese
4 potatoes, cold, boiled
2 pimentos

Wash salt codfish in cold water and shred. Cover with lukewarm water and let stand until soft; drain. Place a layer of potatoes in a buttered casserole, then a layer of codfish covered with strips of pimento and seasoning. Repeat process until ingredients are used. Pour in the tomato sauce, cover with buttered breadcrumbs or grated cheese, and bake until brown. Serves 6. (For tomato sauce, see recipe on page 234.)

SWEET-SOUR DRY CODFISH

(Merluzzo Agro-dolce)

2 lbs. dry cod
½ cup olive oil
½ cup flour
⅔ cup water
1 tsp. basil
1 tsp. fresh mint, chopped
2 tblsp. pinenuts
1 clove garlic
½ cup vinegar
pinch of salt
pinch of thyme

Soak codfish overnight; drain. Cut into serving pieces, wash and dry again. Roll in seasoned flour. Brown garlic in hot olive oil, then fry codfish slowly until light brown and tender. Mix vinegar, pinenuts, water, basil and mint; cook for 5 minutes, then pour over codfish and simmer slowly about 10 minutes. Serve hot. Serves 6.

CODFISH VINCENT

(Merluzzo alla Vincenzo)

3 slices codfish
1 egg, beaten
¼ cup olive oil
salt and pepper
flour
breadcrumbs
lemon slices

Cut fish into small fillets, season and roll in flour, dip in egg and roll in fine breadcrumbs. Fry in hot olive oil until a golden brown. Serve with lemon slices. Serves 6.

BOILED HARD-SHELLED CRAB

(Granchi Bolliti)

Drop crabs one at a time in boiling, salted water, using 2 tblsp. salt to a quart of water; boil 20 to 25 minutes. Drain and wash carefully, tear off claws, pull off hard shells and remove spongy part. Serve the remaining soft shell with the claws.

CREAMED CRAB

(Crema di Granchi)

3 tblsp. olive oil
¼ cup celery, minced
4 tblsp. flour
salt, pepper, paprika
1 tsp. onion, grated
¼ cup green pepper, minced
2½ cups milk
1½ cubs crab, flaked, canned or frozen

Sauté vegetables in hot olive oil 3 minutes; stir in flour, add milk and cook, stirring until thickened. Add seasonings and cook for 4 minutes; stir in crab and cook until thoroughly heated without boiling. Serve on toast. Serves 6.

CREAMED CRAB MEAT

(Crema di Granchi su Crostoni)

2 tblsp. butter
½ cup breadcrumbs
1 pt. crab meat
2 egg yolks, beaten

1 cup cream
½ tsp. dry mustard
salt and cayenne pepper
tabasco sauce

Mix the butter, breadcrumbs, cream and egg yolks in the top of a double boiler, cook until thick; add seasonings, then the crabmeat, then warm through. Serve on croutons or with rice or noodle ring. Serves 4.

CRAB WITH ONION

(Granchi con Cipolle)

4 crabs with claws cracked
1 cup parsley, minced
salt and pepper
1 can tomato sauce
1 cup onion, chopped
1 cup olive oil
3 cups tomatoes
¼ cup basil

Place the cleaned crab with meat still in the shells in a large kettle with onion, parsley and olive oil; season lightly, cover and simmer 20 minutes. Heat tomatoes with tomato sauce and basil and when boiling hot, pour over the crab and simmer 30 minutes. Serve crab with plenty of sauce. Serves 4.

NOTE: This dish served with a tossed green salad and hot Italian bread makes a delicious meal.

BAKED EEL

(Anguilla al Forno)

2 lbs. eel
olive oil
2 cloves garlic, chopped
2 or 3 bay leaves
breadcrumbs
salt and pepper

Skin and cut eel into 2-inch lengths. Heat a little olive oil, add garlic and bay leaves. Season the eel and coat with breadcrumbs, then place in hot olive oil, adding more oil if necessary. Bake eel in a moderate oven (350°F.) until slightly brown and quite tender. Add 1 or 2 tablespoons of water in course of baking. Serves 6.

EEL WITH MACARONI

(Anguilla con Maccheroni)

2 lbs. eel
¼ cup olive oil
1 clove garlic, chopped
1 sprig parsley

1½ tsp. wine vinegar
1 small onion, chopped
1 small carrot, chopped
1 cup marsala wine
salt
1 stalk celery, chopped
2 cloves
1 blade mace
¾ lb. macaroni

Cut cleaned eel into 3-inch lengths, rub with salt, cover with water and let stand for 30 minutes, then dry. Mix olive oil, vinegar, vegetables, herbs and spices, and pour over eel in a deep saucepan to marinate for 1 hour. Add marsala wine and sufficient boiling water to cover and cook gently until eel is tender. Cook macaroni in salted, boiling water; drain and pile on a hot platter. Drain eel, split and remove bones, then arrange on top of macaroni. Strain and press the liquid in which the eel was cooked through a coarse sieve, and pour sauce over eel and macaroni. Serves 6.

EEL STEW

(Stufato di Anguilla)

2 lbs. eel
1 clove garlic, chopped fine
1 glass claret wine
1 pt. oyster water or stock
1 bay leaf
1 large onion, chopped fine
1 tsp. flour
½ pt. button mushrooms
salt and pepper
1 tsp. oregano

Clean, skin, and cut eel into 1-inch pieces. Brown garlic and onion in hot olive oil; stir in flour gradually, add wine, mushrooms, oyster water, and cook slowly for 10 minutes; add seasoning, bring to a boil and add eel; simmer about 1 hour. Serve with fancy croutons. Serves 6.

BAKED FISH

(Pesce al Forno)

Sprinkle cleaned fish with salt and pepper, brush with olive oil if fish is of the dry variety, dip in flour and place on an oiled tin; bake in a hot oven (400°F.) until fish separates easily from the bone, allowing about 12 to 15 minutes to the pound. Baste fish with oil drippings several times while baking. Serve with sliced lemon and minced parsley, or with Pietro's Favorite Fish Sauce (see page 245 for recipe).

BAKED SMALL STUFFED FISH

(Stufato di Pesce)

4 small fish
1 clove garlic, minced
1 tblsp. parsley, minced
1 tblsp. olive oil
1 cup fresh breadcrumbs
1 small onion, minced
2 tblsp. Parmesan cheese, grated
salt and pepper

Open fish along stomachs, clean, wash, and dry thoroughly. Brown onion and garlic in hot olive oil; mix with breadcrumbs, parsley and cheese with seasoning to taste. Rub fish with olive oil and salt, stuff with mixture and place on their backs in an oiled pan; bake about 30 minutes in a hot oven (400°F.). Serves 4.

BOILED FISH

(Pesce Bollito)

2 lbs. fish
1 tsp. salt
½ lemon, sliced
½ tsp. pepper
1 onion, sliced
1 bay leaf

Cover fish with cold water, add salt, onion, lemon, pepper and bay leaf; heat to boiling point and simmer 15 minutes or longer, depending on thickness of fish. When done, lift fish carefully to serving platter. Serve with either lemon slices or sauce. Serves 6.

NOTE: Strain stock and use for fish sauce.

BOILED FISH WITH LEMON SAUCE

(Pesce Bollito in Salsa di Limone)

3 lbs. fish (preferably pike)
1 lemon, juice and rind
2 egg yolks, well beaten
1 tsp. parsley, chopped
¼ cup sugar
salt to taste
1 cup hot fish stock

Boil fish according to preceding recipe. Skin and bone fish and arrange on platter. Mix sugar, grated lemon rind and juice with egg yolks, and gradually pour into the strained, hot fish stock; cook until thick, stirring constantly. Add salt and parsley and pour over fish. Serve cold. Serves 6.

FISH CAKES

(Focaccia di Pesce)

1 cup cold, boiled fish, shredded
1 cup cold, mashed potatoes
1 tsp. sweet basil, chopped
pepper
2 tblsp. olive oil
celery salt
1 egg, beaten

Combine fish, potatoes, seasonings and egg; shape into small cakes, and fry in hot olive oil until nicely browned on both sides. Serves 4.

FISH CASSEROLE

(Pesce in Casseruola)

1 cup pastina
1 tsp. salt
1 cup onion, diced
2 tblsp. olive oil
¼ cup green pepper, diced fine
1 can condensed tomato soup
1/16 tsp. white pepper
½ cup celery, diced fine
2 cups cooked white fish, flaked

Cook pastina for 15 minutes; drain, and combine with tomato soup, salt and pepper. Sauté onion and celery in hot olive oil, then add fish and green pepper. Cover the bottom of a 2 qt. greased casserole with 1/3 of the pastina mixture, add half the fish mixture and cover with another layer of pastina; add the rest of the fish and top with remaining pastina. Bake in a hot oven (425°F.) for 30 minutes or until thoroughly hot. Serves 4 to 6.

TIPSY FISH FILLETS

(Filetto di Pesce Ubriacati)

6 fish fillets
1 bay leaf
1 onion
salt and pepper
2 peppercorns
white wine

Season fillets with salt and pepper, roll and place in a casserole with bay leaf, peppercorns, onion and cover fish halfway with white wine; poach for 15 minutes. Remove fish and make a sauce of:

2 tblsp. butter to each cup liquid remaining from poaching fish
2 tblsp. capers
1 pt. oysters
¼ cup dill pickle, chopped

3 tblsp. parsley, chopped
2 tblsp. pinenuts

Cook the above ingredients a few minutes, pour over fish and return to oven; cook until fish is done. Serves 6.

NOTE: Serve this dish and your popularity is assured.

FISH FILLETS WITH RICE BALLS

(Filetto di Pesce con Polpette di Riso)

4 to 6 fillets of fish
¼ cup flour
1 tsp. salt
½ cup olive oil
1 egg
2 tblsp. water
½ cup breadcrumbs, fine
1 standard recipe rice balls

Dip fillets in salted flour, then in egg diluted with water, and in breadcrumbs. Fry in hot olive oil until well browned on both sides. Serve with rice balls (see pages 35 and 213) and green beans, and you will have a superb lunch. Serves 4.

OVEN FRIED FISH

(Pesce Fritto al Forno)

4 tblsp. olive oil
1 tblsp. salt
2 lbs. fish fillets
3 lemons, sliced
1 cup breadcrumbs
2 tblsp. cheese, grated
1 cup milk
1 tblsp. oregano flakes

Cut fish to serving sizes, dip in salted milk, roll in breadcrumb and cheese mixture; place in a well greased pan, sprinkle with olive oil, and bake in a hot oven (450°F.) about 12 minutes. Serve sprinkled with oregano flakes and covered with lemon slices. Serves 6.

FISH PIES

(Pasticcio di Pesce)

6 slices fish, cut ½ inch thick and cooked
¼ cup olive oil
salt and pepper
1 tblsp. onion, grated
1 pie crust, standard recipe
3 tblsp. parsley, minced

Sprinkle fish with salt and pepper; brush both sides with olive oil mixed with onion. Cut thinly rolled pie crust into portions slightly more than double the size of fish slices. Lay a slice of fish on each portion of pastry, sprinkle with parsley, fold pastry over fish and seal edges together, completely enfolding the fish. Place pie on an oiled baking sheet, bake in a very hot oven (400°) about 10 minutes; reduce heat to 300° and bake 20 minutes longer. Serves 6.

FISH ROLLS

(Involto di Pesce con Funghi)

1 ½ lbs. fish fillets
1 tblsp. olive oil
2 tblsp. onion, minced
1 ½ tsp. salt
pepper
4 tomatoes, peeled and quartered
¼ lb. mushrooms, sliced
½ cup cold water
½ cup white wine

Sauté onion in hot olive oil until transparent. Roll each fillet like a jelly roll, place in skillet with onion, sprinkle with salt and pepper. Arrange tomatoes around fillets with the mushrooms on top, pour in the water and wine; cover and simmer until fish is tender, approximately 10 minutes. Serves 4.

SWEET-SOUR FISH

(Pesce Agro-dolce)

3 ½ lbs. pike or trout
½ cup brown sugar
¼ cup vinegar
¼ tsp. saffron
1 cup hot fish liquid
¼ cup raisins, seeded
½ tsp. onion juice
1 lemon, sliced and seeded

Clean, slice and salt fish and let stand overnight. Boil the fish (see recipe on page 158), then drain and bone, reserving 1 cup of fish liquid. Mix the remaining ingredients and cook until smooth and thick; pour hot over fish. The fish and sauce should taste strong of vinegar and sugar, so more of each may be added if needed. Serve cold. Serves 6.

FLOUNDER MARIA

(Pesce Passera alla Maria)

1 lb. fillet of flounder
salt and pepper
1 sprig parsley
¼ cup flour and water paste
1 carrot, chopped
1 onion, chopped
1 tblsp. butter
head and bones of the fish

Cover head and bones of the flounder with cold water, add carrot, onion, parsley, and bring to boil; cook 45 minutes, reducing broth to 1 cup; strain. Season fillets and place in a large soup plate, pour broth over them, then place another soup plate on top and seal the two plates together with the flour paste to prevent steam escaping. Bake in a moderate oven (350°F.) for 25 minutes. Open at the table and you will find the flavor amazingly delightful. Serves 4.

HALIBUT

(Pesce Passera Pannato)

halibut, sliced
salt and pepper
egg, beaten
olive oil
fine breadcrumbs

Cut halibut into slices or steaks; rub each slice with olive oil, season and roll in breadcrumbs, dip in egg and roll again in breadcrumbs. Fry in hot olive oil for 5 minutes.

BAKED HALIBUT WITH CHEESE

(Pesce Passera al Forno alla Parmigiana)

2 lbs. halibut steaks
½ cup Parmesan cheese
2 tblsp. lemon juice
salt and pepper
4 tblsp. butter
4 tblsp. flour
2 cups milk, hot

Broil halibut steaks about 15 minutes, then break into rather large pieces and place in a buttered baking dish, and sprinkle with lemon juice. Make a white sauce of the butter, flour, milk and seasoning; pour over the fish, add cheese and bake uncovered in a moderate oven (350°F.) for 20 minutes. Serve in baking dish. Serves 6.

BAKED HALIBUT STEAK

(Braciole di Pesce Passera al Forno)

4 halibut steaks
2 bay leaves
½ tsp. allspice
juice of 2 lemons
salt and pepper to taste
4 strips salt pork
½ tsp. peppercorns
2 or 3 cloves
2 tblsp. olive oil

Salt and pepper the steaks and place in a baking dish with a strip of salt pork over each steak; add bay leaves, peppercorns, allspice, cloves and lemon juice and let marinate for 2 hours. Before placing in oven to bake, add olive oil. Bake in a hot (400°F.) oven for 20 minutes. Serve with tomato sauce. Serves 4.

BAKED STUFFED HALIBUT

(Stufato di Pesce Passera al Forno)

3 lbs. halibut with pocket
2 tblsp. onion, minced
2 tblsp. green pepper, chopped
½ cup celery, diced
3 tblsp. olive oil
1 tsp. salt
½ tsp. pepper
¼ tsp. saffron
2 cups breadcrumbs
2 tblsp. cheese, grated

Cook celery, green pepper and onion slowly in hot olive oil until golden brown. Mix breadcrumbs, cheese and seasonings and add the vegetables, mixing well. Stuff fish with this mixture, closing opening with skewers; place fish on rack in baking pan and brush with olive oil. Bake in a hot oven (375°F.) for 25 minutes. Serves 6.

NOTE: Sea bass, bluefish, mackerel and pickerel are all good baked this way.

LOBSTER MARIA

(Aragosta alla Maria)

1 large lobster, boiled
salt and pepper
¼ cup Parmesan cheese, grated
¼ lb. spaghetti, boiled
1 lb. mushrooms, cooked
½ cup breadcrumbs

Mix breadcrumbs and cheese, place half in a buttered casserole. Combine lobster, spaghetti, mushrooms and seasoning and pour over breadcrumb-cheese mixture, then top with remaining breadcrumb-cheese mixture. Pour a cheese sauce (see recipe on page 241) over all and bake in a hot oven (400°F.) for 20 minutes. Serves 4.

BOILED LOBSTER:

Half fill a large kettle with water, let it come to a rolling boil, add ¼ cup salt, slowly slide in live lobster so as not to disturb boiling water, cover and boil rapidly 4 to 5 minutes. Simmer 20 to 30 minutes, the time depending on size of lobster, then lift the lobster out and lay on its claws to drain. With sharp knife or kitchen shears remove soft shell-like covering, crack claws to remove meat.

LOBSTER MARSALA

(Aragosta alla Marsala)

1 large lobster, boiled
2 tblsp. parsley, chopped
½ cup Marsala wine
½ cup breadcrumbs
3 tblsp. garlic olive oil
salt and pepper to taste
3 tblsp. cheese, grated

Cut lobster in half and remove meat from shell without breaking shell. Clean and cut lobster to bite size, brown in garlic oil, adding salt, pepper and parsley. Cover and simmer for 20 minutes, then add wine and simmer a few more minutes. Fill lobster half shells with the mixture, sprinkle with breadcrumbs, add cheese; then brown very lightly in broiler. Serve at once. Serves 2.

NOTE: To boil lobster see preceding recipe.

LOBSTER SAMUEL

(Aragosta alla Samuele)

2 lobsters, boiled, cut bit size
¼ tsp. salt
1 tblsp. catsup
½ cup olive oil
⅛ tsp. pepper
1 tsp. mint leaves

Drop lobsters in boiling water; add salt and heat to boiling point. Reduce heat, cover and simmer for 20 minutes. Drain, with sharp knife remove soft shell-like covering on underside of tail. Make a deep cut through center of flesh and remove dark vein. Place on broiler rack 6 inches apart, sprinkle melted butter over lobsters to prevent drying. Broil about 6 minutes.

Cook green part of lobster, catsup and seasoning in hot olive oil 5 minutes; add lobster, heat and serve. Serves 4.

STEWED LOBSTER

(Aragosta Stufata)

1 lobster, boiled
dash of pepper
½ cup milk
1 tblsp. butter

Cut lobster to bite size, add to milk and heat; turn off fire and add butter and pepper. Serve on toast (crostoni). Serves 4.

NOTE: To boil lobster see page 163.

Be careful to cook lobster just long enough to heat through, as longer cooking renders it tough.

MACKEREL WITH BASIL SAUCE

(Sgombro con Salsa di Basilico)

- 2 lbs. fresh mackerel
- 2 tblsp. olive oil
- 2 tblsp. flour
- 2 tsp. basil, chopped
- salt and pepper
- 2 tblsp. chives, minced
- 3 tomatoes, sliced
- ½ cup red wine
- ½ cup chicken broth
- ½ tsp. oregano

Stir flour into hot olive oil, add wine, oregano, basil and broth; cook until thick. Season the fish and lay in a greased casserole with tomato slices on top, then pour the sauce over them, and sprinkle with chives. Bake in a moderate oven (350°F.) for 40 minutes. Serves 4.

BROILED SALT MACKEREL

(Sgombro Salato Arrosto)

- 3 lbs. salt mackerel
- parsley, chopped
- lemon juice
- pepper
- butter

Soak fish overnight in cold water; drain and wipe dry. Remove head and tail and broil to a light brown on a buttered broiler. To serve, place upon a hot dish, season with pepper, add bits of butter and a sprinkle of parsley and lemon juice. Serves 6.

STUFFED MACKEREL

(Sgombri Ripieni)

- 3 lbs. mackerel
- ½ cup olive oil
- 1 onion, sliced
- 1 tblsp. parsley, chopped
- salt and pepper to taste
- 1 cup breadcrumbs
- ½ cup grated cheese
- ¼ cup mushrooms, chopped
- 1 lemon, sliced
- 1 tsp. fresh basil, chopped

Have fish cleaned and split down center, sprinkle with salt. Heat ¼ cup olive oil and sauté onions, mushrooms and parsley until tender. Mix breadcrumbs, basil, cheese, salt and pepper and add to mushroom mixture, blending well. Stuff the fish with this mixture, sew up the center and place fish in a baking dish with remaining olive oil. Bake about 30 minutes in a moderate oven (350°F.), or until tender. Serve with lemon slices. Serves 6.

OYSTERS IN BLANKETS

(Ostriche in Coperta)

2 doz. firm oysters
red pepper
24 slices bacon, thin
parsley, chopped

Drain and wipe oysters dry; lay each oyster on a thin slice of bacon, add a dash of red pepper, sprinkle with parsley and fold bacon around oyster, then fasten with a toothpick. Brown oysters in a skillet and serve hot. Serves 6.

FRIED OYSTERS

(Ostriche Fritte)

1 lb. oysters
1 tblsp. cold water
1 cup breadcrumbs
½ cup milk
1 egg, beaten
salt and pepper to taste
3 tblsp. cheese, grated
½ cup olive oil

Season breadcrumbs and mix with cheese; dip oysters in milk, roll in the breadcrumb mix, and dip in egg and water mixture, and again in breadcrumbs. Fry in hot olive oil until a golden brown on both sides, and drain on brown paper. Serve with lemon slices and tartar sauce. (See page 245 for Pietro's Favorite Fish Sauce.) Serves 4.

OYSTER ITALIENNE

(Ostriche all'Italiana)

3 tblsp. olive oil
½ tsp. prepared mustard
1 tsp. salt
1 cup celery, minced
½ tsp. pepper
¾ cup milk
1 pt. oysters
½ cup macaroni
1 cup Mozzarella cheese, sliced

Sauté celery in hot olive oil until tender; add milk, seasonings and oysters; cook 3 minutes. Cook macaroni in boiling, salted water until tender; drain. Place macaroni in a greased casserole, cover with oyster mixture, top with cheese; bake in a hot oven (425°F.) about 20 minutes, or until lightly browned. Serves 4.

OYSTER SHRIMP CASSEROLE

(Ostriche con Gamberetti al Forno)

3 tblsp. olive oil
3 tblsp. flour
1 ½ cups milk
¾ tsp. salt
½ tsp. pepper
1 tsp. Worcestershire sauce
2 dashes tabasco sauce
2 cups peas, cooked
1 dozen oysters, drained
1 cup shrimp
pastry dough

Heat olive oil in top of a double boiler, blend in flour; add milk and cook until thick; season. Place peas, oysters and shrimp in layers in a buttered casserole, cover with sauce, top with pastry rolled to ⅛-inch thickness, and seal edges. Bake in a moderately hot oven (375°) about 17 minutes or until brown. Serves 4.

PASTRY DOUGH:

1 cup flour
½ tsp. salt
¼ cup shortening
3 tblsp. ice water

Measure flour after sifting then add salt and blend, cut shortening into flour until flour particles are the size of pea grains. Add water a few drops at a time, tossing around with fork. Add only enough water to press the mixture gently into a shape that can be picked up easily in the hands. Place dough on lightly floured board and quickly press out to desired circle.

BAKED SALMON IN VEGETABLE SAUCE

(Salmone con Legumi al Forno)

2 lbs. salmon steaks
1 tblsp. lemon juice
½ tsp. salt
¼ cup olive oil
3 tblsp. flour
1 tsp. salt
½ tsp. pepper
1 cup peas, cooked
½ cup carrots, cooked and diced
¼ cup celery, cooked and diced

Place salmon steaks in an oiled baking pan, sprinkle with lemon juice and 1 tblsp. olive oil. Heat remaining oil in saucepan, blend in flour, seasonings, and add milk gradually; cook until thickened. Stir in peas, carrots and celery, and pour sauce over salmon; bake about 20 minutes in a moderate oven (350°F.). Serve with parsley and lemon wedges. Serves 6.

SALMON PATTIES

(Focaccette di Salmone)

½ cup pastina
¼ cup celery, finely diced
2 cups canned salmon
1 egg, slightly beaten
¼ tsp. white pepper
⅓ cup olive oil
¼ cup onion, finely diced
3 tblsp. olive oil
¼ cup parsley, minced
1 ½ tsp. salt
breadcrumbs

Cook pastina about 15 minutes; drain. Sauté onion and celery in 3 tblsp. olive oil until tender; add pastina, salmon, parsley, egg and seasonings, mixing thoroughly. Shape into 8 patties; coat on all sides with breadcrumbs and brown in 1/3 cup hot olive oil over moderate heat. Serves 4.

GRILLED SCALLOPS

(Conchiglie di Pesce al Ferri)

1 lb. scallops
1 small onion, chopped
1 clove garlic, chopped
1 tblsp. parsley
salt and pepper

Grill seasoned scallops until tender. Brown onion, garlic and parsley in hot olive oil; pour over grilled scallops. Serves 4.

CREAMED SEAFOODS

(Pesce Misto in Crema)

¼ cup shrimp, cooked
½ cup peas, cooked
1 cup crabmeat, cooked
1 cup white sauce

Stir the shrimp, crabmeat and peas into the white sauce, seasoning to taste. Serves 4.

WHITE SAUCE:

2 tblsp. butter
2 tblsp. flour
½ tsp. salt
1 cup milk

Melt butter in saucepan, add flour and salt, blend until smooth. Stir in cold milk gradually and cook over direct heat, stirring constantly until sauce becomes thick and smooth.

See also page 247.

FRIED SHRIMP

(Granchi Fritti alla Parmigiana)

1 lb. shrimp, cooked
1 egg, beaten
1 cup milk
olive oil
2 tsp. salt
3 tblsp. Parmesan cheese, grated

Remove black vein from shrimp and rinse in cold water; marinate for 20 to 30 minutes in:

½ cup olive oil
1 tsp. salt
½ cup lemon juice
¼ tsp. pepper

Combine eggs, milk and 1 tblsp. olive oil, salt, flour, cheese and beat with egg beater until well blended. Drain shrimp, dip in egg batter and fry in hot olive oil (about ¼-inch deep in pan) until golden brown. Serves 6.

NOTE: Fillet of sole and other fresh or frozen fillets are also excellent cooked this way.

SHRIMP WITH MUSHROOMS AND WINE

(Gamberetti con Funghi e Vino)

½ cup onion, chopped
½ cup mushroom caps
½ cup celery, diced
1 clove garlic, minced
3 tblsp. olive oil
1 tblsp. flour
1 tsp. sugar
½ cup red wine
½ cup water
2 cups tomatoes, canned
2 cups peas
1½ lbs. shrimp, cooked
4 cups rice, cooked
1 tblsp. chili powder

Sauté onions, mushrooms, celery, and garlic in hot olive oil until tender; add flour, salt, sugar, and chili powder mixed with ¼ cup water, and mix well; add wine and remaining water, simmer 15 minutes and add tomatoes, peas, vinegar, and shrimp; heat thoroughly. To serve, pour the shrimp mixture over hot rice. Serves 6.

SHRIMP WITH RICE

(Risotto con Gamberetti)

3 dozen shrimp
2 cups cooked rice
salt and pepper
olive oil
2 pints stock made from shells of shrimp
1 small onion, chopped
flour

Brown onion in hot olive oil until a golden brown, add rice, and stock highly seasoned with salt and pepper, stir well and simmer for about 30 minutes, or until rice has absorbed the stock. Dip shrimp in flour and fry in hot olive oil until a golden color, then add to rice 10 minutes before serving. Serves 6.

SHRIMP STOCK:

3 pints water
1 cup diced celery
1 tsp. whole black pepper
1 tblsp. salt
½ medium onion, sliced
3 dozen shrimp
½ lemon sliced

Heat water to boiling point, add celery, pepper, salt and onion. Simmer 30 minutes. Rinse shrimp in cold water, drop in boiling liquid and simmer for 10 minutes. Remove shrimp, strain liquid. You will have 2 pints of shrimp stock.

SHRIMP STEWED IN TOMATO SAUCE

(Gamberetti Stufati in Salsa di Pomidoro)

1 lb. shrimp, cooked and shelled
salt and pepper
tomato sauce

Cook shrimp in tomato sauce (see recipe on page 234) until tender, approximately 30 minutes. Season and serve. Serves 4.

NOTE: Stewed shrimp combines very well with hot boiled rice, noodles, etc.

FILET OF SOLE WITH VINEGAR SAUCE

(Filetto di Sogliola Marinato)

2 lbs. filet of sole
1 or 2 onions, chopped
1 tblsp. raisins
flour
1 tblsp. pinenuts or other nuts
½ cup vinegar
¼ cup olive oil
salt

Brown onions in hot olive oil. Sprinkle sole with flour and salt; add to onions with raisins and nuts, cook until fish is brown, and add vinegar; simmer about 1 hour. Serves 4.

FILET OF SOLE IN WINE SAUCE

(Filetto di Sogliola in Vino)

- 8 medium sized filet of sole
- 1 tsp. green onion, chopped
- 3 fresh mushrooms
- 1 bay leaf
- 1 cup white wine
- 2 tblsp. olive oil
- 1 tsp. parsley, chopped
- 1 stalk celery, chopped
- ½ cup consomme
- Parmesan cheese, grated

Brown onion, parsley, mushrooms, and celery in hot olive oil lightly; add bay leaf, consommé and wine, and bring to a boil; add fish and simmer 10 minutes. Lift out fish carefully and place in a casserole. Boil sauce down to about 1 cup, pour over fish, sprinkle with cheese, and bake in a hot oven (450°) 10 minutes. Serve garnished with parsley and lemon slices. Serves 6.

NOTE: This dish can be prepared ahead of time up to the baking process, and kept in the refrigerator. It makes an excellent Friday meal served with a tossed salad, hot Italian bread and fruit.

SQUID WITH ONIONS

(Calamaretti con Cipolle)

- 1 lb. squid
- ¼ cup olive oil
- 3 onions, sliced
- salt and pepper

Clean squid and cut into 1-inch lengths. Cook onion and squid in hot olive oil, covered, until tender and onion is brown, approximately 20 minutes. Season to taste and serve. Serves 4.

TO CLEAN SQUID:

Remove heads and tentacles, empty sac, wash thoroughly. Remove outer veiling by dousing in hot water, the veiling will pull off easily; rinse again in cold water. You now have a clean white fish. The tentacles are also edible. To clean these, remove eyes, douse tentacles in hot water, pull off veiling and cups. Wash thoroughly and cut up.

SQUID WITH TOMATOES

(Calamaretti con Pomidoro)

3 lbs. squid
6 tblsp. olive oil
1 tblsp. parsley, chopped
1 clove garlic
1 ½ cups tomatoes, chopped
¾ cup red wine
salt and pepper
1 tblsp. basil, chopped

Clean squid according to preceding directions, rinse many times. Brown garlic in hot olive oil; add squid, cover and cook slowly for 10 minutes; add seasonings and wine, cook 5 minutes and add tomatoes, basil and parsley; cook until tender, about 20 minutes longer. Serve hot. Serves 6.

BAKED TROUT WITH SARDINES

(Trotto al Forno con Sardelle)

2 to 3 lbs. trout
1 cup sour cream
cayenne pepper
1 cup cheese, grated
½ cup butter
½ lb. sardellen, or sardines packed in brine
cracker crumbs

Split trout and remove center bone. Place trout skin-side down on a buttered platter, cover with butter, sour cream and sardellen, which has been soaked in water, boned and chopped fine; sprinkle with cracker crumbs, pepper and cheese. Bake in a hot oven 30 minutes (400°F.). Serve on same platter. Serves 6 to 8.

TUNA CASSEROLE WITH ALMONDS

(Tonno al Forno con Mandorle)

1 cup macaroni shells
½ cup onion, chopped
¼ cup green pepper, chopped
3 tblsp. olive oil
2 tblsp. flour
1 ¼ cups milk
1 10½-oz. can cream of chicken soup
¼ cup pimento, chopped
1 cup tuna, flaked
¼ cup almonds

Cook macaroni; drain. Sauté onion and green pepper in hot olive oil until tender; add flour and blend, then mix in milk and cook over low heat until thick, stirring constantly. Stir in chicken soup and remaining ingredients, then combine with macaroni; pour into a greased casserole. Garnish with almonds and bake in a moderate oven (350°F.) for 30 minutes. Serves 4.

TUNA WITH WINE

(Tonno al Vino Bianco)

1 lb. canned tuna fish, drained
2 onions, chopped
1 or 2 stalks celery, chopped
1 or 2 carrots
1 clove garlic, chopped
¼ cup olive oil
¼ cup white wine

Cook vegetables in hot olive oil until tender; add tuna and white wine, and simmer for about 30 minutes. Serves 4.

TUNA WITH MARSALA

(Tonno al Marsala)

1 7-oz. can tuna fish
2 tblsp. Marsala wine
3 tblsp. olive oil
1 tblsp. capers
½ lb. shrimp
2 anchovies
3 potatoes, boiled
¼ cup mayonnaise
1 doz. ripe olives

Mix tuna, anchovies, olive oil and hot potatoes; sieve through colander to make a smooth paste; add wine and place in a mold or square pan to cool for 2 hours. Unmold tuna mixture onto a serving platter, spread with a mixture of mayonnaise and capers, and garnish with olives and shrimp. Serves 4.

TUNA FISH PIE WITH CHEESE ROLLS

(Pasticcio di Tonno con Involti di Cacio)

½ cup green pepper, sliced
2 slices onion
3 tblsp. olive oil
6 tblsp. flour
½ tsp. capers
1 large can tuna fish, drained
½ tsp. salt
2 cups milk
1 tblsp. lemon juice
cheese rolls, one standard recipe

Brown green pepper, capers and onion in hot olive oil, blend in flour and salt; add milk slowly, stirring constantly until thick and smooth, then add tuna and lemon juice. Place in a baking dish and over top place cheese rolls (see recipe on page 317). Serves 8.

TUNA RICE PATTIES

(Pasticcini di Riso con Tonno)

1 can tuna, medium size
2 cups rice, steamed (page 212)
1 egg, slightly beaten
2 tblsp. onion, chopped
2 tblsp. parsley, chopped
2 tblsp. flour
1 tsp. salt
olive oil

Blend tuna with steamed rice; combine with egg mixed with onion, parsley, flour and salt. Shape into small flat cakes and fry in hot olive oil until golden brown. Serves 4 to 6.

TUNA SURPRISE

(Tonno al Forno)

5 slices bread
½ cup cheese, grated
2 cups milk
1 med. sized can tuna
3 eggs
1 tsp. salt

Trim crusts from bread, and cube. Arrange half the cubes in a layer on the bottom of a greased casserole. Drain oil from tuna and flake the meat onto top of bread, sprinkle with cheese, then add remaining bread cubes. Beat eggs, add milk and salt, then pour over tuna mixture. Bake in a 325°F. oven for 1 hour. Serve with mushroom sauce (see recipe on page 238), if desired. Serves 6.

WHITE BAIT OMELET

(Ghiozzi in Frittata)

½ lb. white-bait
salt and pepper
½ cup olive oil
1 tsp. minced parsley
6 eggs, beaten

Wash white-bait thoroughly in several waters, drain and dry with a cloth; season with salt and pepper, sprinkle with parsley. Season eggs, add fish and stir together, then pour into heated olive oil and stir until eggs are set. Brown the omelet on both sides, using a pancake turner to turn; slide from pan to a hot platter. Serves 6.

FILET OF WHITING

(Filetto di Nasello con Finocchi)

1 lb. filet of whiting
Parmesan cheese, grated
olive oil
salt and pepper
finocchio, finely minced or coarsely grated

Dip filets in olive oil; grill until tender. To serve, season with salt and pepper to taste, dust with cheese and fennel. Serves 4.

CHAPTER NINE

Vegetables

ASPARAGUS WITH CHEESE

(Asparagi alla Parmigiana)

1 bunch fresh asparagus
3 tblsp. olive oil
4 tblsp. Parmesan cheese, grated
salt and pepper

The best way to separate the woody fiber from the tender spears is to break the spears as low down the stalks as possible. The stalk will break with a snap where the woodiness begins. The lower woody part may be trimmed off, diced and cooked to make soup.

Only enough water should be used to cook the asparagus until tender. (About 15 minutes.)

Cook asparagus in small amount of salted water about 15 minutes and drain. Combine asparagus with olive oil, salt, pepper and top with grated cheese. Bake in slow oven (300°) until slightly browned. Serves 4.

ASPARAGUS WITH GARLIC

(Asparagi all'Aglio)

¼ cup Parmesan cheese, grated
1 lb. asparagus
salt and pepper
hot garlic oil

Select asparagus with tightly closed buds; discard tough ends and scales. Tie asparagus into small bunches, stand in rapidly boiling, salted water and cook for 10 minutes; cover tips of asparagus with inverted half of a double boiler and steam 15 minutes; drain. Serve with hot garlic oil as a dressing. Serves 4.

ASPARAGUS WITH LEMON AND OIL

(Asparagi all'Olio e Limone)

1 lb. asparagus
3 tblsp. olive oil
juice of ½ lemon
salt and pepper

Cook asparagus about 15 minutes in as little water as possible with salt until tender. To serve, sprinkle with olive oil, lemon juice and pepper. Serves 4.

ASPARAGUS MILANESE

(Asparagi alla Milanese)

1 lb. asparagus
Parmesan cheese, grated
4 eggs, beaten
salt and pepper

Cook asparagus in small amount of salted water, about 20 minutes, drain. Arrange asparagus in a buttered baking dish, cover with eggs and seasoning; sprinkle with cheese and place under broiler until eggs are done and cheese a golden brown. Serves 4.

MOM'S ASPARAGUS

(Asparagi alla Mama)

1 lb. asparagus
½ cup Parmesan cheese
4 eggs
2 tblsp. olive oil

Cook asparagus until tender; drain and arrange in ovenproof serving dish. Place whole eggs fried soft in olive oil over asparagus, sprinkle with cheese and brown lightly in broiler. You will notice a delicious, nutty flavor. Serves 4.

BAKED ARTICHOKES

(Carciofi al Forno)

4 med. artichokes
2 cloves garlic
salt and pepper
6 tblsp. olive oil
1 tsp. parsley, chopped

Remove stems of artichokes and snip off the sharp tips of leaves, loosening leaves slightly. Crush the garlic, mix with parsley, salt and pepper to taste and place between the loosened leaves. Place artichokes in a small baking dish and pour 1½ tblsp. olive oil over each artichoke, adding a cup of water to the baking dish. Cover and simmer over a low fire until leaves are tender, adding more water if needed. When artichokes are tender, uncover, place pan in oven for 5 minutes, and serve hot. Or, if desired, artichokes may be served cold. Serves 4.

BOILED ARTICHOKES

(Carciofi Bolliti)

3 large artichokes
4 quarts boiling water
3 tblsp. salt
2 tblsp. vinegar

Remove outer leaves and points of artichokes; place in boiling water to which salt and vinegar have been added, and cook until leaves pull out easily, about 20 to 30 minutes; drain. Cut into halves lengthwise and remove white fuzzy fibre or "choke". Serve cold with vinaigrette sauce, tartar sauce or filled with your favorite salad filling.

NOTE: If artichokes are small, use 6 in making the above recipe, and do not cut in half. Can be served hot with melted butter.

ARTICHOKES CALABRESE

(Carciofi alla Calabrese)

4 large artichokes
½ cup Parmesan cheese, grated
¼ cup olive oil
salt and pepper
1 cup breadcrumbs
1 tsp. parsley, chopped
½ cup water

Discard stems and outer leaves of artichokes, and trim tips of remaining leaves by cutting across the top of the artichoke. Open leaves of artichoke by pounding it on top. Make a filling of breadcrumbs, cheese, parsley, salt and pepper; stuff between the leaves of artichokes pressing mixture in with butt of the palm. Place artichokes in a saucepan, add olive oil and a little water; cover and simmer 1 hour, adding more water if necessary. Serves 4.

NOTE: The Italian way with artichokes is very heavy on olive oil, the standard approach being to fit the artichokes tightly into a pan, and then to pour in enough oil to cover. To save oil and still achieve flavor, oil can be mixed with the stuffing. The artichokes can then be, in effect, steamed (with a little oil) once oil has been placed inside the leaves.

FRIED ARTICHOKES

(Carciofi Fritti)

8 small artichokes, fresh (about 1½ inches high)
olive oil
salt and pepper

Remove outer leaves of artichokes and trim tips of leaves with sharp scissors, fry cones in deep hot olive oil, seasoned with salt and pepper. When well fried, about 15 minutes, remove from oil; arrange on a serving dish with leaves pushed slightly back from center to resemble small flowers. As the whole of small artichokes are edible, the chokes need not be removed. Serves 4.

FRIED ARTICHOKES WITH BATTER

(Carciofi Fritti con Salsa)

4 artichokes
2 tblsp. water
½ tsp. oregano
½ tsp. salt
1 tsp. onion, grated
1 egg
½ cup flour
¼ tsp. pepper
1 tsp. vinegar
olive oil

Cook artichokes until tender; cool, quarter and fry in hot olive oil until a golden brown. Beat egg and water, add flour gradually, onion, vinegar, and seasoning. Dip artichokes in plain flour, shake well, dip in batter and fry in olive oil to a golden brown. Serves 4.

HEARTS OF ARTICHOKES

(Cuori di Carciofi all'Acciuga)

1 large can artichoke hearts
juice of 1 lemon
½ cup olive oil
salt and pepper
1 2-oz. can anchovies
lettuce leaves
1 tblsp. capers
1 green pepper, chopped
2 eggs, hard-boiled and chopped

Marinate artichoke hearts in lemon juice, olive oil, salt and pepper for 1 hour. To serve, place an artichoke heart on a lettuce leaf, top with capers, chopped pepper, egg and a rolled anchovy. Serve with small sandwiches. Serves 4.

ARTICHOKES WITH LEMON

(Carciofi al Limone)

4 artichokes
1 tblsp. lemon juice
salt and pepper
2 tblsp. olive oil
1 tsp. parsley, minced
1 cup meat broth

Discard outer leaves, and drop artichokes immediately into cold water to prevent discoloring (a little lemon juice in the water will help avoid discoloration), and let stand for about

5 minutes. Then remove from water and set upright and close together in a saucepan, sprinkle with lemon juice, seasoning and parsley. Pour the meat broth over them and simmer for 30 minutes, basting now and then. When artichokes are tender, lift out and thicken liquid with a little flour, if desired, and pour over artichokes to serve.

ARTICHOKES WITH MUSHROOMS

(Carciofi con Funghi)

4 artichokes
1 small onion, chopped fine
3 tblsp. white wine
3 tblsp. olive oil
pinch of oregano
salt and pepper
4 large mushrooms, chopped fine
4 strips bacon
3 tblsp. water
2 tblsp. tomato paste
½ cup breadcrumbs

Boil artichokes 20 minutes in salted water; drain. Cook onions and mushrooms in hot olive oil 5 minutes; add tomato paste and cook over a low fire a few minutes. Spread leaves of artichokes, remove choke and sprinkle with salt and pepper; fill with mushroom mixture. Place artichokes close together in a baking pan, add wine and water; cook 10 minutes in a moderate oven (350°), basting twice. Serves 4.

ARTICHOKES WITH OLIVES

(Carciofi con Olive)

4 artichokes
3 eggs, hard-boiled, sliced
8 black olives, chopped
½ cup sour cream
flour
olive oil
6 tblsp. cheese, grated
3 tblsp. tomato paste
1 tsp. oregano
lemon juice
salt and pepper

Discard outer leaves of artichokes, slice the remaining bud lengthwise, and cut out choke; sprinkle with lemon juice. Oil and flour a baking dish; spread a layer of artichokes on bottom and cover with egg, olives, oregano, tomato paste, seasoning, and top with remainder of artichokes and sour cream; bake in a moderate oven (350°F.) about 30 minutes; uncover and bake 10 minutes. Serves 4.

STUFFED ARTICHOKES

(Carciofi Ripieni)

4 artichokes, trimmed
12 anchovy filets, in oil
6 cloves garlic
2 tblsp. parsley, chopped
3 carrots, chopped
salt and pepper
3 large onions, chopped
few strips of bacon
1 stalk celery, chopped
4 tblsp. olive oil
pinch of oregano, basil, and marjoram

Boil artichokes 20 to 30 minutes in salted water, until they are slightly tender but still quite firm; drain thoroughly and remove center leaves and choke. Pound anchovy and garlic together in a mortar and fill artichokes with mixture. Mix onions, carrots, parsley, celery, herbs, seasoning; place on bottom of a saucepan, arrange artichokes on top with a strip of bacon over each artichoke; add olive oil and a little water, cover and simmer gently about 45 minutes, beating occasionally. To serve, remove bacon, arrange artichokes and vegetables on a hot dish, and strain a little sauce over them. Serves 4.

ARTICHOKES WITH WHITE WINE

(Carciofi al Vino Bianco)

4 artichokes
2½ cups vegetable stock
4 tblsp. olive oil
6 tblsp. white wine
2 tblsp. parsley, chopped
salt and pepper

Heat olive oil with parsley for 3 minutes, add vegetable stock, and bring to a boil. Spread leaves of artichokes and remove choke; add artichokes to stock, cover and simmer 20 minutes. Add seasoning and wine; simmer until artichokes are tender, by testing with a fork.

VEGETABLE SOUP OR STOCK:

2½ lbs. meaty shank bone
2 tblsp. oil
8 cups water
½ bay leaf
¼ tsp. marjoram
¼ cup sliced onion
1 tblsp. salt
1 cup diced potatoes
½ cup diced celery
½ cup diced carrots
1 cup endive
½ cup green beans

Have butcher crack bone. Dice meat from the bone and brown in oil. Add bone, water, onion, salt and spices tied in a piece of muslin. Cover and simmer about 2 hours. Strain soup, reserving meat. Skim excess fat from stock. Add remaining ingredients except endive.

Boil until vegetables are tender, add endive and cook about 10 minutes longer. Serve with the chopped meat, sprinkle with grated Parmesan cheese. For a vegetable stock— Mash vegetables and strain through a fine cheese cloth.

BEAN AND CHESTNUT LOAF

(Pane di Fave e Castagne)

1 pt. cooked beans, cold
2 eggs, well beaten
2 tblsp. tomato paste
1 cup chestnuts, mashed
1 cup breadcrumbs
1 tblsp. onion, chopped
salt and pepper
1 lb. Italian sausage, small

Combine all ingredients except sausage; shape into a loaf and bake in moderate oven (325°F.) for 25 minutes. Serve with broiled sausages. Serves 6.

KIDNEY BEANS

(Fagioli all'Uccelletto)

1 lb. kidney beans
4 tblsp. olive oil
2 tblsp. tomato pulp
2 sage leaves
salt and pepper

Boil beans in salted water until tender; drain thoroughly. Heat olive oil with sage leaves until very hot; add beans, salt and pepper, and cook until oil has been absorbed, stirring occasionally. Blend in tomato pulp, and serve hot. Serves 4.

KIDNEY BEANS WITH GARLIC

(Fagioli Bolliti all'Aglio)

1 lb. kidney beans, canned or dried
parsley, chopped
3 tblsp. olive oil
salt to taste
1 clove garlic
¼ tsp. marjoram
¼ tsp. chili pepper

Boil beans in salted water until tender, drain; sauté in hot olive oil with garlic, parsley, marjoram and chili pepper. Season to taste. Serves 6.

NOTE: If dried beans are used, soak overnight. This dish especially delicious if you can find the white kidney beans called cannellini at your local Italian grocer. (Also available in cans.)

KIDNEY-LIMA BEAN CASSEROLE

(Fave Miste)

- 1 can green lima beans
- 1 cup cooked ham, diced
- 1 tsp. Worcestershire sauce
- 1 small onion, sliced into thin rings
- 1 can red kidney beans
- 1 can cream of mushroom soup, condensed
- 1 med. green pepper, sliced

Drain beans, reserving ¼ cup of red kidney bean liquid. Combine beans and ham in a casserole, and cover with a mixture of cream of mushroom soup, Worcestershire sauce and red kidney bean liquid. Arrange pepper slices and onion rings on top of beans, and bake in a moderate (350°F.) oven until bubbling hot. Serves 8.

BAKED LIMA BEANS

(Fave al Forno)

- 1 lb. lima beans, dried
- ¼ lb. salt pork
- 2 tblsp. flour
- salt and paprika
- 2 tblsp. olive oil

Soak beans for 2 hours in lukewarm water to cover; drain. Add fresh warm water with salt pork, and bring quickly to boil; simmer 1 hour or until beans are tender, adding salt and paprika. Brown flour in hot olive oil, combine with beans and 1 cup of bean liquid in casserole; bake in a moderate oven (325°F.) about 30 minutes, adding more bean liquid, if required. Serves 6.

LIMA BEANS WITH TOMATO SAUCE

(Fave con Salsa di Pomidoro)

- 2 cups lima beans, cooked
- 1 onion, sliced
- 3 stalks celery, chopped
- 3 Italian sausages, cut in half
- Parmesan cheese, grated
- 1 cup tomato sauce
- 2 tblsp. parsley, chopped
- ½ tsp. salt
- breadcrumbs

Combine lima beans, tomato sauce (see recipe on page 202), onion, parsley, celery and salt; pour into an oiled casserole and sprinkle with a mixture of breadcrumbs and cheese. Top with sausage and bake in a moderate oven (350°F.) for 20 minutes. Serves 4.

SNAP BEANS WITH LEMON JUICE

(Fagiolini al Sugo di Limone)

1½ lbs. snap beans
1 tomato, sliced
1 egg, hard-boiled
2 cups vegetable stock
salt and pepper
chives, chopped
juice of 1 lemon
4 tblsp. olive oil
1 tsp. sugar
1 clove garlic, cut
parsley, chopped

String and cut beans to desired lengths. Rub bottom of saucepan with garlic, add olive oil, parsley, salt and sugar; cook over a low heat 5 minutes, stirring frequently; add beans and cook 5 minutes; add soup stock, cover and simmer until beans are tender. Uncover, add lemon juice and cook until liquid has evaporated and beans are brown; season with pepper and garnish with egg and tomato. Serve hot or cold sprinkled with chives. Serves 6.

STRING BEANS WITH TOMATOES

(Fagiolini con Pomidoro)

No. I

1 lb. green string beans
1 onion, chopped
3 tomatoes, strained
2 tblsp. olive oil
1 tsp. parsley, chopped
salt and pepper

Cook string beans until tender; drain, and while still warm, fry in hot olive oil with onion, parsley and seasoning. As the beans dry, add the juice of tomatoes, cook down slowly 15 minutes. Serve hot. Serves 6.

No. II

1 lb. string beans
1 cup tomatoes, strained
2 tblsp. butter
2 tblsp. flour
1 tsp. salt
¼ tsp. pepper
1 tsp. sugar

Cut off ends of beans, string and break into 1-inch pieces, cook in boiling, salted water until tender, then remove all but ½ cup of liquid. Heat butter, add flour, seasoning and tomatoes; cook to a smooth sauce and pour over beans; cook slowly about 15 minutes. Serve hot. Serves 6.

BROCCOLI WITH PARMESAN CHEESE

(Broccoli alla Parmigiana)

- 1 large bunch broccoli
- 2 tblsp. sweet vermouth
- 4 tblsp. olive oil
- Parmesan cheese, grated

Boil broccoli about 10 minutes in salted water. Heat olive oil, add wine and simmer 2 minutes. To serve, place broccoli on a serving dish, cover with wine sauce and sprinkle with cheese. Serves 6.

BROCCOLI WITH LEMON

(Broccoli al Limone)

- 1 bunch broccoli
- 1 clove garlic (optional)
- salt and pepper to taste
- juice of 1 lemon
- 3 tblsp. olive oil

Select broccoli that is a good dark green with tightly closed buds; wash well and cut off tough ends of stalks. If the broccoli is rather thick, split lengthwise and tie into small bunches. Place upright in an open kettle of rapidly boiling, salted water with flowerettes out of water. Boil for 10 minutes. Then cover with an inverted half of a double boiler and continue boiling for 15 minutes to steam tips; drain when tender. Serve with a sauce made of olive oil, lemon juice, garlic, salt and pepper. Serves 6.

BRUSSELS SPROUTS WITH CHESTNUTS

(Cavoli di Brusselle con Castagne)

- 1 qt. Brussels sprouts, cooked
- ½ lb. chestnuts, blanched
- ½ cup butter
- 1 tblsp. flour
- 2 tsp. sugar
- 1 tsp. salt

Cover chestnuts with salted, boiling water; cook gently until water has evaporated and chestnuts are tender. Brown flour in 2 tblsp. butter, add sugar, salt and 1 cup of liquid from sprouts;

cook, stirring constantly until thick and smooth. Combine chestnuts and sprouts with sauce, heat and serve. Serves 6.

CABBAGE WITH CHESTNUTS

(Cavoli con Castagne)

1 small cabbage, finely shredded
1 cup chestnuts, blanched
¼ cup raisins
1 cup water
1 tsp. salt
1 tblsp. sugar
2 tblsp. olive oil
1 tblsp. flour
¼ cup vinegar
¼ tsp. pepper

Place cabbage in a colander over another pan; pour over it boiling water to which vinegar has been added and let steam 10 minutes. Brown cabbage in hot olive oil with salt and pepper; cover and simmer 10 minutes. To the vinegar water add sugar, raisins and chestnuts; cook until chestnuts are tender. Sprinkle flour over cabbage, add to chestnut mixture and cook a few minutes. Serve hot. Serves 6.

CABBAGE IN WINE

(Cavoli con Vino)

1 medium white cabbage, cut up
1 cup tomatoes, quartered
1 medium onion, chopped
½ cup wine
¼ cup cheese, grated
2 tblsp. olive oil
1 tblsp. fennel seed
¼ tsp. lemon juice
salt to taste

Cook onion and cabbage in hot olive oil about 10 minutes; add fennel seed, tomato and salt, cover and cook 15 minutes. Pour in wine and lemon juice; cook 10 minutes. Serve sprinkled with cheese. Serves 6.

BOILED CARROTS

(Carote Bollite)

2 bunches carrots, cut up
½ tsp. nutmeg
4 tblsp. olive oil
salt to taste

Boil carrots in a small amount of water until almost tender, about 15 minutes; drain. Mix in olive oil, nutmeg and salt; cook until tender. Serves 8.

BAKED CAULIFLOWER

(Cavolfiori al Forno)

No. I

1 head cauliflower
1 cup thin white sauce
paprika
breadcrumbs
butter

Cook cauliflower in salted, boiling water about 20 minutes, or until tender; drain. Place on a serving dish, sprinkle with breadcrumbs mixed with butter; brown in a hot oven. Cover with white sauce (see recipe on page 247), sprinkle with paprika and serve. Serves 6.

No. II

1 large cauliflower
4 tblsp. olive oil
salt and marjoram to taste
Parmesan cheese, grated
1 egg, hard-boiled and sliced
4 tblsp. tomato paste

Cook cauliflower in salted, boiling water about 20 minutes or until tender; drain. Place in a greased baking dish; cover with olive oil blended with tomato paste and seasoning; bake in a moderate oven, covered, 15 minutes, then uncover and bake 10 minutes. Serve garnished with egg and cheese. Serves 6.

BOILED CAULIFLOWER

(Cavolfiori Bolliti)

1 head cauliflower
¼ tsp. salt
2 qts. boiling water
1 cup tomato sauce

Remove green leaves and stalk from cauliflower; soak head down in cold, salted water 10 minutes; drain. (If desired, separate cauliflower into flowerettes.) Cook cauliflower in boiling, salted water about 20 minutes, or until tender; drain. To serve, place on a hot serving dish, season, and cover with tomato sauce (see recipe on page 234). Serves 6.

NOTE: Try using the green leaves of cauliflower with spaghetti by boiling until tender; add spaghetti with enough more water to cook. Most of the water will be absorbed in the cooking. Drain, and serve sprinkled with grated cheese.

CAULIFLOWER PIETRO

(Cavolfiori alla Pietro)

1 medium cauliflower
½ onion, minced
1 clove garlic, minced
1 large tomato, chopped
½ cup chicken broth
salt and pepper
Parmesan cheese, grated
3 tblsp. olive oil

Wash cauliflower in water to which a tablespoonful of vinegar has been added; drain well. Separate into flowerettes and boil 10 minutes in salted water. Brown onion and garlic in hot olive oil, add tomato, chicken broth and seasoning; boil 10 minutes, and add cauliflower; cover and simmer until tender. Serve sprinkled with cheese. Serves 6.

CAULIFLOWER WITH TOMATOES

(Cavolfiori al Pomidoro)

1 head cauliflower
2 or 3 cloves garlic
2 or 3 tblsp. tomato sauce
olive oil
parsley, chopped
Parmesan cheese, grated

Divide cauliflower into small clusters and blanch in boiling, salted water for 10 minutes; drain. Heat a little olive oil with garlic and parsley until hot; add cauliflower and brown slightly. To serve, add tomato sauce (see recipe on page 234) and sprinkle with grated cheese. Serves 6.

CHESTNUT PUREE

(Purea di Castagne)

1 pt. chestnuts, blanched
salt and pepper
scalded milk

Cook chestnuts in boiling, salted water until tender; drain. Mash or rice chestnuts, season to taste, and add sufficient milk to moisten; beat until light. Serve with meat, fish or fowl Serves 6.

ONION CASSEROLE

(Cipollata)

3 carrots, sliced
1 lb. chestnuts, blanched
1 lb. Italian sausage
3 turnips, quartered
8 small white onions
½ lb. mushroom buttons

3 artichokes, quartered
1 qt. strong veal gravy (page 126)
1 stalk celery, chopped
salt and pepper

Combine the above ingredients in a large saucepan and cook for 30 minutes. Serves 6 to 8.

NOTE: This dish is very, very Italian. As it will keep several days, the recipe can be doubled, and it will be enjoyed to the last bit.

COLLARDS

(Trunzo)

2 lbs. collards, cubed
1 clove garlic, cut
1 cup vegetable stock
3 tblsp. Parmesan cheese, grated
1 medium onion
1 cup tomato juice
3 tblsp. olive oil
salt, pepper and marjoram

Heat olive oil in pan rubbed with garlic; add tomato juice with vegetable stock, and bring to a boil; add collards and whole onion, cover and simmer 10 minutes. Remove onion, add seasoning; simmer until tender (20 minutes). Serve sprinkled with cheese. Serves 6.

CORN PUDDING

(Podingo di Frumento)

2 cups milk
¼ onion, diced
2 eggs, well beaten
2 tsp. salt
⅛ tsp. white pepper
½ cup pastina (star shaped)
2 tblsp. olive oil
2 cups corn, whole kernel
1 tsp. celery salt

Heat milk in a double boiler, add pastina and cook 15 minutes, stirring frequently the first 5 minutes. Sauté onion in hot olive oil until tender; mix with pastina, corn, eggs and seasonings, and turn into a well oiled deep baking dish; bake in a moderate oven (350°F.) until firm. Serves 6.

BAKED EGGPLANT

(Melanzane al Forno)

1 large eggplant
2 tblsp. olive oil
1 tblsp. cheese, grated
2 tblsp. breadcrumbs

1 tsp. oregano
¼ onion, cut fine
1 egg yolk
salt and pepper

Parboil eggplant in salted, boiling water until tender but firm; cut in half crosswise, scrape out inside but have skin unbroken. Brown onion in one tablespoonful olive oil; add mashed eggplant pulp, breadcrumbs, seasonings, egg yolk, and mix well. Fill eggplant shells with mixture, place shells in baking pan; bake in a moderate oven about 30 minutes (350°F.). Baste frequently with olive oil until nicely browned. Serves 6.

EGGPLANT BALLS

(Polpette di Melanzane)

1 large eggplant
2 green peppers, chopped
¾ cup breadcrumbs
1 tsp. paprika
2 tblsp. olive oil
tomato sauce
1 onion, grated
2 eggs
2 tsp. salt
1 tblsp. cheese, grated
flour

Pare and cut-up eggplant, cover with boiling water and cook until tender; drain and cool. Mix onion, peppers, 1 egg, ½ cup breadcrumbs, salt, paprika, and cheese with eggplant; roll into balls, dip in flour, second beaten egg, and roll in breadcrumbs; fry in hot olive oil. Serve covered with tomato sauce (see recipe on page 234). Serves 6.

EGGPLANT CASSEROLE

(Melanzane in Casseruola)

1 small eggplant
3 tblsp. Parmesan cheese, grated
3 eggs, beaten
salt and pepper to taste
2 tblsp. garlic oil
1 lb. beef, chopped
tomato sauce

Peel and slice eggplant, dip in egg, roll in flour, season, and fry slowly in garlic oil until a light brown; remove eggplant and brown the meat. Place a layer of eggplant in a casserole, sprinkle with cheese, add a layer of meat, then tomato sauce. Continue alternating layers of ingredients until used up, then bake in a moderate oven for 25 minutes. Serves 6. (For tomato sauce see recipe on page 234.)

EGGPLANT WITH CHEESE

(Melanzane con Formaggio)

6 slices eggplant
½ cup cream
1 tomato, sliced
salt and pepper
1 cup breadcrumbs
1 mild onion, sliced
6 slices Scamozza cheese
olive oil

Peel and cut eggplant into 2-inch thick slices; dip each slice in breadcrumbs, then into cream, and then again into breadcrumbs. Fry in hot olive oil until a golden brown. Place eggplant in a baking dish with each slice topped with onion, tomato and cheese; season and bake in a pre-heated oven (350°F.) about 25 minutes. Serves 6.

EGGPLANT WITH EGGS

(Melanzane con Uova)

1 large eggplant, sliced thick
¼ cup olive oil
salt and pepper
1 clove garlic, minced
4 tblsp. Parmesan cheese, grated
1 onion, sliced
1½ cups tomato juice
½ tsp. sugar
3 eggs, hard-boiled and sliced

Fry eggplant slices in hot olive oil until golden brown; remove eggplant. Use the same oil to brown onion and garlic; add tomato juice, sugar, salt and pepper. Arrange half the eggplant in a buttered baking dish, cover with sliced egg, half the cheese, and half the tomato sauce; repeat process, using remaining ingredients. Heat in a moderate oven 15 minutes, and serve. Serves 4.

FRIED EGGPLANT

(Melanzane Fritte)

1 med. eggplant
½ cup flour
⅓ cup olive oil
1 tsp. salt

Pare and cut eggplant into thin slices; sprinkle with salt and stack in a colander, with a heavy weight placed on top to press out the juice; let stand about 1 hour. Squeeze dry and dredge slices with flour; fry slowly in hot olive oil until crisp and brown. Serves 4.

NOTE: If desired, the eggplant slices may be dipped in beaten egg and breadcrumbs before frying in olive oil. This dish makes an excellent meat substitute.

POTTED EGGPLANT

(Melanzane alla Graticola)

1 large eggplant
4 tblsp. milk
lemon juice
½ cup Parmesan cheese, grated
salt and pepper to taste

Parboil unpeeled eggplant 5 minutes; drain. Cut eggplant into ½-inch slices and place in a shallow baking dish, sprinkle with lemon juice and seasoning. Mix milk with cheese and pour over eggplant; broil in a moderate oven about 20 minutes or until cheese is a golden brown. Serves 4.

EGGPLANT RELISH

No. I

(Caponatina)

1 peck fresh tomatoes
1 lb. seedless raisins
1 small bottle capers
2 cups wine vinegar
salt and pepper
1 lb. ripe green olives, pitted and cut in half
¼ lb. pinenuts
4 bunches celery with greens, cut into 1-inch pieces
1 cup sugar
4 eggplants, cubed

Fry eggplant in deep oil; drain. Cook tomatoes 15 minutes and strain. Add olives, raisins, pinenuts, capers, celery and seasoning; cook until celery is tender, then add wine vinegar, sugar and cook 10 minutes more. Combine sauce with eggplant, stir a minute or so; while hot pour into sterile jars and seal.

No. II

(Melanzane Saporose)

1 large eggplant
1 small head lettuce
1 clove garlic, minced
pinch of oregano
juice of ½ lemon
2 med. tomatoes, sliced
4 tblsp. mayonnaise
1 tsp. parsley, minced
1 clove garlic, minced
salt and pepper

Impale eggplant on a wooden fork to hold it securely, and brown over a low fire about 15 minutes or until it looks like charcoal. Chop eggplant, unpeeled, coarsely and add lemon juice, then chop until fine; add seasoning to taste, parsley, garlic and mayonnaise; blend into eggplant. Serve in a nest of lettuce with tomatoes. Serves 6.

ROMAINE EGGPLANT

(Melanzane alla Romagna)

- 1 med. sized eggplant, cut into thick slices
- 1 egg, beaten
- ¼ Scamozza cheese, sliced
- ¼ cup onion, minced
- 1 tsp. salt
- 6 tblsp. olive oil
- 1 cup tomato sauce

Dip eggplant slices in egg to which salt has been added, sauté slowly in hot olive oil until golden brown on both sides. Arrange eggplant in stacks of three in a baking dish, with slices of cheese between and on top; cover with tomato sauce (see recipe on page 234) and bake in a moderately hot oven (375°F.) about 25 minutes, or until cheese is slightly browned on top. Serves 4.

ROSA'S FAVORITE EGGPLANT

(Melanzane alla Rosa)

- 1 large eggplant
- ½ onion, grated
- 1 green pepper, chopped fine
- ½ tsp. salt
- ½ cup Parmesan cheese, grated
- ½ cup olive oil
- ⅛ tsp. pepper
- ½ tsp. oregano
- 2 slices bacon (fried crisp and chopped)
- 4 fresh tomatoes, peeled and chopped
- 1 cup cashew nuts, chopped
- ½ cup breadcrumbs, fried in olive oil
- ⅛ tsp. paprika

Peel and slice eggplant thin; brown lightly in hot olive oil, and place in casserole. Brown onions and green pepper lightly in same olive oil; mix with bacon, tomatoes, half the nuts, and spread over eggplant. Mix remaining nuts with breadcrumbs and seasonings, and sprinkle over eggplant; cover with cheese and bake in a moderate oven (350°F.) about 40 minutes, or until bubbly and brown. Serves 4.

EGGPLANT SICILIAN STYLE

(Melanzane alla Siciliana)

1 large eggplant, sliced thin
1 cup Parmesan cheese, grated
2 eggs
4 tblsp. milk
salt and pepper
olive oil for deep frying
1 tsp. parsley, minced
1 dash cayenne pepper
1 clove garlic, minced
flour
breadcrumbs

Mix cheese, 1 egg, milk, parsley, and cayenne pepper into a paste, and add garlic. Make sandwiches of the eggplant by spreading a slice with paste and topping with another slice; dredge in seasoned flour, dip in beaten egg mixed with a few drops of water, and roll in breadcrumbs; fry in deep, hot olive oil until a golden brown. Drain on absorbent paper, and serve garnished with parsley. Serves 4.

STUFFED EGGPLANT

(Melanzane Ripiena)

2 large eggplants
2 tblsp. olive oil
½ cup onion, chopped fine
1 tblsp. parsley, chopped
2 tblsp. green pepper, chopped
½ lb. ground beef
2 cups cooked rice
½ cup breadcrumbs, toasted
1 tblsp. butter
salt and pepper

Parboil eggplant about 15 minutes; drain. Cut in half lengthwise, scrape out pulp to within ½-inch of skin and chop fine. Sauté onion, parsley and pepper in hot olive oil about 5 minutes; add beef and pulp, and simmer until meat is browned; remove from heat and add rice and seasoning. Salt and pepper inside of eggplant shells and fill with meat mixture, top with breadcrumbs and dot with butter. Place on a baking sheet and bake in a hot oven (400°F.) about 15 to 20 minutes. Serves 6.

STUFFED EGGPLANT WITH SPAGHETTI

(Ripieno di Melanzane con Spaghetti)

½ cup tubettine spaghetti
¼ cup onion, chopped fine
1 cup tomatoes, diced
½ tsp. salt
2 tblsp. cheese, grated
1 large eggplant
2 tblsp. olive oil
1 cup left-over meat, ground
1/16 tsp. pepper

Cook and drain spaghetti. Cut eggplant in half, lengthwise, and scoop out pulp without breaking shell; dice and sauté pulp in hot olive oil, add tomatoes and cook 5 minutes; add meat, seasonings and spaghetti, mixing well. Fill eggplant shells generously with mixture; sprinkle with cheese and place in a baking dish containing ⅛-inch of hot water. Bake in a moderately hot oven (375°F.) about 20 minutes or until cheese is browned. Serves 4.

EGGPLANT WITH TOMATO

(Melanzane al Pomidoro)

2 medium eggplants
½ lb. ground beef, browned
1 egg, hard-boiled
salt and pepper
tomato sauce (see page 234)
1 cup breadcrumbs
3 tblsp. Parmesan cheese, grated
1 egg, beaten
2 tblsp. olive oil

Cut eggplant in half lengthwise, scoop out and parboil pulp about 10 minutes or until mushy. Mix pulp with breadcrumbs, seasoning, beef, cheese, hard-boiled egg; fill eggplant shells. Brush tops of filled shells with egg, fry a minute or two in hot olive oil to seal, place in a casserole with tomato meat sauce, cover and bake in a moderate oven (350°) about 45 minutes. Serves 4 to 6.

NOTE: Serve this dish with a mixed green salad, Italian bread and wine, you will receive many compliments. Fruit, cheese and crackers complete the dinner.

FENNEL

(Finocchio all'Italiana)

2 heads fennel (finocchio)
¼ cup olive oil
1 egg, hard-boiled
2 tblsp. breadcrumbs
1 tblsp. Parmesan cheese, grated
salt and paprika

Cut off tops of fennel, quarter and cook until tender in boiling, salted water; drain. Place fennel in a buttered baking dish with cut sides up; cover with olive oil and a mixture of breadcrumbs, eggs, and cheese. Brown in a hot oven, adding a dash of paprika and sprinkle of parsley. Serves 4.

FENNEL WITH TOMATO

(Finocchio con Pomidoro)

2 bunches fennel (finocchio)
¾ cup water
4 tblsp. tomato paste
parsley, chopped
1 fresh pimento, chopped
6 tblsp. Parmesan cheese, grated
1 tblsp. olive oil
salt and paprika to taste

Mix tomato paste with water and heat to a boil. Peel fennel and slice directly into boiling liquid; cover and simmer 10 minutes. Cook pimento in hot olive oil 5 minutes, then add to fennel with seasoning; simmer until fennel is tender. Serve sprinkled with parsley and cheese. Serves 6.

BRAISED LETTUCE

(Lattuga alla Pietro)

2 heads lettuce, quartered
½ cup breadcrumbs
salt and pepper
3 tblsp. butter
3 tblsp. cheese, grated

Boil lettuce in the smallest amount of salted water about 5 minutes; drain. Arrange in a shallow baking dish, dot with butter, and sprinkle with breadcrumbs mixed with cheese, salt and pepper; bake in a hot oven (450°F.) about 15 minutes. Serves 4.

MIXTURE

(Mescolanza)

2 small eggplants, halved
salt and pepper
3 eggs
1 cup breadcrumbs
4 onions, sliced
3 cups lamb, cooked and minced
½ cup meat gravy
1½ cups tomatoes, strained
½ tsp. sugar
½ tsp. paprika
1 cup corn
3 tblsp. cream

Parboil eggplant in salted, boiling water about 10 minutes; drain, and season with pepper. Dip eggplant in one egg slightly beaten with 1 tblsp. water, roll in breadcrumbs and fry in hot olive oil until light brown. Fry onion in hot olive oil until yellow; season with salt and pepper. Place a layer of eggplant in an oiled baking dish, cover with onions, add a layer of meat with gravy, and top with a layer of eggplant. Strain tomatoes, season with salt, sugar, paprika; pour over eggplant, and bake in a moderate oven (350°F.) about 20 minutes. Beat remaining eggs slightly, add cream, corn, salt and pepper; beat together, and pour over eggplant. Replace eggplant in oven, turn off heat and allow to remain 10 minutes; place under broiler and brown slightly. Serves 4.

NOTE: This is a good way to use left-over meat and gravy.

MUSHROOMS WITH CHICKEN LEFT-OVERS

(Funghi con Pollo)

- 1 lb. large mushrooms
- 1 tblsp. onion, minced
- 3 tblsp. chicken, minced
- ½ cup chicken stock
- butter
- 2 tblsp. garlic oil
- 2 tblsp. breadcrumbs
- 1 tblsp. parsley, minced
- 4 tblsp. cheese, grated

Remove stems from mushrooms leaving a hollow center. Chop stems fine; cook in garlic oil and add onion, breadcrumbs, chicken, parsley, chicken stock and mix well. Fill mushroom centers with mixture, cover with cheese and breadcrumb mixture and dot with butter. Bake in a moderate (350°F.) oven for 15 minutes. Serves 4.

MUSHROOMS AND GARLIC

(Funghi all'Aglio)

- 1 lb. mushrooms, peeled
- 2 lbs. tomatoes, quartered
- 2 or 3 cloves garlic
- 2 tblsp. olive oil
- 2 or 3 sprigs marjoram
- salt and pepper

Simmer tomatoes, garlic, salt and pepper, without adding any water, over a low fire about 1 hour, until tomatoes are reduced to a pulp, crushing now and then with a spoon to extract the juice; rub through a sieve, and you have what the Italians call "sugo di pomidoro", which is used extensively in Italian cooking. Mix the "sugo", olive oil and marjoram; add mushrooms and bring to a boil; simmer gently about 30 minutes. Serves 4.

MUSHROOMS ISADORO

(Funghi alla Isadoro)

- 1½ lbs. mushrooms, sliced
- 1 clove garlic
- 1 med. onion, chopped fine
- ½ cup wine

3 tblsp. olive oil
salt and cayenne pepper
1 tblsp. flour

Cook mushrooms and onion in hot olive oil about 5 minutes, stir in flour and seasoning; add garlic and wine, cover and simmer over a low fire 10 minutes. Remove garlic and serve. Serves 6.

SMOTHERED MUSHROOMS

(Funghi Affogati)

½ lb. mushrooms
3 tblsp. olive oil
½ clove garlic, crushed
salt and pepper

Wash, dry and cut mushrooms in half; marinate for 2 hours in olive oil, garlic and seasoning, stirring occasionally. Fry gently in skillet, shaking pan to prevent burning; reduce heat when brown, cover and let smother a few minutes. Serve on toast. Serves 4.

MUSHROOM STEW

(Stufatò di Funghi)

1 lb. mushrooms
4 potatoes, diced
2 onions, sliced
½ cup celery, diced
1 tsp. basil
2 tomatoes, peeled and quartered
1 green pepper, diced
2 carrots, diced
¼ cup olive oil
3 tblsp. parsley, chopped
salt and pepper
1 tsp. oregano

Brown each vegetable separately in hot olive oil, place in saucepan then add water and seasoning; simmer until vegetables are tender; add mushrooms and continue cooking 10 minutes more. Serve hot with chunks of Italian bread. Serves 6.

STUFFED ONIONS

(Cipolle Ripiene)

2 lbs. medium onions
1 cup left-over, cooked meat, chopped
⅓ cup green pepper, chopped
1 tblsp. olive oil
1 cup breadcrumbs
1 cup milk
¼ tsp. oregano
½ tsp. parsley, minced
½ cup browned crumbs
salt and pepper to taste

Peel onions carefully to preserve shapes. Wash and cut a slice from the top of each onion. Pierce each onion through center in several places. Boil onions until almost tender, drain and push out centers. Combine meat, green peppers, breadcrumbs and olive oil, add seasonings and stuff onion cups. Place in an oiled baking dish. Pour milk around onions. Cover top with browned crumbs. Bake in a moderate oven (375°) until tender and the tops are a golden brown, about ½ hour. Serves 6.

NOTE: To retain the sweet flavor of onions they should always be boiled in a large open saucepan with plenty of water. The boiling should be gentle to prevent layers from falling apart. With a sharp knife make several gashes around onion.

BROWN CRUMBS:

Heat 3 tblsp. of olive oil in skillet, add ½ cup fine breadcrumbs and stir over medium heat until crumbs are toasted to a golden brown.

LIMA STUFFED ONIONS

(Cipolle Ripiene di Fave)

- 2 cups dried lima beans
- 8 large onions
- ¼ tsp. sweet basil
- ¼ lb. Provoloni cheese, diced
- 1 tblsp. salt
- 4 tblsp. olive oil
- ⅛ tsp. pepper
- ½ cup breadcrumbs

Soak lima beans overnight in sufficient water to cover. Do not drain, but add enough more water to cover well, salt and simmer about 1½ hours. Cook whole, peeled onions in ½ cup boiling water; cut a slice from top of each onion, remove centers by pushing from bottom with thumb; place onion shells in greased baking dish. Chop onion centers and add to lima beans with olive oil, basil, pepper and cheese, blending well. Fill onion shells with bean mixture, placing the remaining mixture around the onions; top with breadcrumbs and bake in a moderate oven (350°F.) about 20 minutes or until breadcrumbs are browned. Serves 4.

PEAS WITH HAM

(Piselli al Prosciutto)

- 1 lb. peas
- 1 tblsp. olive oil
- a few strips (to taste) of Italian ham (prosciutto)
- 2 or 3 tblsp. stock
- salt and pepper

Cook peas in a covered saucepan or casserole with olive oil, stock, seasoning and a few, thin strips of ham; simmer until very tender. Serves 6.

BLACK-EYED PEAS WITH SAUSAGE

(Piselli con Salsiccia)

1 lb. (2 cups) black-eyed peas, dried
1 tblsp. salt
1 tblsp. bacon fat
¼ tsp. basil
1 lb. Italian sausage, sliced
1 large onion, minced
1 can (No. 2) tomatoes
1 tsp. black pepper

Soak peas overnight in sufficient water to cover. Do not drain after soaking, but add salt and more water to cover well; simmer 1½ hours. Brown sausage and onion in hot bacon fat; add peas, tomatoes, pepper, basil and salt to taste; simmer about 20 minutes to blend flavors well. Serve in soup plates or individual casseroles. Serves 4.

BAKED PEPPERS

(Peperoni al Forno)

4 green peppers
olive oil

Quarter peppers, remove seeds and membrane; arrange in a baking dish, sprinkle with olive oil, and bake in a moderate (350°F.) oven about 30 minutes. Drain. Serves 4.

BAKED PEPPERS WITH CHEESE

(Peperoni al Forno alla Parmigiana)

6 large green peppers
3 eggs, beaten
2 cups milk
2 tblsp. curry powder
2 tblsp. Parmesan cheese, grated
½ tblsp. soy sauce
1 cup rice, cooked
½ tsp. salt
dash of pepper

Cut off stem ends of peppers, remove membrane and seeds; parboil in boiling, salted water 5 to 10 minutes. While peppers are boiling, beat together eggs, milk, curry powder, cheese, soy sauce, and seasoning; add rice and fill peppers. Bake in a moderate (350°F.) oven about 1 hour Serves 6.

FRIED PEPPERS WITH EGGS

(Peperoni Fritti con Uova)

6 green peppers
4 eggs, beaten
¼ cup olive oil
1 onion, sliced

Cut peppers into slices after removing seeds and membrane; brown in hot olive oil with onions, add eggs and cook until done. Serves 4.

NOTE: Served with a salad, this dish makes a very tasty lunch.

STUFFED GREEN PEPPERS

(Peperoni Ripieni)

6 large green peppers
4 tblsp. cheese, grated
1 tsp. black pepper
½ tsp. garlic salt
2 slices salami, diced
1½ cups breadcrumbs
1 tblsp. salt
1 tsp. oregano
1 egg, hard-boiled, chopped
¼ cup olive oil

Cut around the pepper stems and remove seeds and pulp from peppers, leaving shell unbroken. Mix together cheese, pepper, garlic salt, salami, breadcrumbs, salt, oregano and egg; fill pepper shells. Brown peppers in hot olive oil, remove and arrange in casserole.

SAUCE:

1 onion, chopped fine
4 cups water
fennel seeds
1 tblsp. sugar
1 cup tomato paste
oregano, celery salt, garlic salt
½ cup wine vinegar

Mix above ingredients in olive oil peppers were browned in; simmer 30 minutes, and pour over peppers. Bake in a moderate oven (350°F.) about 1 hour. Serves 6.

See also pages 227 and 234.

PEPPERS STUFFED WITH CHICKEN

(Peperoni Ripieni con Pollo)

6 green peppers
6 anchovies, cut small
4 tomatoes, chopped
¼ cup breadcrumbs
3 tblsp. cheese, grated
½ cup olive oil

½ lb. chicken, cooked and chopped
salt and pepper
oregano, basil and paprika

Slice tops with stems from peppers and remove seeds and membrane. Mix anchovies, tomatoes, chicken, cheese, bread-crumbs and herbs; stuff peppers and replace pepper tops, using toothpicks to anchor them. Arrange in baking pan, cover with olive oil, and sprinkle with salt, paprika and cheese. Bake in a moderate (350°F.) oven about 30 to 45 minutes. Serves 6.

PEPPERS STUFFED WITH MEAT

(Peperoni Ripieni con Carne)

No. I

12 sweet green peppers
½ lb. beef, ground
½ lb. crackers, rolled
¼ lb. Romano cheese, grated
3 eggs, hard-boiled, chopped
tomato sauce
½ cup pinenuts
½ lb. pork, ground
½ cup olive oil
½ cup seedless raisins
salt and pepper

Brown meat in 2 tblsp. hot olive oil; season with salt and pepper, add raisins, cracker crumbs, cheese and eggs. Remove stem-ends and pulp of peppers, fill shells with meat mixture, replace stem-ends and hold in place with toothpicks. Heat remainder of olive oil and fry stuffed peppers until slightly brown; cover with tomato sauce and bake in a moderate oven (350°) for 45 minutes. Serves 6.

TOMATO SAUCE:

2 6-oz. cans tomato paste
6 cans water
1 medium onion, chopped
3 tblsp. olive oil
salt and pepper
¼ tsp. oregano

Brown onion in olive oil, add tomato paste, water, salt, pepper and oregano, simmer for 1 hour.

See also page 234.

No. II

2 cups ground beef, cooked
2 tblsp. onion, grated
½ cup potatoes, mashed
½ tsp. salt
½ cup catsup
1½ cups gravy or soup stock
⅓ cup Parmesan cheese, grated
6 green peppers
paprika

Mix meat, onion, potatoes and seasoning with enough gravy or thickened soup stock to moisten. Cut off the caps of the peppers, remove membrane and seeds; cook 2 minutes, drain and rinse with cold water. Fill peppers with meat mixture, arrange on rack in baking pan, and bake in a moderate oven (350°F.) about 45 minutes. Sprinkle with cheese and paprika about 15 minutes before peppers are done. Serves 6.

PEPPERS STUFFED WITH SPAGHETTI

(Peperoni Ripieni con Spaghetti)

- 12 green peppers
- 1 No. 3 can tomatoes
- 3 tblsp. Parmesan cheese, grated
- ½ tsp. pepper
- ¼ cup breadcrumbs
- 3 cups left-over meat, ground or chopped fine
- 1 lb. spaghetti
- salt to taste

Cut peppers lengthwise, remove seeds; parboil 5 minutes, then drain and salt insides. Cook spaghetti in salted, boiling water until tender; drain, and mix with tomatoes, meat, breadcrumbs, cheese and seasoning. Lay pepper halves in an oiled baking pan; fill half of the peppers with spaghetti mixture, replace remaining halves over filling; sprinkle with olive oil. Place pan with peppers in another pan containing a cup of water; bake in a moderate oven (350°F.) about 30 minutes. Serves 8.

VARIED STUFFED PEPPERS

(Peperoni con Ripieni Varii)

- 6 large green peppers
- 1 large onion, chopped
- 1 clove garlic, minced
- 3 tblsp. olive oil
- 1 qt. tomatoes, forced through a sieve
- 2 eggs, beaten
- 1 tsp. salt
- ½ tsp. pepper
- ½ tsp. sugar
- 4 slices stale bread
- 1 cup Parmesan cheese, grated
- 6 eggs, whole

Cut peppers in half lengthwise and remove seeds and membrane; parboil 5 minutes. Brown onion and garlic in hot olive oil, add tomatoes, salt, pepper and sugar; heat and pour into a shallow baking pan. Dip bread slices into cold water, squeeze dry, mix with cheese and beaten eggs; fill peppers, and arrange in the tomato sauce. Bake in a moderate (350°F.) oven 25 minutes, then break the 6 whole eggs into sauce and continue baking until eggs are set. Serve from casserole. Serves 6.

RICE WITH OKRA

(Riso con Okra)

1 lb. okra, small
2 cups boiling water
1 clove garlic
1 tsp. salt
2 tblsp. olive oil
1 cup rice, cooked

Wash and cut off stems of okra. Add garlic to boiling, salted water with okra; cook 20 minutes and drain. Remove garlic, add seasoning and olive oil. Serve with cooked rice. Serves 6.

NOTE: If okra are large with hard pods, cut into ½-inch pieces.

BOILED ROMAINE

(Lattuga Romagna Bollita)

1 head romaine (or outer leaves of 3 heads)
olive oil
garlic
salt and pepper

Wash romaine, cut larger leaves in half, and boil in ½ cup salted water; season with garlic, olive oil, salt and pepper. Makes a tasty dish, and is an excellent way to use the large, outer leaves of romaine. Serves 2.

SPINACH WITH GARLIC

(Spinacci all'Aglio)

3 lbs. spinach
3 tblsp. garlic oil
salt and pepper

Wash spinach well; place in dish containing garlic oil, toss around until leaves are well coated with oil, season and serve. Serves 8.

SPINACH MARIANA

(Spinacci alla Mariana)

¼ cup butter
¼ cup flour
1½ cups milk
3 eggs, lightly beaten
3 cups spinach, cooked
salt and pepper

Make a white sauce of butter, flour and milk; add eggs, and season. Chop spinach fine and add to white sauce; pour into a buttered mold, cover and bake in a pan of hot water in a moderate oven (350°F.) for 1 hour. Serves 6.

SPINACH MARIA

(Spinacci alla Maria)

1 lb. spinach
juice of 1 lemon
2 tblsp. olive oil
salt and pepper to taste

Wash and pack spinach into a saucepan with salt and sufficient water to prevent burning; cook about 10 minutes. Chop spinach and add olive oil, pepper and lemon juice. Serves 4.

NOTE: Endive, lettuce, asparagus and any of the green leaf vegetables can be fixed this way.

ROMAN STYLE SPINACH

(Spinacci alla Romana)

1 lb. spinach
salt and pepper
3 tblsp. olive oil

Cook spinach 10 minutes in two cups of water and, without draining, add hot olive oil with seasoning, mixing well. Serve hot. Serves 4.

STEAMED SPINACH

(Spinacci Affogati)

2 lbs. spinach
2 cloves garlic, minced
4 tblsp. olive oil
salt and pepper

Brown garlic in hot olive oil; add thoroughly washed spinach, salt and pepper to taste, and cover tightly. Steam spinach over a low fire until well cooked, turning occasionally. Serves 6.

SPINACH WITH TOMATOES

(Spinacci con Pomidoro)

1 lb. spinach
3 tblsp. olive oil
1 small can tomatoes
½ tsp. salt
⅛ tsp. pepper

Boil spinach until tender; drain, and chop fine. Brown garlic in hot olive oil; add tomatoes, spinach and seasoning; cook 15 minutes. Serves 4.

TOMATO CASSEROLE

(Pomidoro in Casseruola)

1 onion, sliced	1 green pepper, sliced
½ lb. spaghetti, broken	¼ tsp. pepper
1 tsp. salt	2 tblsp. olive oil
1 cup small lima beans, cooked	½ cup Parmesan cheese, grated
1 can tomatoes	

Brown onion in hot olive oil, add tomatoes, peppers, lima beans; simmer. Cook spaghetti about 8 minutes in boiling, salted water; drain. Combine spaghetti with vegetable mixture, season and turn into a baking dish that has been rubbed with olive oil, sprinkle with cheese and bake about 20 minutes in a moderate (350°F.) oven. Serves 4.

STUFFED TOMATOES

(Pomidori Ripieni)

6 tomatoes	½ cup rice
3 cups broth or stock	2 tblsp. olive oil
6 anchovies	1 clove garlic
dash of pepper	few sprigs of mint

Boil rice in broth or stock until cooked; add anchovies, pepper and mint, and fill centers of hollowed out tomatoes. Heat garlic and olive oil; add filled tomatoes and bake in a moderate oven (350°F.) about 20 minutes.

TOMATOES STUFFED WITH SPAGHETTI

(Pomidori Ripieni di Spaghetti)

1 cup short, elbow spaghetti	4 large ripe tomatoes
¼ cup onion, chopped	¼ cup celery, chopped
2 tblsp. olive oil	½ cup left-over meat, chopped
½ tsp. salt	1/16 tsp. pepper

Cook spaghetti; drain. Slice off tops of tomatoes about ½ inch thick, scoop out centers and dice. Sauté onion and celery in hot olive oil; add spaghetti, tomato pulp, meat and seasoning, mix well. Fill tomato shells with spaghetti and meat mixture; replace tops of tomatoes and arrange in a shallow baking dish containing about ¼ inch of hot water. Bake in a moderately hot oven (375°) about 25 minutes or until tender. Serves 4.

VEGETABLE CASSEROLE

(Casserola di Verdura)

½ cup pastina
¼ cup onion, diced
1 pint milk
2 tsp. salt
¼ tsp. pepper
1 cup celery, cooked and diced
10 tblsp. olive oil
6 tblsp. flour
1 cup carrots, cooked and diced
1 cup peas, cooked
¼ tsp. onion salt
½ cup breadcrumbs

Cook pastina 15 minutes; drain. Sauté onion in 2 tblsp. hot olive oil until tender; combine with pastina and vegetables in a greased casserole. Make a white sauce of 2 tblsp. olive oil, flour, milk and seasonings; pour over vegetable mixture, stirring gently. Brown breadcrumbs in 6 tblsp. hot olive oil, and sprinkle over vegetables; bake in a hot oven (425°F.) about 30 minutes, or until thoroughly hot and crumbs are golden. Serves 4.

CREAMED VEGETABLES

(Crema di Legumi)

4 tblsp. olive oil
1 tsp. salt
2 cups milk
4 tblsp. flour
¼ tsp. pepper
3 cups cooked vegetables (carrots, peas, lima beans, celery or onions)

Season olive oil, heat and blend in flour; remove from fire and add milk slowly, mixing to a smooth sauce. Cook sauce until thickened, stirring to prevent lumpiness; add vegetables and heat through. Serves 6.

VEGETABLES WITH EGG

(Frittata con Legumi)

4 egg yolks
1 tblsp. parsley, chopped
2 cups cooked vegetables, assorted

salt and pepper
Parmesan cheese, grated
1 clove garlic, minced
3 tblsp. olive oil

Beat egg yolks; mix with vegetables, seasoning, garlic, parsley (or other herbs) and cheese. Heat olive oil in a shallow casserole, pour in vegetable mixture (Frittata) and bake in a moderate oven (300°), 15 to 25 minutes, or until firm. Serve cut into wedges. Serves 4.

NOTE: The Frittata can be made of any left over cooked vegetables, such as spinach, artichoke hearts, zucchini, string beans, peas, green lima beans or whatever you have.

VEGETABLE MEAT OMELET

(Frittata di Verdura e Carne)

3 cups vegetables and meats, cooked
3 tblsp. olive oil
6 eggs, beaten
salt and pepper

Combine vegetables, meats and eggs in hot olive oil; cook until set. When edges begin to brown, turn with a pancake turner, and cook until done. Serves 4.

NOTE: Frittata differs from ordinary omelets in that it is more like a pancake fried in olive oil, which gives it a nut-like flavor. Any left over vegetables can be used and/or meats. such as ham, tongue, kidneys, fish, etc.

MIXED VEGETABLES

(Verdure Miste)

1 egg, beaten
2 artichokes, boiled and sliced
1 cauliflower, boiled and sliced
lemon slices
parsley, salt and pepper
3 tblsp. Parmesan cheese, grated
2 zucchini, steamed and sliced
½ lb. spinach, boiled and sliced
breadcrumbs

Dip cold sliced vegetables into egg, then into breadcrumbs mixed with cheese, salt and pepper; fry in hot olive oil until tender. Serve arranged on a warm platter garnished with parsley and lemon slices. Serves 6. (See cooking directions for each vegetable, especially for steamed zucchini, page 211.)

ZUCCHINI AUGUSTINO

(Zucchini alla Augostino)

1 lb. zucchini, sliced across
3 tblsp. Parmesan cheese, grated
2 eggs, beaten
½ cup breadcrumbs
1 tsp. sweet basil
salt and pepper

Dip zucchini in eggs seasoned with basil, salt and pepper· roll in breadcrumbs and cheese mixed. Fry in hot olive oil until golden brown. Serves 6.

ZUCCHINI WITH CHEESE

(Zucchini con Formaggio)

3 medium zucchini, sliced thick
2 small pickles, chopped
4 tblsp. olive oil
flour
2 firm tomatoes, sliced
½ cup sour cream
4 tblsp. Parmesan cheese, grated
salt and pepper

Dredge zucchini in seasoned flour; cook in 3 tblsp. olive oil for 4 minutes. Use remaining olive oil to grease a shallow baking pan, cover bottom with half the zucchini, top with pickles and half the grated cheese; cover with rest of zucchini, spread with sour cream, and tomato slices, and sprinkle with remaining cheese. Broil under moderate heat about 20 minutes. Serves 4.

FRIED ZUCCHINI

(Fritto di Zucchini)

2 lbs. zucchini, sliced across into circles about 3/16 of an inch thick
3 tblsp. onion, minced
½ cup green pepper, minced
½ tsp. salt
⅛ tsp. garlic powder
2 slices bacon, minced
1 cup tomato sauce
½ tsp. thick, meat sauce
¼ tsp. pepper

Cook zucchini, covered, in about ½-inch of boiling, salted water until tender; drain. Sauté bacon, onion and green peppers until bacon browns lightly; add remaining ingredients, and simmer about 10 minutes. Serve at once covered with tomato sauce (see recipe on page 202). Serves 6.

ZUCCHINI MARGHERITA

(Zucchini alla Margherita)

4 small zucchini, halved
6 black olives
3 tblsp. olive oil
3 tblsp. Parmesan cheese
juice of 1 lemon
1 large onion, chopped fine
1 clove garlic
3 tblsp. cracker crumbs
2 tblsp. tomato paste
salt and black pepper

Scoop out zucchini centers and chop fine; blend with onion, crumbs, tomato paste and seasoning to a smooth paste. Salt and rub zucchini halves with garlic; stuff with paste mixture, cover with cheese, dot with olive oil and pitted olives. Place in a baking dish and bake uncovered in a moderate oven (350°F.) about 20 minutes. Serves 6.

MOM'S FAVORITE ZUCCHINI

(Zucchini alla Mama Maria)

4 onions, sliced
1 clove garlic, minced
2 tblsp. olive oil
1 small can tomatoes, chopped
1 lb. zucchini, sliced
salt and pepper

Sauté garlic and onion in hot olive oil until golden brown; add tomatoes, and simmer 20 minutes; add zucchini, simmer a few minutes until tender. Season and serve. Serves 6.

ZUCCHINI SAMUEL

(Zucchini Fritti alla Samuele)

1½ lbs. zucchini, sliced
1 clove garlic
½ cup olive oil
1 cup breadcrumbs
¼ cup cheese, grated
1 egg, well beaten
salt and pepper

Dip zucchini in egg, roll in breadcrumbs mixed with cheese and seasoning; fry in hot olive oil on both sides, slowly. Serves 6.

NOTE: Makes an excellent meat substitute.

SMOTHERED ZUCCHINI

(Affogato di Zucchini)

2 cups zucchini, diced about 1 inch
2 tblsp. olive oil
1 stalk celery, sliced thin
1 small tomato, peeled and sliced
3 tblsp. broth or stock
salt and pepper

Cook zucchini 5 minutes in hot olive oil, add remaining ingredients, reduce heat and continue cooking 5 minutes more. Serves 4.

STEAMED ZUCCHINI

(Zucchini Affogati)

6 med. sized zucchini, sliced
¼ cup olive oil
salt and pepper
½ cup water
½ onion, chopped

Brown onion in hot olive oil, add water and zucchini cover and steam until tender. Season and serve. Serves 4.

ZUCCHINI WITH TOMATO

(Zucchini con Pomidoro)

4 tblsp. olive oil
1 onion, minced
basil, salt and pepper
2 large tomatoes, peeled and sliced
6 zucchini, sliced

Brown onion lightly in hot olive oil; add tomatoes, and cook 3 or 4 minutes; add zucchini with seasoning, cover, and cook 15 minutes. If zucchini gets too dry while cooking, add a little boiling water. Serves 4.

CHAPTER TEN

Rice

METHOD FOR BOILING OR STEAMING RICE

Wash rice thoroughly through several cold waters until last rinse water is clear, drain. Have actively boiling water ready in a 5 quart saucepan, allowing 2½ quarts of water to 1 cup of rice. Add 2 teaspoons salt to each quart of water. Drop rice in slowly so that boiling does not stop. Allow to boil rapidly until grains of rice are entirely soft when pressed between thumb and finger (from 15 to 25 minutes). To prevent rice from sticking to the pan, stir lightly with fork from time to time. When done, pour rice into a colander and rinse with hot water. Cover colander with a cloth and set over pan of hot water over low heat for 10 minutes. This swells and separates the grains as well as steaming.

To make rice snowy white, add 1 teaspoon lemon juice to cooking water. One cup raw rice makes 2 cups steamed rice.

PLAIN RICE

(Risotto)

No. I

1 cup rice
¼ cup butter
1 onion, chopped
1 qt. meat broth
salt and pepper
½ tsp. saffron
1 cup white wine, heated
1 cup Parmesan cheese, grated
1 lb. fresh mushrooms, quartered
3 tblsp. olive oil

Brown rice in butter, add onions and fry a few minutes; add a pint of meat broth, and boil rapidly. While rice is boiling, gently shake the pan to prevent it from sticking, as the broth evaporates. Add remaining broth, and seasonings; continue boiling, reducing heat as liquid absorbs; add cheese, wine and saffron mixed with a little water, mix gently; set over steam until dry and fluffy. Sauté mushrooms in hot olive oil and season. Pile rice in center of serving dish, arrange mushrooms in a ring around it and serve. Have grated cheese in a wooden bowl with a wooden spoon, and let each person sprinkle cheese over his portion of the rice and mushrooms. Serves 6.

NOTE: This is an ancient dish of Tuscany, where it is known as Tridura.

No. II

- 2 cups rice
- 1 or 2 onions, chopped
- 8 tblsp. butter
- 2 cups Parmesan cheese, grated
- 4 tblsp. beef marrow
- 3 or 4 tblsp. white wine
- 3 cups beef or chicken stock
- pinch of saffron
- salt and pepper to taste

Brown onion in heated beef marrow and 4 tblsp. butter; add rice, stir well, and cook 15 minutes. Bring stock to a boil, add to rice with wine, saffron, salt and pepper; simmer gently 20 to 30 minutes, stirring occasionally. Just before serving, sprinkle with cheese and remaining butter, melted. Serves 6.

NOTE: By combining 1½ to 2 cups sliced mushrooms after onions are slightly brown and cooking 5 minutes before adding the rice, you have an excellent dish. In this instance, the wine and saffron are omitted.

RICE BALLS

(Arangini)

- 1 lb. rice
- 1 lb. ground beef
- ½ cup Parmesan cheese, grated
- ¼ cup minced parsley
- 1 tblsp. salt
- cracker crumbs
- 1 egg, beaten
- 1 tblsp. olive oil
- 2 eggs, hard-boiled and chopped
- ½ tsp. pepper

Boil rice in salted water until cooked, drain and mix with beaten egg. Brown the ground beef in olive oil, then mix with cheese, hard-boiled eggs, parsley, pepper and salt. Make a dent in a handful of rice (rinse hands in cold water to keep from sticking) and fill with beef mixture, then mold into a ball. Dip rice balls in cracker crumbs and fry in deep olive oil until golden brown. Drain on brown paper. Makes 8 rice balls. Serves 6.

RICE CASSEROLE

(Riso al Forno)

3 cups rice, cooked
¼ cup olive oil
2 cups milk
¼ cups almonds, chopped
½ cup Parmesan cheese, grated
2 tblsp. green pepper, minced
4 tblsp. flour
1 tsp. salt
3 eggs, hard-boiled and sliced
parsley

Brown green pepper in hot olive oil, blend in flour, and add milk gradually, stirring until thickened; add salt, nuts, cheese, and heat through, mixing well. Pack the hot rice into oiled custard cups to mold; turn out onto hot platter, and cover the molded rice with the hot sauce. Serve garnished with egg and sprigs of parsley. Serves 6.

CHEESE RICE BALLS

(Polpette di Riso e Formaggio)

2 cups rice, cooked
2 eggs, beaten
1 cup breadcrumbs
seasoning to taste
¼ lb. Mozzarella cheese, cubed
½ cup Parmesan cheese, grated
flour
olive oil

Shape the cooked rice into cylinders or balls; place a cube of Mozzarella cheese in the center of each, and dip in flour, egg, and breadcrumbs; fry in hot olive oil. Serve hot. Serves 4.

RICE DAD LOVED

(Riso Preferito da Papa)

3 cups cooked rice
1 cup onion, minced
1½ tsp. salt
1 bay leaf
Parmesan cheese, grated
2 cups tomatoes
3 tblsp. olive oil
½ cup green pepper, minced
5 slices salami, cut into strips

Fry onion in hot olive oil until transparent; add salt, green pepper, tomatoes, and bay leaf; simmer 15 minutes. Remove bay leaf, add rice and salami strips; cook 10 minutes. Serve sprinkled with cheese. Serves 6.

FRIED RICE

(Riso Fritto)

1 cup cooked rice
4 strips bacon, broiled and cut up
1 cup left-over cooked meat
2 eggs, scrambled
1 onion, minced
salt and pepper to taste

Brown the onion in bacon drippings, add meat, rice, bacon, and scrambled eggs seasoned to taste; fry until consistency desired. Serve with your favorite salad and red wine—makes a complete dinner. Serves 4.

RICE AND CHICKEN LIVERS

(Riso con Fegatini di Pollo)

1 cup rice
1 pinch saffron
½ cup Parmesan cheese, grated
seasoning to taste
1 lb. chicken livers
3 tblsp. olive oil
1 ½ cups chicken stock
parsley, chopped

Heat chicken stock, add rice, cover and bring to a boil; add a good pinch of saffron, and when rice is nearly done, stir in cheese and seasoning; cover tightly and put aside. Sauté livers in hot olive oil 5 minutes. Arrange rice in a ring on a warm platter with chicken livers in the center. Garnish with parsley. Serves 4.

RICE MARGHERITA

(Riso alla Margherita)

½ lb. rice, boiled
6 tblsp. Parmesan cheese, grated
olive oil
salt and pepper
4 eggs
2 eggs, beaten
breadcrumbs

Cool rice, add 4 eggs, cheese and seasoning, mix well; shape into balls about the size of golf balls, dip into beaten eggs and breadcrumbs; fry in hot olive oil until golden brown. Serves 6.

NOTE: These rice balls can be stuffed with cubes of cheese (Scamozza) or Italian sausages. They will enhance the flavor.

RICE MARIANA

(Riso alla Marianna)

2 cups rice
1 clove garlic
½ cup olive oil
5 cups stock, meat or chicken
Parmesan cheese, grated
1 can mushrooms, chopped
2 tblsp. parsley, minced
2 cups tomatoes, canned
salt and pepper to taste

Soak rice in cold water 30 minutes; drain. Brown mushrooms, garlic and parsley in hot olive oil; add tomatoes, cover and simmer 30 minutes. Cook rice in ½ cup of stock until stock is absorbed; repeat adding stock until rice is tender. Stir in tomato mixture with seasoning, and cook 30 minutes. Serve sprinkled with cheese. Serves 8.

RICE MILANESE

(Risotto alla Milanese)

1 cup rice
½ onion, minced
¼ cup butter
½ cup Marsala wine
½ tsp. saffron
3 tblsp. cheese, grated
salt and pepper
meat broth

Wash rice thoroughly in several waters, drain and dry in a towel. Fry onion slowly in half the butter until a golden brown; add rice and cook 5 minutes, stirring constantly; add half the Marsala wine with sufficient boiling broth to cook rice, season and cook rapidly until grains swell; reduce heat and finish cooking until rice is nearly dry. Uncover, and add remaining butter, Marsala wine and saffron that has been mixed smooth with a little broth. Set rice over steam or in an open oven until dry and fluffy. Serve sprinkled with cheese. Serves 6.

MOM'S FAVORITE RICE

(Riso alla Mama)

tomato meat sauce
½ lb. rice, cooked
¼ cup Parmesan cheese, grated
1 small can mushrooms
breadcrumbs

Combine rice and cheese with tomato meat sauce (see recipe on page 240); mix well. Line a large buttered mold or casserole with breadcrumbs, fill with rice mixture, and cover top with breadcrumbs; bake in a slow oven until brown on top. Serves 6.

RICE WITH MUSHROOMS

(Riso con Funghi)

1 lb. mushrooms
1 onion, chopped
6 black olives, chopped
½ cup peas
4 tblsp. olive oil
seasoning to taste
1 cup rice
3 cups soup stock
½ cup red wine
½ cup tomatoes, cut
4 tblsp. Parmesan cheese, grated

Cook rice in 2 tblsp. hot olive oil 5 minutes, stirring constantly; place in a double boiler with soup stock, wine, and onion; cook 15 minutes. Sauté mushrooms in remaining olive oil, with tomatoes and olives; add seasoning and rice, and continue cooking until rice is tender. Serve sprinkled with cheese. Serves 6.

BAKED RICE WITH MUSHROOMS

(Riso al Forno con Funghi)

1 cup rice
2 onions, chopped
2 chicken livers
1 cup tomatoes, strained
4 tblsp. olive oil
4 large mushrooms
½ can tomato paste
salt and pepper

Boil rice until tender. Brown onion in hot olive oil, add tomato paste, tomatoes and mushrooms; cook 15 minutes. Add seasoning and rice, pour into an oiled baking dish, and bake in a hot oven (450°F.) about 30 minutes. Serve piping hot sprinkled with grated cheese. Serves 6.

NEAPOLITAN RICE

(Risotto Napolitana)

1 cup rice, uncooked
1 large onion, minced
1 clove garlic, minced
salt and pepper to taste
3 cups chicken broth
2 tblsp. olive oil
¼ tsp. saffron
¼ tsp. rosemary
¼ tsp. oregano
¼ tsp. dried mint leaves

In deep saucepan heat oil, add onion, garlic and rice. Cook until rice is light brown, stirring constantly; add rest of ingredients, lower heat, cover and simmer until rice is done, 20 minutes. Stir from time to time to prevent sticking and cook until moist but not runny. Serve with grated cheese. Serves 4.

ORANGE RICE

(Riso al Sugo d'Arancia)

3 tblsp. butter (duck or chicken fat may be used)
⅔ cup celery, diced with leaves
2 tblsp. onion, chopped
1 cup orange juice
1 cup rice
½ tsp. thyme
1½ cups water
2 tblsp. orange rind, grated
1¼ tsp. salt

Cook celery and onion in melted butter until onion is tender, but not brown; add water, orange rind, orange juice and salt, bring to a boil, and add rice slowly; cover, reduce heat and cook 25 minutes or until tender. Makes 6 servings.

NOTE: Orange rice is delicious served in place of potatoes with ham, duck, chicken, etc.

PEAS WITH RICE

(Piselli con Riso)

2½ cups peas, cooked
4 tblsp. olive oil
salt to taste
1½ cups rice, cooked
5 tblsp. Parmesan cheese
dash of saffron

Heat rice and peas mixed, add olive oil and seasoning; blend. Serve hot, sprinkled with cheese. Serves 6.

See also Rice with Okra, page 204.

RICE WITH SAUSAGE BALLS

(Polpette di Riso e Salsiccia)

2 qts. soup stock
1 lb. Italian sausage
1 small cabbage, sliced
1 large bunch turnips
2 cups rice
½ tsp. saffron
1 tblsp. Parmesan cheese, grated
salt and pepper to taste

Boil rice in hot soup stock with slices of sausage until rice is tender. If turnip and cabbage are to be used, these must be half-cooked by frying slices of the vegetables in hot olive oil before adding to the soup stock and cooking until tender. Add cheese shortly before removing rice from fire. Serves 6.

CHAPTER ELEVEN

Cheese and Eggs

CHEESE ELEANORA

(Formaggio alla Eleanora)

1 onion, sliced
1 cup tomato sauce
½ lb. Scamozza cheese, cubed
2 eggs
¼ tsp. pepper
2 tblsp. Parmesan cheese, grated
6 tblsp. olive oil
¼ tsp. marjoram
3 slices bread, cubed
½ tsp. salt
½ cup breadcrumbs
6 skewers

Cook onion in 2 tblsp. hot olive oil until brown and tender, add tomato sauce and marjoram; simmer 3 minutes. Place alternate cubes of cheese and bread on skewers, starting and ending with cubes of bread. Mix eggs, salt and pepper; dip skewers into the mixture coating bread and cheese on all sides; roll in Parmesan cheese and breadcrumbs mixed, and brown on all sides in hot olive oil. Serve with hot tomato sauce. Serves 6.

CHEESE CELEBRATION

(Formaggio Festivo)

2 cups Parmesan cheese, grated
3 eggs, beaten frothy
1½ tsp. salt
8 slices Italian bread, cut thin
½ cup celery, sliced
3 tblsp. parsley, minced
3 cups milk
1 tsp. hot sauce
2 tsp. onion, minced
1 can tuna fish
3 tblsp. mayonnaise
anchovies

Spread 4 slices of bread with a mixture of tuna fish, celery, parsley, and mayonnaise; cover with remaining slices and cut sandwiches into 4 triangles. Arrange triangles in a buttered dish with layers of cheese. Combine milk and seasoning with eggs, and pour over triangle sandwiches; let stand 30 minutes, then bake in a moderate oven (350°F.) 30 minutes or until puffy and well browned, but firm to the touch. Serve hot with anchovies over top. Serves 4.

SAUCE FOR EGGS

(Salsa per Uova)

2 tblsp. olive oil
6 ripe olives, chopped
2 cups tomatoes
2 tblsp. capers
½ onion, chopped
1 small green pepper, chopped
1 can mushrooms, sliced
¼ tsp. cayenne

Cook onions, olives, and green pepper in hot olive oil a few minutes; add tomatoes and cook until liquid evaporates; then add remaining ingredients. Use this sauce over any type of eggs. It is especially good over eggs Giuseppe (see recipe on page 222).

BAKED EGGS

(Uova al Forno)

6 eggs, separated
1 cup milk
⅛ tsp. pepper
1 tblsp. flour
1 tsp. salt
3 tblsp. olive oil

Fold stiffly beaten whites of 3 eggs into beaten egg yolks, add seasoning and blended milk and flour; pour into an oiled baking pan, and bake in a hot oven. When omelet has set, pour remaining stiffly beaten egg whites over top and return to oven to brown lightly. Serve at once. Serves 4.

EGGS CATHERINE

(Uova alla Caterina)

2 tblsp. olive oil
3 eggs
1 tsp. salt
1 bay leaf
1 onion, chopped
½ can tomatoes, drained
1 tsp. sugar

Heat oil, add onions, and cook a few minutes, then add the tomatoes, bay leaf, salt and sugar, and heat. When hot, break eggs gently into mixture so as not to break yolks. Cover and cook until eggs are set. Serve hot. Serves 3.

CHEESE OMELET

(Frittata alla Parmigiana)

6 eggs
½ cup Parmesan cheese, grated
salt and pepper to taste
3 tblsp. parsley, chopped fine
2 tblsp. olive oil

Beat egg vigorously, add seasonings and parsley, then beat again. Fold in the grated cheese. Heat olive oil in a skillet, then pour in eggs and let cook without disturbing until edges are a light brown. Turn over with a pancake turner and brown. Serve hot. Serves 4.

EGGS FRANCESCA

(Uova alla Francesca)

2 tblsp. olive oil
2 tblsp. green pepper, chopped
1 cup tomatoes, strained
8 eggs, beaten
2 tblsp. onion, chopped
1 can mushroom caps
2 tblsp. capers

Simmer onions and green pepper in hot olive oil until soft; add mushrooms, capers and tomatoes; heat through, and stir in eggs, scrambling well. Serve on toast. Serves 4.

BAKED EGGS WITH GREEN BEANS

(Uova con Fagiolini al Forno)

2 cups green beans
4 tblsp. olive oil
6 tblsp. flour
½ cup breadcrumbs
1 tsp. parsley, minced
6 eggs, hard-boiled
1 tblsp. onion, minced
3 cups milk
½ cup Parmesan cheese, grated
salt and pepper to taste

Cook onion in hot olive oil until it turns yellow; mix in flour, milk, and stir over a moderate heat until thick and smooth, add seasoning. Butter a shallow dish, and arrange alternate layers of beans, eggs, and sauce, ending with a layer of sauce on top; sprinkle with a mixture of breadcrumbs and cheese. Bake in a moderate oven (350°F.) about 25 minutes, or until mixture bubbles. Serves 6.

EGGS HUNTER STYLE

(Uova alla Cacciatora)

4 chicken livers, cut small
¼ cup white wine
4 tblsp. tomato purée
salt and pepper to taste
2 tblsp. olive oil
3 tblsp. onion, chopped
4 eggs
dash of garlic salt

Season chicken livers with salt, pepper, and garlic salt, and brown lightly in hot olive oil; remove livers, pour in wine, add onion and simmer until onion is soft; add tomato purée, and cook 10 minutes. Add livers to sauce, break eggs over them, cover, and cook about 4 minutes. Serve hot on toast. Serves 4.

EGGS GIUSEPPE

(Uova alla Giuseppe)

4 eggs, separated
⅛ tsp. pepper
1 tblsp. olive oil
½ tsp. salt
3 tblsp. hot water
½ cup parsley, chopped

Combine thickly beaten egg yolks with salt, pepper, parsley, and water; mix well, and fold in stiffly beaten egg whites. Cook eggs in hot olive oil until set and browned on bottom. Finish by browning top in a hot oven. Serves 3.

EGGS MARGHERITA

(Uova alla Margherita)

6 eggs, beaten
½ tsp. hot sauce
1 tblsp. pimiento, chopped
½ tsp. salt
2 tblsp. chives, chopped fine

Combine eggs, hot sauce, pimiento and salt in a double boiler; cook until lightly set, stirring away from bottom of pan frequently until eggs are done. Serve on toast garnished with chives. Serves 4.

EGGS WITH PEPPERS

(Uova Peperoni)

5 tblsp. olive oil
6 eggs
3 peppers, sliced
¼ tsp. fresh ground pepper
½ cup Italian cheese, grated
1 clove garlic
salt

Beat eggs until frothy, and blend in cheese and ground pepper. Sauté green peppers with garlic in hot olive oil until tender; lower flame, fold in eggs and stir until eggs are done. Serve hot. Serves 6.

EGGS AND SAUSAGE

(Uova e Salsiccia)

1 lb. Italian sausages
salt and pepper to taste
3 eggs, beaten
¼ cup wine

Split sausages in half, and fry slowly in wine to withdraw the juices. When sausages are cooked, drain all but about 2 tblsp. of the juice; pour eggs over sausages and cook until eggs are done. Serve hot. Serves 4.

CHAPTER TWELVE

Dressings and Sauces

Salad Dressings

ANCHOVY DRESSING

(Salsa d'Acciughe)

1 small can anchovies, with oil
3 tblsp. wine vinegar
1 tblsp. olive oil
salt and pepper

Mash anchovies in their oil; add olive oil, vinegar and seasoning, mix well. Serve on tossed salad sprinkled with cheese.

ENDIVE DRESSING

(Salsa di Endivia)

½ cup olive oil
1 tsp. pepper
¼ cup wine vinegar
¼ cup Parmesan cheese, grated

Blend ingredients just before using. This amount sufficient for 1 head of endive.

GARLIC OIL DRESSING

(Salsa d'Aglio)

1 cup garlic oil
1 tsp. dry mustard
½ cup wine vinegar
½ tsp. salt
1 tsp. oregano

Combine ingredients in a jar, and shake well. This dressing will keep as long as 3 weeks in a cool place. Use on tossed salads.

GORGONZOLA DRESSING

(Salsa con Formaggio di Gorgonzola)

½ cup olive oil
½ tsp. salt
4 tblsp. wine vinegar or lemon juice

1 tsp. sugar
dash of paprika
6 tblsp. Gorgonzola cheese, broken into small pieces

Combine all ingredients, except cheese, in a glass jar, and shake until well blended. Add dressing slowly to cheese, mixing well.

HERB DRESSING

(Salsa di Erbe)

3 tblsp. sweet basil
6 tblsp. vinegar
1 clove garlic
½ tsp. pepper
3 tblsp. oregano
⅔ cup olive oil
½ tsp. salt

Combine above ingredients in a quart jar and shake well. Keep in a cool, but not cold, spot in refrigerator. A very good dressing for any vegetable salad.

IMPERIAL WINE DRESSING

(Salsa con Vino Imperiale)

4 tblsp. olive oil
½ tsp. salt
2 tblsp. white wine
1 tsp. lemon juice
½ tsp. paprika

Blend above ingredients together, and beat until the mixture thickens. Excellent on tomato salad.

ITALIAN SALAD DRESSING

(Salsa all'Italiana)

¼ cup sugar
1½ tsp. salt
1 tsp. mustard
1 tsp. paprika
1 tsp. oregano
1 cup catsup
1 cup olive oil
½ cup vinegar
1 clove garlic
1 onion, chopped fine

Combine ingredients in a quart jar, cover tightly and shake until well mixed. Let stand for 2 hours and strain. Will keep in refrigerator for a long time.

LEMON SALAD DRESSING

(Salsa con Limone)

½ cup olive oil
¼ tsp. each of salt, celery salt, pepper, basil, and oregano
juice of 2 lemons

Blend above ingredients together well. A distinctive dressing for tossed salad.

NOTE: If desired, any tangy cheese and anchovy may be added.

See also page 158 for Lemon Sauce.

LIVORNO SAUCE

(Salsa alla Livornese)

8 anchovies
1 cup mayonnaise
1 tblsp. lemon juice
1 tsp. parsley, minced

Mince anchovies to a paste, and combine with mayonnaise, lemon juice and parsley; beat together. Serve cold.

MAYONNAISE

(Maionese)

2 egg yolks
¼ tsp. pepper
1/6 tsp. dry mustard
2 cups salad oil
½ tsp. salt
¼ tsp. paprika
3 tblsp. white wine vinegar

Beat egg yolks with dry seasonings, add vinegar, and beat again; add oil gradually while beating, making the dressing thick and creamy.

MOM'S FAVORITE SALAD DRESSING

(Salsa alla Mama)

3 parts olive oil
¼ tsp. mustard
salt to taste
1 part wine vinegar
coarse black pepper

Mix dry ingredients in a bowl with 2 ice cubes, then add oil. When well blended, remove ice and add vinegar, a few drops at a time. Add to salad greens, tossing until every leaf is thoroughly coated.

OLIVE OIL DRESSING

(Salsa Liquida per Insalada)

¾ cup olive oil, marinated with garlic for 1 hour
salt, pepper and oregano
⅓ cup wine vinegar

Blend ingredients well just before using with tossed salads.
See also page 90.

TARTAR SAUCE

(Salsa di Tartaro)

⅔ cup mayonnaise
1 tsp. onion, grated
1 tsp. chopped chives
1 tsp. chopped parsley
2 drops tabasco sauce
1 chopped sweet pickle
1 tsp. capers
1 tblsp. chopped celery

Combine ingredients and mix just enough to blend. Keep chilled until ready to serve. Makes about 1 cup.
See also page 248.

VINAIGRETTE SAUCE

(Salsa di Aceto alla Francese)

2 tsp. onion, grated
4 tblsp. vinegar
⅔ cup olive oil
2 tsp. chopped green pepper
2 tsp. chopped pimento
2 tsp. chopped parsley
¼ tsp. salt
¼ tsp. pepper
½ tsp. mustard
2 hard-boiled eggs, riced

Combine ingredients and beat well. Makes about 1 cup.
See also page 201.

Spaghetti Sauces

ANCHOVY SAUCE

(Salsa di Acciughe)

No. I

½ cup olive oil
1 2-oz. can anchovies, rolled or plain
2 cloves garlic, chopped
1 cup water

Heat olive oil with garlic to a boil, add anchovies until dissolved, then add water and cook 5 minutes. Serve over freshly boiled spaghetti.

NOTE: For a more festive dish, add ½ lb. fresh mushrooms when adding the water, and cook slowly about 10 minutes.

See also page 125.

No. II

3 tblsp. garlic olive oil
1 tblsp. parsley, chopped
pepper
1 can tomato paste
1 doz. anchovies, cut up

Heat garlic oil, add tomato paste, parsley, add anchovies. Cook slowly for 30 minutes. Makes an excellent addition to plain spaghetti with breadcrumbs.

BEEF AND MUSHROOM SAUCE

(Salsa di Bue con Funghi)

½ cup onion, diced
½ cup parsley, chopped
6 tblsp. olive oil
1 peppercorn
⅛ tsp. nutmeg
1½ tsp. salt
1 cup mushrooms, sliced
3 tblsp. tomato paste
2 cloves garlic, diced
1 bay leaf
3½ cups tomatoes, peeled and chopped
1 whole clove
⅛ tsp. red pepper
¼ tsp. pepper
½ lb. ground beef, browned

Sauté onion, garlic, parsley, and bay leaf in hot olive oil until brown; add tomatoes, peppercorn, clove, nutmeg, red pepper, salt and pepper, and simmer 30 minutes. Remove bay leaf, peppercorn, and whole clove from sauce, and add mushrooms, beef, tomato paste; simmer 15 minutes.

CHOPPED BEEF SAUCE

(Salsa di Carne di Bue Sminuzzato)

¼ cup onion, diced
4 tblsp. olive oil
¼ cup parsley, chopped
¼ tsp. pepper
3½ cups tomatoes, peeled
4 tsp. olive oil
1 clove garlic, diced
1 sprig basil, chopped
2 peppercorns, crushed
2 tsp. salt
½ lb. lean beef, chopped
3 tblsp. tomato paste

Sauté onion and garlic in 4 tblsp. olive oil until brown; add basil, parsley, peppercorns, salt, pepper and tomatoes, simmer 30 minutes. Sauté the beef in 4 tsp. oil, add tomato paste, and combine with onion mixture; simmer 15 minutes.

CONTI'S SAUCE

(Salsa alla Conti)

2 mushrooms, minced
2 anchovies
2 tblsp. butter
1 cup broth
2 tblsp. wine vinegar
2 tblsp. Marsala wine
½ tsp. mustard
1 dash cayenne
1 tblsp. capers
salt

Heat butter, add anchovies and mushrooms; simmer slowly until brown. Add broth, vinegar, and wine, and simmer about 20 minutes; add seasoning and capers. Serve with spaghetti.

HOT SAUCE

(Salsa Calda)

1 tblsp. butter
12 anchovies
1 tblsp. olive oil
6 or 8 cloves garlic, sliced thin

Pound anchovies and garlic together, add olive oil and butter, and mix well, while bringing to a boil.

CALVES LIVER SAUCE

(Salsa di Fegato di Vitello)

3 tblsp. olive oil
1 onion, chopped
1 lb. calves liver, sliced
1 tblsp. flour
1 cup tomatoes, chopped
1 cup soup stock
salt and pepper

Brown onion in hot olive oil; remove onion and reserve. Scald liver in boiling water 5 minutes, and slowly cook in the olive oil 10 minutes. Mix flour with enough water to make a paste, and add to liver with tomatoes, stock, salt, pepper and onion; cook 20 minutes. When serving with spaghetti, arrange liver slices on top.

For kidney sauce, see pages 63-64.

SPAGHETTI SAUCE MARIA

(Salsa alla Maria)

1 clove garlic, minced
1 onion, minced
⅓ cup olive oil
½ cup celery, chopped
1 lb. ground beef
1 cup red wine
1 cup peas, canned
3½ cups tomatoes
¼ tsp. pepper
salt to taste
pinch of basil
1 bay leaf
pinch of oregano

Fry onion and garlic in hot olive oil until a golden brown, add celery and meat, stirring until meat is brown; add remaining ingredients, except peas, and cook slowly for 2 hours. Add peas and heat through to serve.

See also sauce under Baked Stuffed Tufali, page 90.

MEAT SAUCE

(Salsa di Carne)

No. I

1 No. 3 can tomatoes
1 lb. veal and pork, ground
1 onion, chopped
3 tblsp. parsley, minced
¼ cup olive oil
salt and pepper

Brown meat and onion in hot olive oil. Heat tomatoes to boiling point, add to meat with parsley and seasoning. Simmer 30 minutes.

No. II

¼ cup onion, chopped
¼ cup olive oil
1 6-oz. tomato paste
1 tsp. dry mustard
1/16 tsp. pepper
2 tblsp. parsley, chopped
3 cups left-over roast meat, diced
2 cups beef stock, seasoned
½ tsp. salt
2 tblsp. celery leaves, finely chopped

Sauté the left-over meat in olive oil until well browned; add the remaining ingredients and simmer for about 30 minutes. This is an excellent sauce to use over shell macaroni.

MEAT SAUCE WITH SPAGHETTI

(Salsa di Carne per Spaghetti)

1 ½ lbs. round steak, sliced thin
1 ½ lbs. pork, sliced thin
2 tblsp. salt
2 tblsp. garlic salt
2 tsp. accent (optional)
1 Bermuda onion
2 cans tomato paste
4 cups water
1 tblsp. pepper
2 tsp. celery salt
2 tblsp. olive oil

Cut meat into about 2-inch pieces and place a slice of onion on each piece; roll and hold together with toothpicks. Brown meat in hot olive oil, add tomato paste diluted with water, seasonings; simmer about 2 hours.

NOTE: To make this dish attractive, place spaghetti in center of serving dish surrounded with sprigs of parsley, and cover with sauce; arrange meat on top and sprinkle generously with grated Parmesan cheese.

See also page 65.

MEAT SAUCE ELEANORA

(Salsa alla Eleanora)

1 lb. ground beef
3 tblsp. olive oil
1 6-oz. can tomato paste
1 bay leaf
½ tsp. fennel seed
1 tblsp. sugar
1 onion, minced
1 clove garlic
3 cups water
½ tsp. oregano
salt and pepper

Brown onion, garlic, and meat in hot olive oil; remove garlic, add tomato paste, water, bay leaf, and other seasonings; simmer 1 hour.

MEAT SAUCE WITH MUSHROOMS

(Salsa di Carne con Funghi)

1 large onion, sliced thin
½ clove garlic, sliced thin
¼ cup olive oil
1 lb. ground beef
1 ½ tsp. salt
1 bay leaf
3 cloves
1 tsp. fennel seed
1 tsp. oregano
1 tsp. sugar

¼ tsp. pepper
½ cup parsley, chopped
½ lb. mushrooms, chopped
2½ cups tomatoes
1 can tomato paste

Brown onion and garlic in hot olive oil, add beef and fry until brown; combine with all ingredients, except mushrooms, and simmer for 1½ hours. Add mushrooms with their juice about 5 minutes before sauce is done. Add a little water if sauce is too thick.

MILANESE SAUCE

(Salsa alla Milanese)

1 lb. round steak
¼ lb. lean pork
1 clove garlic
1 No. 3 can tomatoes
salt and pepper
¾ cup olive oil
1 large onion, chopped
1 6-oz. can tomato paste
1 cup water
oregano and fennel seed

Have meat coarsely ground. Brown garlic in hot olive oil, and remove when brown; add onions and meat to olive oil and brown; add tomatoes, tomato paste, water and seasonings to taste; simmer 2 hours.

MINT TOMATO SAUCE

(Salsa di Pomidoro con Menta)

2 lbs. fresh tomatoes
¼ cup olive oil
3 stalks celery, minced
1 clove garlic, minced
1 tblsp. parsley, minced
salt and pepper
2 tsp. mint leaves, minced
1 large can plum tomatoes, strained
1 carrot, minced
1 onion, minced
1 tblsp. fresh basil, minced
1 bay leaf

Brown onion and garlic in hot olive oil; add carrot, celery, mint, basil, bay leaf, parsley, salt and pepper. Cook and strain fresh tomatoes; add to other vegetables with plum tomatoes, and cook 30 minutes. This recipe makes sufficient sauce for 1 lb. of spaghetti.

MUSHROOM SAUCE FOR SPAGHETTI

(Salsa di Funghi per Spaghetti)

1 No. 3 can tomatoes
1 onion
1 carrot
2 stalks celery
salt, pepper and oregano
¼ cup olive oil
3 sprigs parsley
1 can mushrooms
1 can tomato paste

Cook tomatoes, bringing to a boil. Grind all vegetables through a meat chopper, reserving the liquid from mushrooms. Brown vegetables in hot olive oil; add with mushroom liquid to tomatoes, and cook slowly 1 hour.

RIGATONI SAUCE ELEANORA

(Salsa alla Eleanora per Rigatoni)

1 small onion, minced
3 tblsp. olive oil
9 cups water
1½ tsp. oregano
1 bay leaf
⅓ cup sugar
1 clove garlic, minced
3 6-oz. cans tomato paste
½ tsp. red pepper
2 tsp. fennel seed
1 tsp. salt
1½ lbs. chopped beef, browned

Brown onion and garlic in hot olive oil, add tomato paste, water, seasonings, and meat; bring to a boil, then simmer for 1 hour. A super sauce to serve over rigatoni.

SQUID SAUCE

(Salsa Calamare)

1 lb. squid
4 tblsp. olive oil
1 small onion (chopped)
½ tsp. oregano
3 cans tomato paste
6 cans water
1 cup sherry wine
salt and pepper to taste

Clean squid (see page 171), wash thoroughly, cut into 1-inch pieces, dry and brown in olive oil together with chopped onion. Add tomato paste, water and seasonings—simmer about 1 hour, add wine and simmer 1 hour longer. Serve with freshly boiled and drained spaghetti—sprinkle with Parmesan cheese. Serves 6.

FRESH TOMATO PASTE

(Salsa di Pomidoro Freschi)

5 lbs. fresh tomatoes
½ cup water
salt and pepper to taste
3 stalks celery with leaves, chopped

Combine ingredients and cook until soft; strain. Brown 1 medium onion in 4 tblsp. olive oil, add strained tomatoes and simmer for 1 hour. Season to taste.

TOMATO SAUCE WITH ANCHOVIES

(Salsa di Pomidoro con Acciughe)

6 anchovies, minced
1 lump of butter
3 cups water
1 tblsp. olive oil
1 can tomato paste
pepper

Heat olive oil, add anchovies, pepper, and butter. Do not boil. Dilute tomato paste with water, and add to olive oil; simmer for 1 hour.

NOTE: This sauce is best used over long, thin spaghetti, and sprinkled with breadcrumbs browned in olive oil.

TOMATO SAUCE WITH FENNEL SEED

(Salsa di Pomidoro con Fiore di Finocchio)

1 small onion, chopped
1 clove garlic, chopped
¼ cup olive oil
1 stalk celery, chopped
1 bay leaf
pinch of oregano
6 cups water
salt and pepper to taste
½ tsp. fennel seed
2 cans tomato paste
pinch of basil

Brown onion, garlic and celery in hot olive oil. Dilute tomato paste with water, add seasonings and herbs, and add to olive oil; simmer until consistency desired, or approximately 1 hour.

See also page 201.

TOMATO SAUCE GRAZIA

(Salsa di Pomidoro alla Grazia)

1 qt. tomatoes, strained
1 clove garlic, chopped
1 can tomato paste
1 onion, chopped

3 tblsp. olive oil
salt and pepper
1 bay leaf
oregano and fennel seed

Brown onion and garlic in olive oil, add tomatoes, tomato paste, and seasonings to taste; simmer 1 hour or until thickened to taste. Serve over spaghetti.

SHRIMP TOMATO SAUCE

(Salsa di Pomidoro ai Gamberetti)

¼ cup onion, diced
¼ cup olive oil
1 ½ tsp. salt
1 lb. shrimp, cleaned
½ clove garlic, diced
3 ½ cups tomatoes, peeled
¼ tsp. pepper
½ 6-oz. can tomato paste

Brown onion and garlic in hot olive oil; add tomatoes, salt and pepper; simmer about 30 minutes, and add tomato paste and shrimp; simmer 10 minutes.

NOTE: This is a feast served over 1 pound linguine spaghetti.

PEPPINO'S TOMATO SAUCE

(Salsa di Pomidoro alla Peppino)

¼ cup garlic oil
1 med. eggplant, peeled and cut into cubes
3 tblsp. green olives, chopped
3 anchovies, chopped
6 large tomatoes, peeled and chopped
2 green peppers
3 tblsp. capers
parsley, basil, salt and pepper

To hot garlic oil add tomatoes and eggplant, cooking until eggplant is tender. Add roasted peppers, skinned and cut into strips, to eggplant with seasonings, olives, capers, anchovies, and simmer slowly until thickness desired.

TOMATO TUNA SAUCE

(Salsa di Pomidoro e Tonno)

1 can tuna fish
3 tblsp. parsley, chopped
salt and pepper to taste
¼ cup garlic oil
1 tblsp. capers

Brown parsley and capers in hot garlic oil, add tomatoes and cook for 30 minutes. Flake tuna fish with a fork and add to tomato sauce with salt and pepper; cook uncovered until thick.

NOTE: Serve this sauce over 1 lb. spaghetti, cooked, with a salad and you have a full meal.

VEAL BONE SAUCE

(Salsa di Ossobuco)

1 veal shin bone
1 onion, chopped
1 small can mushrooms
½ glass red wine
1 bay leaf
1 No. 2 tomatoes
1 carrot
2 stalks celery
3 tblsp. garlic olive oil
salt and pepper to taste

Roll the shinbone, which has been sawed into small pieces, in flour, and brown in hot garlic oil; add onion, carrot and celery. When vegetables start to brown, add mushrooms, tomatoes and seasoning, cook slowly 45 minutes. Add wine and continue cooking 15 minutes. Serves 6.

TOMATO SAUCE WITH WINE

(Salsa di Pomidoro con Vino Rosso)

1 cup tomato purée
½ cup celery, chopped
¼ cup parsley, chopped
1 onion, chopped
1 tblsp. sugar
1 cup tomato paste
½ tsp. garlic salt
2 bay leaves
salt and pepper
½ cup red wine

Combine ingredients, and simmer slowly about 1 hour, stirring regularly to keep from sticking to pan.

Meat Sauces

BARBECUE SAUCE

(Salsa all'Americana)

1 cup onion, diced
1 cup tomatoes, chopped
1 cup celery, diced
2 tblsp. olive oil
1 cup green peppers, diced
2 tblsp. brown sugar

½ tblsp. dry mustard
salt and pepper to taste
2 cups any clear soup
1 cup catsup

Fry onion slightly in olive oil, add remaining ingredients, and cook slowly for 1 hour, reducing the liquid about one half.

See also page 113.

WHITE WINE BARBECUE SAUCE

(Salsa con Vino Bianco)

1 cup white wine
½ cup olive oil
1 large onion, grated
1 tsp. salt
dash of cayenne
½ tsp. rosemary
2 tblsp. wine vinegar
1 large onion, grated
1 clove garlic, crushed
½ tsp. pepper
½ tsp. thyme

Combine ingredients, stirring until well blended; marinate overnight. Use generously to baste broiled chicken or meats.

NOTE: This sauce will keep a week if garlic is removed after overnight marinating.

BEEF LIVER SAUCE

(Salsa di Fegato di Bue)

⅓ cup flour
1½ lbs. beef liver, sliced thin
⅓ cup onion, diced
3½ cups Italian tomatoes, peeled
¼ tsp. pepper
½ tsp. salt
¼ cup olive oil
1 clove garlic, diced fine
1 tsp. salt
⅓ cup tomato paste

Sift flour and ½ tsp. salt together. Dredge liver in flour, sauté in hot olive oil until well browned on both sides, and add onions and garlic; cook 2 minutes, and add tomatoes, 1 tsp. salt and pepper; cover, and simmer 20 minutes, then add tomato paste, and simmer 10 minutes or until sauce thickens.

BROWN SAUCE

(Salsa Bruna)

3 tblsp. olive oil
1 sprig parsley, chopped
6 peppercorns
½ small onion, chopped
1 tsp. oregano
4 tblsp. flour

2 cups beef stock
salt and pepper
1 bay leaf

Brown onion, parsley, peppercorn in olive oil, stir in flour and cook, then add beef stock. Boil for 2 minutes and add oregano, salt and pepper to taste. Strain, if desired.

CONSOMME SAUCE

(Salsa di Minestra)

1½ tblsp. butter
1 10½-oz. can consommé
½ tsp. oregano
1½ tblsp. flour
1 bay leaf
2 tblsp. red wine

Brown flour slowly in hot melted butter; stir in consommé gradually, add bay leaf and oregano; simmer 20 minutes, then strain and add wine.

MINT SAUCE

(Salsa di Menta)

¼ cup fresh mint
⅓ cup cider vinegar
¼ cup sugar
pinch of baking soda

Chop mint leaves fine, heat vinegar and sugar to boiling and pour over chopped mint leaves, add soda, cover and let cook. Serves 6.

MUSHROOM SAUCE

(Salsa di Funghi)

1 cup brown sauce (page 237)
1 can mushrooms with liquid

Combine brown sauce with mushroom liquid, then add the mushrooms, sliced. Serve hot with steak.

RUBY SAUCE

(Salsa Rossa)

1 cup red wine
1 onion, chopped
¼ cup wine vinegar (red)
pinch of rosemary
1 cup olive oil
1 clove garlic, minced
pinch of red pepper
salt to taste

Mix ingredients in a jar and let stand 24 hours before using. Use for basting meats and poultry. This brings out the true flavor.

SCALLOPINE SAUCE

(Salsa per Scallopine)

1 onion, minced
1 stalk celery, minced
1 carrot, grated
1 cup tomato paste
1 tsp. lemon juice
½ tsp. rosemary
½ green pepper, minced
2 tblsp. olive oil
1 turnip, grated
2 cups water
½ tsp. oregano
salt and pepper to taste

Brown onion, pepper, and celery in olive oil, then add remaining ingredients and simmer for 1½ hours or until sauce has thickened.

STEAK BUTTER

(Salsa di Burro per Carne)

½ clove garlic
1 tsp. chives, minced
1 tsp. lemon juice
¼ tsp. black pepper
½ cup butter
1 tsp. basil
½ tsp. hickory salt

Rub bowl with garlic then discard; place butter in bowl and cream; work in remaining ingredients, blending well. Use as a spread for hot steak, chops, broiled kidneys, etc.

SWEET-SOUR SAUCE

(Salsa Agro-dolce per Carne)

2 tblsp. butter
2 tblsp. flour
½ tsp. salt
2 tblsp. sugar
¼ tsp. pepper
¼ cup vinegar
1 cup hot vegetable liquid

Brown flour in melted butter; add seasonings, liquids and sugar, and cook until smooth. Serve hot with meat balls.

See also pages 113, 114, and 147.

SWEET SOUR NUT SAUCE

(Salsa Agro-dolce con Noci)

¼ lb. pinenuts, chopped
½ lb. pistachio nuts, chopped
2 squares chocolate, unsweetened
2 tblsp. sugar
½ cup white wine vinegar
½ oz. candied lemon peel, chopped
½ oz. candied orange peel, chopped
2 tblsp. currants
3 tblsp. currant jelly
1 cup pan gravy from meat

Combine ingredients and simmer about 30 minutes, season to taste. Serve with roasts or game.

TOMATO SAUCE WITH LAMB

(Salsa di Carne d'Agnello)

2 lbs. lamb shoulder, cut into small pieces
1 med. onion, cut fine
1 qt. water
1 tsp. celery leaves, chopped
1 tsp. oregano
⅓ cup olive oil
1 can tomato paste
1 tsp. parsley, chopped
¼ tsp. pepper
1 tsp. salt

Brown onion in olive oil, add meat and cook until brown then place in a 4 quart kettle with tomato paste, water, parsley, celery, salt and pepper; simmer for 2½ hours, or until thick.

TOMATO MEAT SAUCE

(Salsa Liquida di Pomidoro)

1 small onion, chopped
1 clove garlic, minced
2 tblsp. olive oil
1 large tomato, chopped
1 cup meat broth
1 tsp. parsley, chopped
salt and cayenne

Fry onion and garlic in hot olive oil until golden brown; add tomato and fry a few minutes; add broth, and simmer until sauce thickens, then add seasoning. Serve sprinkled with parsley.

Vegetable Sauces

CHEESE SAUCE

(Salsa di Formaggio)

4 tblsp. butter
1 cup milk
⅛ tsp. pepper
4 tblsp. flour
¼ tsp. salt
½ cup Parmesan cheese, grated

Heat milk, and add blended butter and flour; stir constantly until thick; add cheese and seasonings; stir until well blended. Serve over cauliflower, or broccoli.

EGG SAUCE

(Salsa di Uova)

6 eggs, hard-boiled, diced
1 tblsp. butter
4 tblsp. parsley, chopped fine
1 cup cream
salt and paprika
1 tsp. mint leaves, chopped fine

Combine eggs, butter, parsley, cream, salt, and paprika in top of a double boiler, heat and mix thoroughly. Before serving add parsley and mint leaves. Serve hot over cauliflower, asparagus or fish.

VEGETABLE SAUCE

(Salsa all'Italiana per Legumi)

3 shallots, chopped
1 tblsp. butter
3 fresh mushrooms, chopped
¼ cup white wine
1 cup rich brown gravy
salt and pepper
1 tsp. parsley, minced

Fry shallots in butter, but do not brown; add mushrooms and continue frying until a light brown. Add wine, gravy, and seasonings, and simmer for about 20 minutes. To serve, add parsley.

PARMESAN SAUCE

(Salsa alla Parmigiana)

1 small onion, minced
1 small carrot, grated
salt and pepper
½ tsp. mustard

1 tsp. flour
1 cup meat broth
2 tblsp. cheese, grated
2 tblsp. butter

Fry onion and carrot in butter, add flour and brown; add broth with seasonings, and boil 5 minutes. Place over steam, add cheese, and stir until cheese is well blended into the sauce.

SWEET-SOUR SAUCE

(Salsa Agro-dolce)

½ cup sugar
1 tblsp. flour
½ cup hot water
1 cup soup stock
¼ cup vinegar
½ tsp. salt
⅛ tsp. pepper

Brown sugar and flour in hot skillet, stir; gradually add hot water, hot soup stock, vinegar and seasoning. Serve hot over string beans, spinach or artichokes.

Fish Sauces

OLIVE SALAD DRESSING

(Salsa d'Oliva)

1 slice dried bread
1 clove garlic, crushed
2 doz. pinenuts
2 tblsp. capers
2 anchovy fillets
⅓ cup vinegar
2 egg yolks, hard-boiled
12 ripe olives, pitted
1 tsp. parsley, minced
1 cup olive oil
salt and pepper

Remove crusts from bread, rub center with garlic, sprinkle with sufficient vinegar to moisten; combine with pinenuts, capers, anchovy, egg yolks, olives, and parsley, and grind fine through food chopper. Work mixture into a paste with a wooden spoon, then put through a coarse sieve; stir in olive oil until absorbed, adding more vinegar if needed, and season to taste; mix thoroughly. An excellent dressing for seafood salads.

ALMOND SAUCE

(Salsa di Mandorla)

⅓ cup almonds, slivered
¼ cup butter
juice of 3 lemons

Brown the butter, add almonds and lemon juice. Serve this sauce over fish and delight your taste buds.

BUTTER SAUCE

(Salsa di Burro)

1 green pepper, minced
½ tsp. salt
1 tsp. paprika
4 tblsp. butter

Mix ingredients to a smooth paste, and use over any broiled meats.

CAPER SAUCE

(Salsa di Capperi)

No. I

2 tblsp. capers, chopped
2 tblsp. olive oil
2 tsp. flour
salt and pepper
2 tblsp. vinegar
2 tsp. parsley, chopped
⅔ cup meat broth
oregano

Stir flour into hot olive oil gradually, and cook until light brown; add remaining ingredients with broth last, stirring well; simmer 15 minutes.

No. II

1 cup brown sauce (page 237)
½ cup capers

Drain capers, rinse well under running water; add to hot brown sauce. This sauce is delicious with most fish.

CLAM SAUCE

(Salsa di Vongole)

1 No. 3 can tomatoes
1½ lbs. clams, shelled
pinch of salt, pepper, oregano
2 tblsp. parsley, minced
¼ cup garlic oil

Heat garlic oil, add tomatoes and cook for 15 minutes. Then add clam juice and seasonings, simmer 20 minutes; add clams and parsley. Serve.

FISH SAUCE

(Salsa per Pesce)

1 ½ cups brown sauce
2 tblsp. olive oil
2 tblsp. onion, chopped
2 tblsp. green pepper, chopped
½ tsp. paprika
½ cup mushrooms
1 small can tomatoes
1 tblsp. capers
½ tsp. salt

Make a brown sauce (page 237) and add onion browned in hot olive oil, add tomatoes, mushrooms, peppers, capers and seasonings; simmer 20 minutes.

SAUCE FOR BASTING FISH

(Salsa per Pillottare)

¼ cup olive oil
⅛ tsp. pepper
1 tsp. oregano
½ tsp. salt
1 tsp. parsley, chopped fine
2 tblsp. lemon juice

Mix above ingredients well, and use to baste fish while broiling. Delicious!

ITALIAN FISH SAUCE

(Salsa all'Italiana)

1 cup mushrooms, sliced
2 tblsp. olive oil
1 cup tomato sauce
2 tblsp. parsley, chopped
1 small onion, chopped
¼ cup white wine
1 cup brown sauce
1 tblsp. butter

Cook mushrooms and onions in olive oil until onions are golden brown; add wine and cook 5 minutes. Add sauces and bring to a boil; let boil 2 minutes. Remove from fire and add parsley and butter.

PIETRO'S FAVORITE FISH SAUCE

(Salsa alla Pietrino)

6 sardines
2 tblsp. olive oil
2 tblsp. flour
1 cup broth
1 tblsp. fresh sweet basil, chopped
juice of ½ lemon
salt and pepper
2 egg yolks, beaten
½ cup white wine

Soak sardellen in cold water about 30 minutes; drain, chop and rub through a sieve. Blend flour and broth into hot olive oil until smooth and thick; add lemon juice, wine and sardellen; cook slowly about 10 minutes, season to taste and gradually stir in egg.

FISH SAUCE WITH SHERRY

(Salsa al "Sherry" per Pesce)

½ cup garlic oil
1 tblsp. celery, chopped
2 cups tomato sauce
1 tblsp. paprika
3 cups water
1 tsp. basil
1 tblsp. parsley, chopped
1 tblsp. green pepper, chopped
2 tblsp. salt
½ cup sherry
1 6-oz. can capers
1 tsp. oregano

Sauté parsley, celery, pepper in olive oil until brown, then add remaining ingredients, except water, and cook for 15 minutes; add water and cook for 1 hour.

GENOESE SAUCE

(Salsa alla Genevese)

1 head of a fish
1 tblsp. carrot, minced
1 sprig sweet basil
1 clove
4 peppercorns
1 tblsp. butter
1 small onion, sliced
½ cup claret
juice of 1 lemon
1 tblsp. parsley, minced

Cover fish head with cold water, add all other ingredients except claret, lemon juice and parsley. Bring to a boil; simmer for 30 minutes and strain. This should make 2 cups of liquid. Add claret and cook 10 minutes. To serve, add lemon juice and parsley.

GREEN SAUCE

(Salsa Verde)

1 bunch parsley, minced
½ small onion, minced
1 egg yolk, hard-boiled, chopped
lemon juice
salt and pepper to taste
2 stalks celery, chopped fine
1 tsp. capers
olive oil
½ tsp. oregano
½ tsp. dry basil

Combine parsley, celery, onion, capers, seasoning and egg, gradually mixing in olive oil and lemon juice until you have a thick sauce.

See also Basil Sauce in Mackerel recipe, page 165.

PARSLEY BUTTER

(Burro Prezzemolato)

1 tblsp. butter
1 tsp. parsley, minced
1 tsp. mint leaves, chopped
1 tsp. lemon juice
¼ tsp. salt
1 tsp. sweet basil, chopped

Cream butter, then add remaining ingredients, mixing well. Good served over broiled fish or steak.

SPECIAL MEAT OR VEGETABLE SAUCE

(Salsa Speciale per Carne o Legumi)

1 small onion
2 tblsp. flour
⅛ tsp. pepper
brown sauce (page 237)
2 tblsp. olive oil
½ tsp. salt
1 cup hot water

Brown onion in hot olive oil, add flour and brown; add hot water, brown sauce, and seasoning; cook about 5 minutes. Use with meat or broccoli, green beans, etc.

See also page 167.

MUSHROOM AND TOMATO SAUCE

(Salsa di Funghi e Pomidoro)

3 tblsp. olive oil
2 6-oz. cans tomato paste
1 tblsp. oregano
1 clove garlic, minced
6 cups water
1 bay leaf

2 tblsp. sugar
1 can button mushrooms
salt and pepper to taste

Brown garlic in olive oil, add tomato paste, water, mushrooms and seasonings; simmer until consistency desired.

SQUAB SAUCE
(Salsa per Piccionetto)

⅓ cup butter
4 tblsp. flour
2 cups boiling water
¼ tsp. salt

Blend flour with half the butter, and add boiling water gradually until sauce starts to boil; simmer until thick and smooth. When squab are ready to serve, add remaining butter to sauce with salt, and beat before serving.

THICK WHITE SAUCE
(Salsa Grossa Bianca)

4 tblsp. olive oil
4 tblsp. flour
1 cup milk
salt and pepper

Heat olive oil, blend in flour, milk and seasoning; cook until thickened.

THIN WHITE SAUCE
(Salsa Fina Bianca)

1 tblsp. olive oil
1 tblsp. flour
1 cup milk
salt and pepper

Heat olive oil, blend in flour, gradually add milk, and bring to a boil; reduce heat and simmer 3 minutes; add seasonings. To keep warm, cover tightly and place saucepan in a pan of hot water.

MEAT OR FISH SAUCE
(Salsa per Carne o Pesce)

1½ cups brown sauce (page 237)
2 tblsp. onion, chopped
½ cup mushrooms
1 tblsp. capers
½ tsp. paprika
2 tblsp. olive oil
2 tblsp. green pepper, chopped
1 small can tomatoes
½ tsp. salt

Brown onions in hot olive oil, and combine with remaining ingredients. Cook for 20 minutes. Serve on steak or fish.

SAUCE ELEANORA. *See page 285.*

SAUCE FOR SEAFOODS

(Salsa per Pesce Misto)

1 ½ cups chili sauce
½ cup sour pickles, ground
1 tblsp. lemon juice
½ cup celery, ground
2 cups mayonnaise
½ tsp. Worcestershire sauce

Mix ingredients, blending well. Keep in a cool place for use when needed.

TARTAR SAUCE

(Salsa alla Tartaro)

1 cup mayonnaise
1 dill pickle, chopped fine
1 pimiento, cut fine
juice of 1 thick slice of lemon

Combine above ingredients, and let stand 2 hours before using. See also page 227.

MINCED VEGETABLE SAUCE

(Salsa di Verdure Chioppate)

1 cup olive oil
2 tblsp. parsley, minced
2 tblsp. green pepper, minced
2 cups tomato sauce
1 ½ tblsp. paprika
6 cups water
2 tblsp. garlic, minced
2 tblsp. celery, minced
4 cups tomatoes
4 tblsp. salt
1 cup red wine
¼ cup basil

Heat olive oil and brown onion, garlic, parsley, celery, and green pepper; add tomatoes, tomato sauce, salt, pepper, paprika, and wine; cook for 15 minutes, then add water and cook 1 hour. Sufficient sauce to make about 10 servings over shell or fresh fish.

VENETIAN SAUCE

(Salsa alla Veneziano)

1 onion, chopped fine
1 cup fish broth
2 egg yolks
salt and white pepper

½ cup white wine
2 tblsp. butter, melted
2 tblsp. lemon juice
1 tblsp. parsley, minced

Cook onion in broth for 10 minutes; add wine, and heat to boil. Beat butter and egg yolks together and pour the broth over them slowly, while stirring; add seasoning. Place in double boiler and stir until well blended. Before serving, add lemon juice and parsley.

WINE SAUCE

(Salsa con Vino Rosso)

2 tblsp. olive oil
½ green pepper, minced
¼ tsp. hot or sharp peppers, minced
2 tblsp. onion, minced
1 small can tomato sauce
¼ cup red wine

Cook onions and green pepper in hot olive oil until onions are transparent; add tomato sauce, wine and hot peppers.

See also page 153.

NOTE: Try this sauce over fried tuna rice patties (page 173), or other fish.

WHITE WINE SAUCE

(Salsa con Vino Bianco)

1 cup brown sauce (page 237)
½ cup white wine

Heat wine with brown sauce. Serve at once.

See also pages 285-286.

BROCCHINI'S RELISH

(Stuzzicatori dell'Appetito alla Brocchini)

1 bunch carrots, chopped
1 stalk celery, chopped
1 tblsp. olive oil
2 chili peppers, chopped
2 tblsp. liquid mustard
1 tblsp. lemon juice
1 bunch fresh onions, chopped
2 tomatoes, peeled and chopped
1 tblsp. Worcestershire sauce
½ large bottle chili pepper vinegar
1 clove garlic

Mash garlic in a bowl and let stand awhile to flavor. Chop all ingredients very fine, and mix with liquid ingredients in garlic flavored bowl. Serve with meats and salads.

Stuffings

BREAD AND CELERY STUFFING

(Ripieni di Pane e Sedani)

3 cups breadcrumbs
2 cups celery, diced
2 tsp. salt
1 tsp. basil
½ tsp. garlic salt
½ cup onion, minced
¼ cup olive oil
½ tsp. pepper
1 tsp. parsley, minced
¾ cup soup stock

Brown onions and celery in hot olive oil; mix with breadcrumbs, seasoning, parsley, and moisten with soup stock. Add more seasoning if desired, and mix well. This amount will stuff a 5 lb. bird.

STUFFING FOR BAKED FISH

(Ripieni per Pesci al Forno)

1½ cups breadcrumbs
1 egg
¼ cup butter, melted
⅛ tsp. saffron
1 tsp. onion, chopped
1 tsp. parsley, chopped
1 tsp. salt
1 tsp. capers

Combine the above ingredients, mixing well. Sufficient for a 3 lb. fish.

NOTE: If a moist dressing is desired, use stale (not dried) breadcrumbs.

BREAD STUFFING FOR BAKED FISH

(Ripieni di Pane per Pesce al Forno)

4 cups day old breadcrumbs
3 tblsp. onion, chopped
¼ tsp. marjoram
1 tsp. parsley, chopped

½ cup celery, chopped
1 tblsp. olive oil
3 tblsp. water
salt and pepper to taste

Brown celery and onion in hot olive oil. Toss together remaining ingredients then add the browned onion and celery; combine with water and toss again to blend. This makes enough stuffing for a 3 lb. white fish.

CHICKEN CHEESE STUFFING

(Ripieni di Pollo e Formaggio)

2 cups breadcrumbs
½ tsp. salt
1 tblsp. green pepper, minced
¼ lb. salt pork, cubed
¼ lb. chicken livers, chopped
½ cup cheese, grated
1 tsp. pepper
1 clove garlic, minced
2 eggs

Combine ingredients, adding eggs and chicken livers last. Stuff bird. Sufficient for a 3 to 6 lb. chicken.

CHESTNUT STUFFING

(Ripieni di Castagna)

4½ cups chestnuts, shelled, blanched, boiled and mashed
4 cups soft breadcrumbs
1 onion, chopped
1 tsp. oregano
1 tsp. parsley
¼ cup celery, chopped
½ cup melted butter

Brown onion and celery lightly; combine with remainder of ingredients, mix well. Sufficient for a 12 to 14 lb. turkey.

CHESTNUT STUFFING FOR TURKEY

(Ripieni di Castagna per Tacchino)

1 lb. large chestnuts
¼ cup butter
1 tsp. salt
1 egg
6 slices salami, cut into strips
1 pt. breadcrumbs
½ tsp. parsley, chopped
1 small onion, chopped
turkey liver, chopped fine
juice of 1 lemon

Boil chestnuts 20 minutes, remove shells and skins and cook in boiling, salted water until tender; drain. Put chestnuts through ricer and combine with remaining ingredients; mix well, season to taste. This is enough stuffing for a 12 lb. turkey.

CHESTNUT MACARONI STUFFING

(Ripieni di Castagna e Maccheroni)

½ lb. elbow macaroni
2 apples, diced
2 tblsp. butter, melted
salt, pepper and oregano
1 cup prunes, pitted and quartered
1 lb. chestnuts, parboiled and chopped
1 egg

Cook macaroni in boiling, salted water until tender; drain. Mix apples, prunes, chestnuts, macaroni and seasoning with butter and egg; mix well, and stuff fowl. This amount will stuff a 10 lb. bird.

OYSTER STUFFING

(Ripieni di Ostriche)

2 cups oysters
1 tsp. salt
½ tsp. basil
¼ cup olive oil
2 cups breadcrumbs
½ tsp. pepper
½ tsp. thyme
¼ cup Parmesan cheese, grated

Mix ingredients together well. This is sufficient to stuff an 8 lb. bird.

RICE AND FRUIT STUFFING

(Ripieni di Riso e Frutta)

½ cup cooked rice
½ cup prunes, cooked and pitted
½ cup butter
½ tsp. paprika
3 large tart apples, chopped
12 chestnuts, boiled and shelled
½ tsp. cinnamon
¼ tsp. salt

Mix ingredients well. This amount sufficient to stuff a 4 to 5 lb. bird.

RICE STUFFING FOR TURKEY

(Ripieni di Riso per Tacchino)

6 cups wild rice, cooked
2 cups onion, chopped fine
2 tsp. sage
1 lb. Italian sausage meat
1 cup butter, melted
4 cups celery, chopped fine
½ cup olive oil
2 cups pecans, chopped coarse
4 eggs, separated and beaten

Sauté celery and onion in hot olive oil; add rice, sausage, nuts, butter, sage and egg yolks and mix thoroughly. Fold in egg whites, season to taste. This amount is sufficient to stuff a 16 lb. bird.

SQUAB STUFFING

(Ripieni di Piccionetto)

No. I

2 tblsp. butter, melted
¼ cup breadcrumbs
1 egg, beaten
½ cup cream
¼ cup almonds, blanched and chopped
season to taste

Mix breadcrumbs with cream, butter and seasoning, and add almonds. Inasmuch as the insides of squab are salted before the stuffing is inserted, be careful not to get too much seasoning in the dressing. This amount is sufficient to stuff 3 squabs.

No. II

2 tblsp. butter, melted
2 eggs, well beaten
1 cup breadcrumbs
squab livers, chopped
salt and pepper to taste
1 tsp. parsley, chopped

Mix butter, eggs, livers, and seasoning with enough breadcrumbs to make a soft dressing. This amount should stuff 6 birds.

TUBETTINI STUFFING

(Ripieni di Tubettini per Pollo)

1 cup tubettini macaroni
¼ cup celery, chopped fine
chicken giblets, cooked and
1 egg, beaten
¼ cup onion, chopped fine
1 cup mushrooms, sliced

chopped	3 tblsp. olive oil
½ cup parsley, chopped	1 tsp. salt
⅛ tsp. pepper	½ tsp. sage

Cook tubettini in salted boiling water 8 minutes; drain. Sauté onion, celery, mushrooms, and chicken giblets in hot olive oil; add parsley, salt, pepper, sage and egg, mixing thoroughly. Combine with tubettini, mixing well. Will stuff a 5 lb. chicken.

CHAPTER THIRTEEN

Desserts

BURNT ALMOND SAUCE

(Salsa di Mandorle Tostate)

⅓ cup almonds
1 recipe caramel sauce (below)

Pour boiling water over almonds (approximately 1/3 cup), slip off skins, and place in pan in hot oven to roast until crisp and slightly browned. Chop fine and add to caramel sauce.

CARAMEL SAUCE

(Salsa di Caramella)

1 cup sugar
⅓ cup cream
1 tsp. vanilla
½ cup brown sugar
⅓ cup butter

Boil ingredients together to make a thin sauce. Cool and serve over pudding, fruit or ice cream.

CUMQUAT SAUCE

1 cup cumquats
½ cup water
1 cup sugar

Remove membrane from cumquats and add sugar and water; bring to boil and cook gently for 15 minutes. Cool. Delicious served over ice cream.

FIG AND DATE SAUCE

(Salsa di Fichi e Datteri)

¼ cup dates
½ cup almonds, blanched and shredded
¼ cup preserved figs, cut up

Cover dates with boiling water, and let stand about 1 hour, or until puffed; drain, stone and cut into small pieces. Mix dates with figs and the syrup. Add almonds just before serving.

FRUIT SAUCE

(Salsa per Frutta)

½ cup olive oil
3 tblsp. peach juice
½ tsp. salt
1 tblsp. sugar
1 tblsp. lemon juice
3 tblsp. orange juice
1 tsp. paprika

Place all ingredients in a jar and shake well to blend. Serve over sliced oranges.

JELLY SAUCE

(Salsa di Frutta)

1 orange rind, grated
1 cup preferred jelly
1 tblsp. orange juice (optional)

Beat the grated rind of orange with 1 cup of your favorite jelly. If a thinner sauce is desired, add a tablespoon of orange juice. This sauce is used in many ways, such as between layers of plain cake, or as filling for tarts.

SAUCE FOR CAKE MARGHERITA

(Salsa per Cassata alla Margherita)

9 egg yolks, beaten
1 cup orange juice
2 tblsp. water
⅔ cup sugar
1 ½ tsp. gelatine

Add sugar slowly to beaten egg yolks, and beat until light and fluffy; add orange juice and beat until well mixed. Place the mixture in the top of a double boiler, but do not have the water in the bottom pan touching the pan containing the mixture; beat while cooking until custard thickens, and is doubled in quantity, approximately 10 minutes. Mix gelatine and water, and add to custard; place pan in cold water to cool. When cold, use between layers of cake. (For Cassatta alla Margherita, see recipe on page 289.)

SUGAR-COATED ALMONDS

(Mandorle Inzuccherate)

1 lb. almonds, unblanched
2 cups sugar
1 tsp. cinnamon
½ cup water

Boil sugar and water until thick and clear, add almonds and stir with a wooden spoon until nuts crackle. Reduce heat and stir until dry, then spread on a board until cool, using the wooden spoon to separate the nuts.

SPICED FIGS WITH CREAM

(Fichi Speziati con Crema)

1 large can figs
½ pt. heavy cream
2 sticks cinnamon
¼ tsp. ginger
3 tblsp. brown sugar
whipped cream

Place figs in skillet, add sugar, ginger and cinnamon; cook slowly, uncovered, for 15 minutes or until thick. Pour into a bowl, cover and chill. Serve with whipped cream flavored with rum. Serves 6.

CANDIED FRUIT AND NUT SLICES

(Fette di Frutta Candita con Noci)

½ lb. mixed candied fruit
¼ lb. raisins, seeded
¼ lb. dates, stoned
1 cup pecan meats
2 tblsp. brandy
½ cup chocolate shot

Mix ingredients together and knead. Form into a roll and cover with the chocolate shot. Cut into slices.

MIXED FRUIT

(Frutti Misti)

½ cup raspberries, chilled
½ cup pineapple, chilled
½ cup sugar
½ cup wine
½ cup peaches, chilled
½ cup strawberries, chilled
whipped cream

Combine fruits with sugar; let stand 15 minutes in a cool place. Fill tart shells with mixture and top with whipped cream flavored with your favorite wine. Serves 6.

FRUIT WHIP

(Crema Battuta con Frutta)

¼ cup cornstarch
¼ cup sugar
1 tsp. orange flavoring
1 tsp. lemon flavoring

¼ tsp. salt
2 cups milk
1 tblsp. orange rind, grated
2 egg whites
2 tblsp. powdered sugar

Combine cornstarch, ¼ cup sugar and salt in the top of a double boiler; stir in milk, and cook over boiling water until thickened, stirring constantly; cover, and cook 10 minutes, stirring occasionally. Remove from fire; cool, and add orange rind and flavoring. Beat egg whites stiff with powdered sugar, and fold into the cornstarch mixture; chill until set. Serves 4.

GRAPE CREAM

(Crema d'Uva)

1 tblsp. gelatine
1 cup grape juice
½ tsp. lemon juice
¾ cup cream, beaten stiff
¼ cup cold water
dash of salt
½ cup sugar

Soak gelatine in cold water, dissolve over hot water and add grape juice, salt, lemon juice and sugar. Chill, and when mixture begins to thicken, fold in whipped cream. Pile into dessert glasses and leave in refrigerator until ready to serve.

FROSTED GRAPES

(Gelato d'Uva)

1 cup water
Tokay or Malaga grapes
1 cup sugar

Boil water and sugar together 5 minutes. Dip small bunches of grapes into syrup, sprinkle with sugar and place on rack until hardened; chill. A wax paper may be placed under the rack to catch drippings. Use as a garnish for desserts.

GRAPE CREAM WITH ALMONDS

(Crema d'Uva con Mandorle)

½ cup grape jelly
dash of salt
2 tblsp. almonds, blanched, toasted and chopped fine

½ pt. cream, beaten stiff
¼ cup powdered sugar
whole grapes

Rub grape jelly through a sieve, and add chopped almonds and salt. Combine whipped cream with powdered sugar, and reserve ½ cup. Line 6 or 8 individual molds with cream, and fold jelly mixture into remaining whipped cream carefully, then pour into center of molds; cover top with reserved whipped cream and freeze without stirring. Garnish with grapes. (See Frosted Grape recipe on page 258.)

GRAPE SURPRISE

(Sorpresa d'Uva)

3 cups grape juice
¼ cup lemon juice
2 tsp. grated lemon rind
2 tblsp. sugar
1 egg white
pinch of salt

Beat the egg white with salt until frothy, add sugar and lemon rind gradually while beating. Place the mixture in a large bowl and add the juices, then beat until frothy. Pour into frosted glasses that have had the rims rubbed in wine, and serve. Serves 4.

GLAZED NUTS OR FRUITS

(Noci o Frutti Invetriati)

2 cups sugar
⅛ tsp. cream of tartar
1 cup boiling water
1 lb. fruits or nuts

Combine sugar, boiling water and cream of tartar in a saucepan and stir until sugar is dissolved. Heat to boiling and let boil, without stirring, until syrup begins to turn a light yellow color, or when a few drops poured into cold water become brittle. Remove saucepan and place in pan of cold water to stop boiling, then quickly place in pan of hot water to keep syrup from hardening. Now quickly dip fruits or nuts, a few at a time, in the hot syrup and remove them with a fork or winespoon to oiled paper.

Glazed fruits should be attempted only in clear, cold weather. Oranges and tangerines are separated into sections and allowed to dry a few hours or overnight before dipping. When dipping both fruits and nuts, dip fruits first and then the nuts, but do them quickly.

SLICED ORANGES AND APPLES WITH WINE

(Aranci e Mele Afettate al Marsala)

Slice oranges and apples very thin, mix, dust with powdered sugar, and add a generous amount of Marsala wine. Let stand an hour before serving.

PEACH COMPOTE

(Composta di Pesche)

6 ripe peaches
6 tblsp. powdered sugar
1 cup red wine
1 stick cinnamon (1-inch)

Pare and slice peaches, sprinkle with powdered sugar and set aside. Combine wine, cinnamon and lemon peel in a saucepan; boil 4 or 5 minutes, and strain over peaches. Cover and let chill 2 hours before serving. Serves 4.

PEACHES DON ISADORO'S

(Pesche alla Don Isidoro)

Peel and slice one or two large peaches; place in a dessert glass and cover with your favorite wine. Serve at once. Be sure to have both peaches and wine chilled.

STUFFED PEACHES

(Pesche Ripiene)

fresh peaches, peeled
crushed almonds
white wine or sherry
cake crumbs
sugar

Cut not too ripe peaches in half; place in a casserole and fill cavities with cake crumbs and almonds, and sprinkle with sugar; cover with white wine or sherry, and bake in oven. Serve cold with a zabaglione sauce (see recipe on page 271).

PEARS IN WINE

(Pere al Vino)

1 cup water
1 cup sugar
4 Bartlett pears
4 whole cloves
1 cup wine

Cook sugar and water together until syrupy, stirring until sugar is dissolved. Peel pears, but leave whole with stems on. Add wine and cloves. Simmer gently until pears are tender, about 20 minutes. Let chill in syrup. Serve cold with sponge cake. Can be served with cream. Serves 4.

STRAWBERRIES IN WINE

(Fragole al Vino)

1 qt. strawberries
¼ cup sugar
½ cup white wine

Sprinkle hulled berries with sugar, and cover with wine; chill. You will find the berries delicious and different. Serves 4.

NOTE: For variation, try a liqueur instead of wine and omit the sugar; or a little champagne and sugar served ice cold. Or you might like a little lemon or orange juice with a spoonful of sugar, and let stand several hours.

ITALIAN CANDY

(Torroni)

2 lbs. honey
3 lbs. nuts, chopped
1 lb. sugar
1 orange peel, sliced thin

Cook honey and sugar until brown, add nuts and orange peel and cook until thick. Spread on a board that has been dampened, and cut into pieces while still warm. Smaller quantities can be made if desired. Wrap in squares of wax paper.

CHESTNUTS

(Castagne)

In Italy everyone knows the nutritional value of chestnuts, and the numerous ways they can be prepared. Chestnuts are high in nutritive value, containing protein, fat, sugar and starch equal to approximately 682 calories to the pound.

Chestnuts are not only very tasty, but they are easy to digest, justifying the picturesque Italian name of "Bread of the Mountain." They play a very important role in the diet of the country people, especially in the winter months, and are used in many delicious dishes, such as stews, stuffings, desserts, and with spaghetti. Chestnuts used with lima, red, or any other beans give an unusual flavor that is very tasty.

As a basic recipe, chestnuts should be shelled, boiled, and skinned before being used in the preparation of a dish.

MOM'S CHRISTMAS CHESTNUTS

(Castagne Servite da Mamma Durante il Natale)

Boil, peel and skin large chestnuts; place in a pan and cover with a not too thick lukewarm simple syrup, and let marinate a few hours, skimming top layer of syrup when it becomes too thick. Remove chestnuts from syrup and spread on a board to dry. Repeat this process for 3 days, and after the last dipping and drying process, roll chestnuts in powdered sugar.

NOTE: Chestnuts prepared in this manner, together with roasted chestnuts (see recipe on page 265), served with wine at an Open House during the Christmas holidays, means hospitality.

BOILED CHESTNUTS

(Castagne Bollite)

Place the chestnuts in a pot, cover them halfway with water, place a lid on tight and boil for 20 minutes. When chestnuts are cooked, pour off the water and leave chestnuts on the fire for a moment in order to dry.

A bay leaf added to the boiling process enhances the flavor, or you might try fennel seeds.

CHESTNUT BALLS

(Polpette di Castagna)

1 cup chestnuts, blanched and mashed
2 tblsp. thick cream
¼ tsp. vanilla
2 egg yolks
1 tsp. sugar
breadcrumbs

Mix chestnuts and cream together well, add 1 egg yolk, sugar and vanilla; shape into balls and dip alternately in breadcrumbs, beaten egg yolk and again in breadcrumbs. Fry in hot olive oil and drain on brown paper, and sprinkle with powdered sugar.

CANDIED CHESTNUTS

(Castagne Candite)

1 lb. chestnuts
½ cup water
1 cup sugar
1 tsp. almond extract

Boil sugar, water and almond extract together until you have a thick syrup; beat well with a wooden spoon until frothy and white. Boil chestnuts about 15 minutes, peel, skin and dip into syrup to coat; remove with a skimmer and let dry.

CHESTNUT CUP CAKES

(Torte di Castagne)

1 cup mashed chestnuts
¼ cup melted butter
½ tsp. vanilla
¼ cup powdered sugar
4 eggs, separated

Mix chestnuts with sugar, butter, egg yolks and vanilla; stir thoroughly. Beat the egg whites until they hold a peak, then fold into the mixture. Bake in fancy cups in a hot oven (450°F.). When cakes are cold, ice with a thin icing and top with nuts.

See also page 274.

CHESTNUT FRITTERS

(Fritelle di Castagne)

1 cup chestnuts, shelled and peeled
1 cup milk
¼ tsp. salt
1 tblsp. butter
powdered sugar
1 tblsp. sugar
¼ tsp. vanilla
3 egg yolks
½ cup breadcrumbs, sifted

Salt milk, add chestnuts, and cook until tender; drain and mash through sieve; add butter, sugar, vanilla and 2 egg yolks, mix well and cool. Roll a spoonful at a time into balls; dip in remaining egg yolk, beaten, and in breadcrumbs; fry in deep fat, and drain. Serve hot, sprinkled with powdered sugar.

CHESTNUT GLACE

(Castagne Invetriate)

1 pt. chestnuts, blanched
¼ bean vanilla
1 cup water
1 lb. sugar

Cook peeled, whole chestnuts covered with boiling water and a little sugar until tender, but not broken; drain. Boil sugar and 1 cup of water with vanilla bean until syrup colors, do not stir. Dip chestnuts in the syrup at once; leave for 5 minutes and remove carefully with a silver fork, and place in a warm sieve in a warm place. Next day, reheat the syrup and repeat the dipping and drying process. When lifting chestnuts from the syrup, be careful they do not break. Roll chestnuts separately in wax paper, or place them in a jar covered with boiling syrup; set aside. They will keep indefinitely.

CHESTNUT ICE CREAM

(Gelato di Crema con Castagne)

3 cups chestnuts
3 cups milk
½ tsp. vanilla
1½ pts. cream
½ lb. candied fruit, cut fine
1½ cups sugar
½ tsp. salt
1½ cups water
6 egg yolks, well beaten
maraschino liqueur

Salt milk, add chestnuts, and cook until tender; drain and put through ricer. Make a syrup of sugar and water, add riced chestnuts and bring to a boil; gradually add egg yolks, stirring well. Remove from stove and stir until cold; add cream and candied fruit that has been dipped in maraschino liqueur; freeze. Serves 8.

CHESTNUTS WITH PRUNES

(Castagne con Susine)

1 pint chestnuts, blanched
¼ cup sugar
cinnamon, if desired
1 pint prunes
juice of ½ lemon

Cook chestnuts in boiling water until tender, but not broken (test with a fork); allow water to evaporate while cooking. Stew prunes and add sugar, lemon juice and chestnuts; cook for a few minutes. Serves 6.

STEWED PRUNES:

1 lb. prunes
2 lemons, sliced
½ cup wine
3 tblsp. sugar

Wash dried prunes quickly in cold water. Place in saucepan and barely cover with water. Set aside to soak for 1 or 2 hours.

Then cook in same water with wine and sliced lemon, cook over low heat until fruit is tender. Serves 6.

When stewing prunes to be used with chestnuts, omit the lemon.

CHESTNUT PUDDING

(Pasticcio di Castagne)

1 lb. chestnuts, blanched
2 cups sugar
1 cup water
1 pt. cream, whipped
1 tblsp. maraschino liqueur

Boil shelled chestnuts until half tender; drain. Boil sugar and water about 10 minutes, add chestnuts, and boil until tender and soft. Rice chestnuts and let cool. Serve pudding topped with maraschino flavored whipped cream. Serves 6.

CHESTNUT AND RAISIN COMPOTE

(Composta di Frutta)

1 lb. chestnuts
2 tsp. olive oil
1 lb. seeded raisins
juice and grated rind of ½ lemon
1 stick cinnamon (1-inch)
¼ tsp. allspice
¼ tsp. cloves
½ cup sugar

Score chestnuts with a sharp knife on flat side; parboil 5 minutes and drain. Place chestnuts in a frying pan with olive oil, and shake over hot fire about 5 minutes; remove brown skins and outer shells, cover with salted boiling water, and cook gently until tender; drain. Cover raisins with water, add lemon juice and rind with spice; simmer until water is nearly absorbed, then add sugar and chestnuts, and cook until well blended; cool. Serves 6.

ROASTED CHESTNUTS

(Castagne Arrostite)

Make a gash on one side of good large chestnuts (any amount), and cook in a pan with a perforated bottom over a moderate fire. When chestnuts are cooked, wrap in a cloth for about 12 minutes. Serve with butter and salt.

STEWED CHESTNUTS

(Castagne Stufate)

Peel and skin chestnuts and place in a pot with a little water, a bay leaf, and a few drops of olive oil to prevent chestnuts from sticking when water boils down; cook over a low fire about 45 minutes. When cooked, chestnuts should be salted slightly.

SUGARED CHESTNUTS

(Castagne Zuccherate)

Roast chestnuts according to recipe on page 265; remove skins and cut into halves. Dip each half in well beaten egg white one at a time; roll in powdered sugar, and lay on paper in a slow oven (250°) to dry. Do not touch until dry and cool.

CHESTNUT SWEET BREAD

(Pandolce di Castagne)

2 cups chestnut flour
½ tsp. salt
water
olive oil
¼ cup walnut meats
⅛ cup almonds
⅛ cup raisins

Mix chestnut flour with a little salt and sufficient water to make a stiff dough; knead in broken walnut meats, bits of blanched almonds, raisins, and form into a round loaf. Cover bottom of frying pan with olive oil; place dough in this and sprinkle with olive oil. Bake in a moderate oven (350°) for about an hour.

PISTACHIO CUSTARD

(Spuma di Pistacchio)

1 tsp. gelatine
1 cup milk
3 tblsp. corn syrup
1 tsp. vanilla
⅓ tsp. almond extract
green food coloring
2 tblsp. cold water
⅓ cup sugar
dash of salt
½ pt. cream, whipped
3 tblsp. pistachio nuts, chopped fine

Soak gelatine in cold water, then dissolve in 1/3 cup scalded milk; slowly add the remaining milk, sugar, corn syrup, salt, and vanilla; strain and chill. When custard begins to stiffen, beat until light, fold into whipped cream with almond extract and nuts; add food coloring delicately and freeze.

ALMOND PUDDING

(Budino di Mandorle)

2 egg yolks
1 cup powdered sugar
rind of 1 lemon, grated
4 egg whites, beaten stiff
juice of 1 lemon
1 cup almonds, grated
2 tblsp. cracker crumbs

Beat egg yolks to a cream with sugar, lemon rind and juice; add almonds with cracker crumbs, and fold in egg white; bake in a moderate oven (350°F.) about 45 minutes. Serve cold with a fruit sauce (see recipe on page 256). Serves 4.

NOTE: A cup of rice may be used in place of almonds, if desired.

MILK OF ALMOND RICE PUDDING

(Pasticcio di Riso e Mandorle)

¼ cup rice
2 cups boiling water
1 tsp. salt
rind of ½ lemon
4 drops almond extract
1 cup almonds, blanched
2 tblsp. cream
¾ cup powdered sugar

Pour washed rice into boiling, salted water with lemon rind and almond extract; cook in double boiler 12 minutes. Pound almonds with cream in a mortar, and strain through a cloth, rubbing all liquid through. Remove rice from fire, discard lemon rind, stir in powdered sugar and almond milk; return to heat, and cook 12 minutes, stirring frequently. Serve hot or cold. Serves 4.

BLACK PUDDING

(Budino alla Mandorla Bruciata)

1½ cups light brown sugar
1½ cups almonds, blanched and chopped
⅛ tsp. salt
6 egg whites, beaten stiff

Heat sugar in a saucepan until it begins to color, stir in almonds, and salt; pour into a buttered dish to cool. When cool, pound to a powder, put through a sieve and fold into egg white; pour into a buttered mold, cover, and place mold in a pan of boiling water. Bake in a moderate oven (350°F.) about 45 minutes. Serves 6.

CHOCOLATE PUDDING

(Pasticcio di Ciocolata)

- 3 cups milk
- 2 tblsp. lemon peel, grated
- 4 squares unsweetened chocolate
- 3 tblsp. candied orange peel, chopped fine
- 1 cup honey
- ¼ tsp. mace
- 4 tblsp. breadcrumbs
- puff paste (see page 293)

Scald milk with lemon peel. Place chocolate in the top of a double boiler, gradually add scalded milk, stirring until smooth; cool, mix in almonds, orange peel, honey, spice and breadcrumbs; cook until well thickened. Line a buttered cake tin with a thin puff paste, fill with mixture and bake in a moderate oven (350°) until set. Serves 6.

CREAM PUDDING

(Pasticcio alla Crema)

- 4 egg yolks
- ¼ cup sugar
- ½ tsp. vanilla
- powdered macaroons
- grated lemon rind
- 3 cups light cream

Beat egg yolks with sugar and vanilla; stir in cream, and pour into buttered custard cups. Set cups in a pan of hot water on top of stove, cover with paper, and boil until custards are firm; remove cups and chill. Before serving, sprinkle with powdered macaroons and grated lemon rind. Serves 6 to 8.

MAMA ODESSO'S PUDDING

(Budino alla Mama Odesso)

- 1 qt. and 1 cup milk
- 10 eggs, beaten lightly
- 2 cups sugar
- 2 tsp. cocoa
- 6 slices white bread, diced
- ½ cup water
- ½ cup rum
- maraschino cherries

Mix milk, eggs, cocoa and 1 cup of sugar; set aside. Make a syrup of water and 1 cup of sugar; bring to a boil and let brown. Line a mold with the syrup, pour in egg mixture, cover with bread, and steam 2 hours. Do not lift cover for full period of steaming time. Unmold, cool, and decorate with cherries; cover with rum and slice. Serves 12.

MOM'S DELIGHTFUL PUDDING

(Budino "Delizia di Mama")

4 egg yolks
2 cups powdered sugar
juice of 1 lemon
1 cup strawberries, fresh
½ pt. heavy cream, whipped
½ cup butter
rind of 1 lemon, grated
6 egg whites, stiffly beaten
½ cup shredded almonds

Combine egg yolks, butter, sugar, lemon rind and juice; cook in a double boiler until thick. Remove from heat, fold in egg white, stir in strawberries and almonds, and bake in glass ovenware in a moderate oven (350°F.) until firm. Chill, and serve with whipped cream. Serves 6.

COTTAGE CHEESE FILLING

(Ripieni di Ricotta)

1 lb. Ricotta cheese
¼ cup chocolate bits
1 tblsp. orange rind, grated
3 tblsp. milk
2 tsp. vanilla

Blend all ingredients together, and place in refrigerator until ready to serve. This makes an excellent filling for cream puffs (see recipe on page 284).

TAPIOCA PUDDING

(Pasticcio di Spuma)

4 cups tapioca
1 qt. milk, scalded
1 cup powdered sugar
4 eggs, beaten
1 tsp. vanilla
½ tsp. salt

Soak tapioca in sufficient cold water to cover for 1 hour; drain, add to scalded milk in a double boiler, and cook 30 minutes. Remove from fire, cool, add sugar and stir 1 minute; add eggs, vanilla and salt, and beat 2 minutes. Butter and sugar 6 cup-sized molds; fill with mixture, and set in a baking pan filled with warm water; bake in a slow oven (325°F.) about 35 minutes. Serve with sago wine sauce (see recipe on page 286).

TIPSY PUDDING

(Pasticcio Ubbriacato)

½ cup shelled almonds
4 egg yolks, beaten
½ tsp. cinnamon
rind of ½ lemon, grated
½ pt. whip cream
¾ cup breadcrumbs
¾ cup sugar
4 egg whites, beaten stiff
2 cups red wine

Put almonds and breadcrumbs through a food chopper. Cream beaten egg yolks with sugar until fluffy, then add grated lemon rind, cinnamon, almonds and breadcrumbs, mix and fold in egg whites. Pour into well greased pan and bake 35 minutes in a moderate oven. Heat the wine and pour slowly over pudding as soon as taken from the oven. Top with whipped cream and chopped almonds. Serves 6.

VIOLET CREAM

(Crema alla Violetta)

½ cup water
2 tsp. gelatine
⅔ cup grapefruit juice with pulp
pinch of salt
violet food coloring
½ cup sugar
2 tblsp. cold water
½ cup grape juice
whipped cream

Cook sugar and water 3 minutes; add gelatine that has been soaked in 2 tblsp. cold water, and beat until thick; add grapefruit juice with pulp, grape juice, and salt, mixing thoroughly; freeze to a mush, stirring occasionally. To serve, place cream in a bowl surrounded by ice; spoon to dessert glasses, and top with whipped cream that has been tinted with violet food coloring. The bowl containing whipped cream should, also, be placed in cracked ice.

WHITE MOUNTAIN

(Monte Bianco)

2 lb. chestnuts
½ pt. heavy cream, whipped
2 tblsp. sugar
2 cups milk
1 tsp. vanilla
rum or brandy

Boil chestnuts, remove shells and skins; place in a double boiler with milk, and cook until mealy; add vanilla, and put through ricer onto a serving platter. Add sugar to whipped cream with rum or brandy to taste, and spread over chestnuts. This is a dessert you will never forget! Serves 8.

WINE PUDDING

(Pasticcio al Vino Rosso)

½ pt. milk
2 eggs, separated
12 macaroons
½ pt. whip cream
8 red cherries
½ cup sugar
1 tblsp. gelatine
⅔ cup red wine
½ cup chopped nuts

Place milk, sugar and beaten egg yolks in a double boiler and cook to a soft custard. Remove from stove and add gelatine that has been soaked in ½ cup cold water. Add crumbled macaroons and wine, then fold in stiffly beaten egg whites. Pour into dessert glasses. To serve, sprinkle with nuts, add a spot of whipped cream and top with a cherry. Serves 8.

WINE CUSTARD

(Zabaglione)

No. I

6 eggs
dash of salt
4 tblsp. powdered sugar
6 tblsp. sherry wine

In a double boiler combine the eggs, sugar and salt, place over hot water and beat constantly for about 8 minutes. Then gradually beat the sherry wine into the mixture, and when stiff enough to hold a spoon upright in the center, pour into tall glasses and serve either cold or hot. Serves 6.

No. II

4 egg yolks
3 tblsp. Marsala wine
4 tsp. sugar

Mix ingredients and beat thoroughly; place in top of a double boiler and cook very slowly, beating continuously until thick as molasses. Remove from heat immediately, and serve in wine glass or cup. Can be served warm or chilled. A delicious dessert! Serves 6.

ANISE SLICES

(Fette all'Anice)

4 cups flour
6 eggs
½ cup sugar
6 drops anise oil
1 cup shortening
1 tsp. baking powder
½ tsp. salt

Combine 5 eggs, salt and sugar and beat until well blended, add sifted flour and baking powder. Soften the shortening and add anise oil, blending well, then mix with batter and knead until dough is smooth and pliable. Roll dough into a loaf about 4 inches wide and ½ inch thick. Brush with remaining egg, sprinkle with sugar and slice into 1-inch slices. Bake on a greased cookie sheet for 15 minutes or until light brown in a moderate oven. Makes about 3 dozen.

RUM BALLS

(Struffali al Rum)

2 cups vanilla wafers, crumbled
2 cups pecans, chopped fine
2 cups sifted powdered sugar
4 tblsp. cocoa
½ cup rum or whiskey
3 tblsp. light corn syrup

Combine dry ingredients, blend in rum and corn syrup, mix thoroughly. Roll into balls the size of a marble, roll in powdered sugar. Store in refrigerator.

FIG BARS MARIA

(Ficato di Maria)

3 lbs. flour
1 cup sugar
6 eggs, beaten
2 tsp. vanilla
1 cup walnuts, chopped
3 lbs. figs, chopped
¾ lb. shortening
8 tsp. baking powder
1 ½ cups milk
1 cup almonds, chopped
1 cup candied cherries, chopped
1 lb. seedless raisins

Cream shortening and sugar together, add eggs, milk and vanilla, mix and gradually add flour with baking powder; knead and roll into sheets, then cut into 3-inch squares. Mix almonds, walnuts, candied cherries, figs and raisins together well; place a tablespoon of the mixture on one half of each square of dough, fold over and pinch together. Bake on a cookie sheet in a moderately hot oven (375°) about 20 minutes.

BOW KNOTS

(Farfallette)

6 eggs
3 tblsp. sugar
3 cups flour
½ tsp. vanilla
½ cup powdered sugar
¼ tsp. salt
2 tblsp. butter
6 drops almond flavoring
3 cups peanut oil

Beat eggs lightly, then add sugar, salt, and flavoring, and blend well. Place flour in a bowl, cut in butter, and blend in egg mixture; then knead until smooth, adding a little more flour now and then if needed. Let set for 30 minutes, then cut dough in several sections, and roll on well floured board until very thin. Cut into strips about 6 inches long and ¾ inches wide, and tie into knots. Fry bow-knots in deep hot oil for about 3 minutes, then drain on brown paper, and sprinkle with powdered sugar. Makes 3 dozen.

ALMOND BREAD SLICES

(Pane di Mandorle)

2 eggs, well beaten
½ cup sugar
½ tsp. vanilla
juice and grated rind of
 1 lemon
1 ⅔ cups flour
¼ cup olive oil (or butter)
¼ cup almonds, blanched
2 tsp. baking powder

Mix eggs and sugar together, add lemon juice and rind with vanilla and 1 cup of flour; mix well, and add almonds cut in half lengthwise, olive oil, remaining flour and baking powder. Knead dough into two long loaves about 2-inches thick; place in oiled and floured pans, and bake in a moderately slow oven (325°F.) from 20 to 30 minutes. Remove from pans when baked, and while still warm cut into ½-inch thick slices.

SPANISH BREAD

(Pane di Spagna)

½ cup shortening
3 eggs
1 cup sugar
2½ cups flour, sifted

1 tblsp. vanilla
pinch of salt
3 tsp. baking powder

Cream shortening with sugar, add eggs, vanilla, and gradually add flour and baking powder; knead and roll dough lengthwise a thickness of about 2 inches. Bake cake roll on a cookie sheet in a moderately hot oven (350°) for 20 minutes; remove from oven, slice about ½-inch widths, place an inch apart on the cookie sheet, and return to oven to brown cut sides. Makes about 2 to 3 dozen.

CHESTNUT CUP CAKES

(Torticelli di Castagne)

1 lb. chestnuts
1 egg yolk, beaten
3 tblsp. whipped cream
¾ cup sugar
¼ cup butter
½ tsp. vanilla

Cook chestnuts in boiling, salted water until skins come off easily, peel, pound with butter and cream in a mortar; and rub through a sieve, being careful not to have the purée too wet. Mix purée, sugar and vanilla; form into small cakes, and place on a buttered baking sheet. Make a slight incision on top of each small cake, brush with egg yolk, and bake in a hot oven (400°) about 20 minutes.

See also page 263.

MARIE'S PINENUT CLUSTERS

(Pignolata di Maria)

2 eggs
2 cups flour
2 tblsp. pinenuts
¼ tsp. salt
½ cup honey
2 cups olive oil
½ cup sugar
colored candies

Pour a cup of flour onto a breadboard, make a well in center and break in eggs and salt; knead, adding more flour from the 2nd cup to make a soft, smooth dough. Cut dough in half for easy handling, and roll in circular pieces about ¼-inch thick; cut into strips ¼-inch wide and roll lengthwise, then again cut into ¼-inch pieces, and sprinkle with flour lightly to prevent sticking. Roll these small pieces of dough in pinenuts, drop in hot olive oil and stir with a wooden spoon until lightly browned; drain on brown paper. Heat sugar and honey over low heat about 5 minutes or until smooth; add browned pieces of dough, swishing them about until well coated, then remove to a platter. Bunch them together into small clusters with a spoon, or form them into a ring and sprinkle with colored candies. Serves 8.

ALMOND COOKIES

(Biscotti di Mandorle)

1 ¼ cups flour
½ cup sugar
¼ tsp. lemon extract
pinch of salt
¼ tsp. baking powder
½ cup shortening
1 egg, well beaten
½ cup almonds, finely chopped (unblanched)

Sift flour before measuring, add baking powder and salt; sift again. Cream shortening with sugar until light; add egg and lemon extract, and mix well. Combine dry ingredients with the creamed mixture, fold in almonds and chill. Roll dough on a lightly floured board to about ⅛th-inch thickness; cut into desired shapes, and bake in a hot oven (425°F.) from 8 to 10 minutes. If a glazed surface is desired, brush once with beaten egg before baking. Makes about 4 dozen cookies.

BASIC COOKIE RECIPE

(Ricetta Base per Biscotti)

4 eggs
1 ⅓ cups shortening
9 tesp. baking powder (or 3 tblsp. and 1 cup sugar)
½ cup milk (approx.)
2 lbs. flour
1 ⅓ cups sugar
1 oz. anise extract

Mix flour, shortening, sugar and baking powder well; add eggs and half the milk, and mix well. Add flavoring and knead dough until silky, adding remainder of milk as needed; roll and cut into desired shapes. Bake in a moderate oven (350°F.) from 10 to 15 minutes.

FROSTING:

1 lb. powdered sugar
1 tblsp. anise extract

Mix sugar and extract, adding enough water to spread easily. Frost cookies when cool. For variety, add a food coloring to the frosting, or sprinkle with colored sugar, chololate jimmies, etc.

CARDAMON COOKIES

(Biscottini di Cardamono)

1 cup butter
1 cup sugar
2 eggs
4 cups flour
1 tblsp. cardamon seed, crushed
rind of 1 lemon

Mix butter and sugar together, add other ingredients and mix well. Roll, cut and bake about 12 minutes in 325° oven.

CHOCOLATE COOKIES

(Biscotti di Ciocolata)

⅓ cup cocoa
1 ⅓ cups sugar
1 tblsp. baking powder
1 tblsp. anise flavoring
1 ½ cups shortening
about ½ cup milk
2 squares bitter chocolate, melted
4 eggs
1 ½ cups roasted peanuts, coarsely chopped
3 ⅓ cups flour

Cream sugar, shortening, and eggs; add cocoa and chocolate, and mix well. Sift flour with baking powder, add to egg mixture, mix, and add flavoring, peanuts; then gradually add milk, mixing thoroughly. Roll dough into small round balls the size of walnuts; bake on a cookie sheet not too far apart, in a moderately hot oven (375°) about 22 minutes.

FROSTING:

1 lb. powdered sugar
juice of 1 lemon
2 squares bitter chocolate, melted

Mix sugar, chocolate, and lemon juice, adding sufficient water to make a soft frosting. Dip the baked cookies into the frosting, and set on wax paper to dry. Will keep fresh about 2 weeks.

FILLED COOKIES

(Biscottini Ripieni)

4 eggs (save 2 egg whites for filling)
1 ½ cups Spry (shortening)
3 ⅓ cups flour
1 tblsp. almond extract
¾ cup (scant) milk
1 cup and 2 tblsp. sugar
1 tblsp. baking powder
yellow food coloring

Mix the eggs, sugar, and shortening well; then add the milk, flour, baking powder, flavoring, and food coloring. Mix to a smooth dough and divide into three parts. Roll out thin, cut into small squares and place a scant teaspoonful of filling in the center of each square, pinch opposite corners together, and sprinkle top with colored sugar. Bake in moderate oven 10 to 12 minutes.

FILLING:

- 2 egg whites
- 3 tblsp. chopped walnuts
- 3 tblsp. sugar

Beat the egg whites stiff, then add sugar and chopped nuts.

GUFANI COOKIES

(Biscottini Gufani)

- 4 eggs
- 1 ½ cups Spry (shortening)
- 3 ⅓ cups flour
- 1 tblsp. anise or almond flavoring
- 1 cup and 2 tblsp. sugar
- ¾ cup milk
- 1 tblsp. baking powder

Mix eggs, sugar, and shortening until creamy; then add the milk, flour, baking powder, and flavoring; and mix well. Divide dough into three sections. Color one section with the red food coloring, another with green food coloring, and leave the other part as it is. Roll dough out and cut into desired shapes. Bake in a moderate oven for about 20 minutes. Makes about 3 pounds and they keep very well.

FROSTING:

- 1 lb. powdered sugar
- red food coloring
- juice of 1 lemon
- green food coloring

Mix sugar with a little water and add lemon juice. Divide frosting into three parts and mix the red food coloring in one part, the green in another and leave one part white. Frost cookies with alternating colors, using red frosting on green cookies, etc.

JACK'S FAVORITE COOKIES

(Biscotti di Giacamo)

- 2 cups flour
- 4 tblsp. powdered sugar
- 2 cups nuts, chopped
- ½ lb. butter
- 1 tblsp. water
- 1 tblsp. almond extract

Cream butter and sugar, add water and extract gradually, then flour and nuts; mix thoroughly with hands, and roll into size of walnuts, then flatten. Place cookies close together on cookie sheet, and bake in a slow oven (300°F.) about 1 hour. When cool, but not cold, roll in powdered sugar. Makes about 4½ dozen.

NUT COOKIES

(Biscotti di Noci)

½ cup shortening
1 egg, separated
1 tsp. vanilla
¼ cup sugar
1 cup flour, sifted
½ cup walnuts, chopped

Cream shortening with sugar, add egg yolk, vanilla, and flour a little at a time, mixing well; roll into size of walnuts with hands, dip into stiffly beaten egg white then walnuts; bake in a moderately hot oven (375°F.) about 10 minutes.

COOKIE SLICES

(Biscotti Affettati)

4 eggs, beaten slightly
1 dessert spoon anise or other flavoring
1 heaping tblsp. baking powder
⅓ lb. butter
1 ⅓ cups sugar
¾ lb. walnuts, coarsely ground
3 ⅓ cups flour

Cream butter and sugar, add eggs, flavoring, and baking powder; cream well, add flour and nuts, and roll into a loaf; bake in a moderate oven (350°F.) about 30 minutes. Cut into slices while still warm.

CREAM CHEESE ICE BOX COOKIES

(Biscottini con Ricotta)

½ cup butter
¼ cup Ricotta cheese
1 ½ cups flour
2 tsp. baking powder
½ cup sugar
½ tsp. salt

Blend butter and cheese thoroughly, and gradually add sifted dry ingredients to make a stiff dough; form into a long roll, chill in ice box overnight, slice thin, and bake on a buttered sheet in a moderate oven (350°F.) about 10 minutes, or until delicately browned. Makes about 3 dozen.

SESAME COOKIES

(Biscottini Sesamo)

1 ⅓ cups flour
1 tblsp. baking powder
1 ½ cups shortening, melted
¾ lb. sesame seeds
1 lb. sugar
4 eggs, beaten
1 tblsp. anise
milk as needed

Blend flour, sugar, and baking powder; add eggs and shortening; and mix with hands; add flavoring and mix to a smooth dough, using milk, if needed. Roll dough out and cut into 1-inch lengths about the thickness of a finger; roll in sesame seeds, and bake in a moderate oven (325°) about 20 minutes.

ALMOND CRISP

(Croccante di Mandorle)

¾ cup almond paste
¾ cup sugar
¾ cup butter
4 egg whites
½ tsp. vanilla
1 cup flour
¼ tsp. salt
blanched almonds

Work the almond paste (see recipe on page 283) with a spoon until it is well blended, then add sugar. Cream butter, add almond paste and blend together until light and fluffy, then add egg whites and beat well. Add vanilla, flour and salt and mix. Drop batter by spoonfuls onto lightly greased cookie sheet about 4 inches apart. Flatten with a spoon and place a whole almond in the center of each. Bake in a 325°F. oven for 10 to 15 minutes. While cookies are still warm, roll around a spoon handle to curl the edges. Makes about 2½ dozen.

DOUGHNUT DROPS

(Spinchi)

No. I

2 eggs
1 tsp. salt
1 ½ cups flour
⅓ cup milk
¼ cup sugar
2 tblsp. butter, melted
4 tsp. baking powder

Beat eggs until light, add sugar, salt and butter. Mix flour and baking powder; combine with eggs and drop by tablespoonfuls into deep, hot fat; fry until brown. Drain on brown paper, and sprinkle with sugar.

No. II

4 cups boiling water
2 tblsp. sugar
½ cup butter
juice and grated rind of
  1 orange
4 cups flour
4 tsp. baking powder
12 eggs, beaten
1 tsp. salt

While water is boiling add butter, sugar, salt, and rind and juice of orange; remove from fire, stir in flour and baking powder gradually to prevent lumpiness; add eggs, and beat until smooth. Drop batter by tablespoonfuls into deep, hot fat and fry until a golden brown; drain on brown paper. Serve sprinkled with powdered sugar.

SWEET DUMPLINGS

(Gnocchi Dolci)

5 egg yolks
2 egg whites
1 tblsp. sugar
1 cup cake flour
¾ tsp. cinnamon
pinch of salt
¼ cup breadcrumbs, sifted
1 cup milk
2 tblsp. butter
1 tblsp. grated orange rind
¼ cup powdered sugar

Mix the egg whites with 3 egg yolks, stir in sugar, flour, salt and milk, and mix thoroughly; strain into a double boiler, and add butter; cook until it starts to thicken, stirring constantly, then cook 5 minutes and remove from heat; pour into a bowl and mix with remaining egg yolks and orange rind. Place mixture on a well floured board, shape into small balls and flatten slightly; drop into boiling water and cook 2 minutes, then move pan to side of stove and allow to stand 5 minutes. Remove dumplings, drain, and arrange in layers on a hot dish sprinkled with powdered sugar, cinnamon and breadcrumbs combined. Brush with butter and serve. Makes about 2 dozen.

EASTER NESTS

(Nidi di Pasqua)

½ cup powdered sugar
cream to blend
1 square chocolate, melted
sponge cake (see page 291)
almond paste (see page 283)

Make a frosting of the sugar and chocolate, using just enough cream to spread easily. Cut a sponge cake into 3-inch rounds (or any size desired) and spread top and sides with the chocolate frosting. With a pastry tube, spread the frosting on the outer top edge of the cake so that you have a hollow in the center. Make little eggs of almond paste (see recipe on page 283) and place three eggs in the hollow on each little cake, then sprinkle the edge of the nest with angelica.

FOPS

(Moscardini)

2 cups sugar	1 cup flour
5 drops anise flavoring	water

Combine sugar, flour, and flavoring with sufficient water to make a stiff dough; roll to desired thickness, working fast, and cut into diamond shapes; let dry overnight. Bake the next day in a slow oven (300°) from 8 to 12 minutes. You will be surprised, upon removing the cookies from the oven, to find they have changed shape. Makes 4 dozen cookies.

CHERRY FRITTERS

(Fritte di Ciliegielle)

1 ⅓ cups flour	1 egg, well beaten
¼ tsp. salt	3 tblsp. sweet butter
1 tblsp. sugar	1 lb. sweet cherries
2 tsp. baking powder	sprinkle of powdered sugar
⅔ cup milk	sprinkle of cinnamon

Sift flour, salt, sugar, and baking powder; then add milk and stir to a smooth batter, and blend in egg. Select big cherries with stems and tie into small bunches at stem ends. Put a few bunches into a frying pan with enough sweet butter to fry them, then drop a small amount of batter around them. When batter is set and nicely browned, remove fritters to a hot plate and sprinkle with sugar and cinnamon. Serve hot.

CORN MEAL FRITTERS

(Frittelle di Polenta)

1 cup milk	1 tblsp. butter
1 tblsp. sugar	1 egg yolk

Mix milk, sugar and salt in a double boiler and bring to a boil, then add corn meal slowly, stirring constantly. Boil gently for 20 minutes, then remove from heat and stir in butter, egg yolk, and lemon rind. Turn mixture onto a dampened board, spread about ½ inch thick, and let cool. Cut into squares, dip in beaten egg, then breadcrumbs, and cook in deep fat until crisp. Drain, then sprinkle with sugar. Serve hot.

1 egg, well beaten
½ cup corn meal
¼ cup sifted breadcrumbs
1 tsp. lemon rind, grated
dash of salt

LADY FINGERS

(Salviardi)

4 eggs
1 tblsp. anise flavoring
pinch of salt
2 cups flour
2 tsp. baking powder
1 cup sugar

Beat eggs with sugar until creamy. Sift flour, salt and baking powder together, and slowly add to egg mixture. Keep beating until smooth and creamy. Butter a cookie sheet, sprinkle it with flour, and drop batter by spoonfuls on it, shaping the batter oblong. Cookies should be about 2 inches apart on the cookie sheet. Bake in a moderate oven for about 10 minutes, or until a delicate brown. Makes about 3 dozen. These keep nicely and are excellent for young children.

MACAROONS

(Biscottini)

1 doz. almond macaroons (see recipe below)
½ pt. heavy cream, whipped
1 cup red wine
2 tblsp. powdered sugar

Soak macaroons in wine, and place on the bottom of a shallow bowl. Combine whipped cream with powdered sugar, and spread over macaroons; place another layer of macaroons over cream, and cover with whipped cream and remaining wine; chill 1 hour. Serves 6.

ALMOND MACAROONS

(Biscottini di Mandorle)

6 egg yolks
2 cups powdered sugar
1½ cups flour, sifted 3 times
6 egg whites, beaten stiff

¼ tsp. salt
1 tsp. orange rind, grated
1½ cups almonds, blanched and ground

Cook egg yolks, sugar, salt and orange rind until thick and creamy; stir in half the flour, fold in half the egg white, then the remaining flour and egg white. Fill a pastry tube with the mixture and squeeze out rounds and ovals about 3 inches in diameter onto a buttered and floured baking sheet. Sprinkle almonds on top, and bake in a moderate oven (350° F.) until a delicate brown. Makes 3 dozen.

CHOCOLATE SURPRISE MACAROONS

(Biscottini Sorpresa)

3 egg whites
¾ cup sugar
3 cups cornflakes
1 cup chocolate chip bits
½ tsp. salt
1 tsp. vanilla or almond flavoring

Combine salt and egg whites, and beat until egg whites hold a peak. Beating constantly, gradually add the sugar, flavoring, cornflakes and chocolate bits. Drop tablespoonsful of batter on greased cookie sheet, and bake in a moderate oven (325°) for 15 minutes. Makes 3 dozen.

FILBERT MACAROONS

(Biscottini alla Nocciole)

4 egg yolks
½ lb. filbert nut meats
½ lb. sugar

Mix egg yolks with the sugar, and add all but 24 nuts, unblanched and ground fine. Chill mixture, then spread on floured board and cut with cookie cutter. Top each with a whole filbert, and bake in a moderate oven (325°) for ½ hour or until crisp.

ALMOND PASTE

(Pasta di Mandorle)

1 cup almonds, blanched
5 egg yolks
2 cups powdered sugar
grated rind of 1 lemon
3¼ cups cake flour, sifted
1½ cups butter
1 egg

Pound almonds, 4 yolks and 1 tblsp. powdered sugar to a paste. Sift flour and powdered sugar onto a pastry board, make a well in the center and add butter, almond paste, egg, and remaining egg yolk with lemon rind; mix well with hands to a stiff consistency, and place in refrigerator 1 hour before using. Serve with your favorite sauce.

WINE PASTRY

(Dolce al Marsala)

1 ½ cups pastry flour
¾ cup butter
¾ cup sugar
1 egg
¼ cup Marsala wine

Cream butter and sugar, add egg and flour and mix to a soft dough, but firm enough to roll out. Use more wine if more liquid is needed.

Cut into squares—top with chopped, cooked figs or any cooked fruits. Pinch edges together, bake in moderate oven until lightly browned. Sprinkle with powdered sugar.

CREAM PUFFS

(Spinge)

¼ lb. butter
¼ tsp. salt
1 cup flour
1 cup water
4 eggs
1 tblsp. sugar
1 tblsp. glaced lemon rind, grated
1 tblsp. glaced orange rind, grated

Boil butter and water together, add flour and salt, stirring until mixture parts from sides of pan; remove from stove, cool, and add eggs 1 at a time, beating vigorously after each addition. Combine with remaining ingredients, blend, and drop a tablespoonful at a time about 3 inches apart on a cookie sheet. Bake in a hot oven (400°F.) for 10 minutes; reduce heat to 325°F. and finish baking, approximately 30 minutes. Upon removing puffs from oven, open them immediately to allow steam to escape. Makes about 16 puffs, which can be filled with a Ricotta cheese filling or custard.

SAUCE ELEANORA

(Salsa alla Eleanora)

2 green onions, chopped
4 egg yolks
1 tsp. mint leaves, chopped
1 tblsp. soup stock
⅛ tsp. paprika
2 tblsp. tarragon vinegar
1 tsp. parsley, chopped fine
4 tblsp. butter
¼ tsp. salt

Add onion to vinegar and bring to a boil, then let simmer until liquid has reduced about one half; strain and cool. Add egg yolks one at a time to the vinegar while stirring; cook slowly until smooth, stirring constantly. Gradually stir in butter, add soup stock and seasonings. Serve with broiled meat or fish.

MARASCHINO SAUCE

(Salsa al Maraschino)

1 cup cream, whipped
¼ cup powdered sugar
3 tblsp. maraschino liqueur

Place the bowl containing cream over a bowl of chopped ice, add maraschino liqueur and beat, adding sugar gradually until it becomes a thick froth.

NOTE: One tablespoonful of rum may be used instead of the maraschino liqueur, if preferred.

MARSALA WINE SAUCE

(Salsa di Vino Marsala)

½ cup flour
1 cup boiling water
1 cup Marsala wine
1½ tblsp. butter
½ cup sugar

Mix flour with a little wine until smooth, and add boiling water, stirring constantly; heat, and add butter in small pieces, cooking 5 minutes; add sugar and wine. Serve.

NOTE: Brandy may be used in place of the wine, if desired.

WHITE WINE SAUCE

(Salsa con Vino Bianco)

1 cup white wine
½ cup water
¼ cup sugar
1 tsp. potato flour

3 slices lemon
⅛ tsp. cinnamon
4 egg yolks, beaten
4 egg whites, beaten stiff

Boil wine, water, lemon, and cinnamon with sugar until well flavored. Moisten flour with a little water, then stir into wine mixture until smooth; pour mixture gradually over egg yolks, stirring constantly to avoid curdling. Return mixture to saucepan, add egg white, and heat, stirring constantly; pour into a sauce bowl, and top with remaining egg white sweetened with sugar.

See also page 249.

SAGO WINE SAUCE

2 oz. sago
1 cup water
½ cup sugar
1 cup claret
juice of 1 orange
2 tblsp. rum

Soak the sago in water 2 hours, then boil in same water until clear; add sugar, claret and orange juice, stirring until mixture thickens; add rum. Serve with cereal puddings.

SWEET RAVIOLI
(Ravioli Dolce)

1 ¾ cups flour
1 ½ tblsp. butter
1 ½ tblsp. shortening
½ lb. Ricotta cheese
water
1 egg white
2 egg yolks
2 tblsp. sugar
½ tsp. vanilla
powdered sugar

Mix flour, butter, shortening, and water to a stiff dough; roll out thin. Combine remaining ingredients, except powdered sugar, to make a filling. Cut the rolled out dough into 2-inch squares; place a teaspoonful of filling in the center of each square, cover with another square of dough, seal edges tight with a fork, and fry in hot fat to a golden brown. Serve sprinkled with powdered sugar.

ITALIAN SWEETS
(Dolci Italiani)

¼ lb. candied cherries
¼ lb. raisins, seeded
¼ lb. candied figs
¼ lb. dates, stoned
¼ lb. almonds
½ lb. walnut meats
¼ lb. pecan meats
powdered sugar

Mix ingredients together; grind or chop fine, and toss onto a board sprinkled with powdered sugar; knead well, press to desired thickness, and cut into small squares. Will keep if packed in layers with wax paper between layers.

ALMOND CAKE

(Torta di Mandorle)

½ cup butter
1 cup sugar
½ tsp. baking powder
½ tsp. nutmeg
2 oz. brandy
2 cups chopped almonds
3 eggs
1 cup flour
½ tsp. cinnamon
dash of salt
2 cups raisins

Cream sugar and butter, add eggs, and mix well. Add all dry ingredients slowly, stirring thoroughly after each addition. Mix in the brandy, nuts, and raisins. Bake in a well greased 9-inch tube pan for 1 hour in a moderate oven (350°).

NOTE: Flour nuts and raisins before mixing for easy distribution through cake. Cake will keep indefinitely in a tightly closed tin if a little brandy is added from time to time.

CHOCOLATE CAKE

(Torta di Ciocolata)

3 eggs, separated
¼ cup sugar
¼ cup almonds, ground
4 squares chocolate
½ cup butter
1 ½ cups flour

Melt chocolate in a double boiler, add butter, sugar, flour, almonds, egg yolks, and mix well. Beat egg whites stiff and fold into mixture; pour into a buttered flat mold, and bake in a slow oven (325° to 350°) about 1 hour. Cake will be moist when cut.

ICING:

¼ cup powdered sugar
rum, coffee, or vanilla flavoring
½ cup butter

Cream butter and sugar, add flavoring, and spread over cake.

CORN MEAL CAKE

(Torta di Farina)

3 cups milk
½ cup butter
¼ cup sugar
rind of 1 lemon, grated

¼ tsp. salt
1 cup corn meal
1 recipe Marsala wine sauce (page 285)
8 eggs, separated
marmalade

Combine milk, 1 tblsp. butter, and salt; scald and stir in corn meal slowly; cook to a smooth paste, remove from heat and cool. Cream remaining butter with sugar, add lemon rind, and beat in the egg yolks thoroughly; add cooled corn meal paste, and fold in stiffly beaten egg whites. Pour 2-inch layer of mixture into a buttered baking dish, spread with marmalade, and add another layer of mixture; alternating mixture and marmalade, and ending with a layer of mixture on top. Bake in a moderate oven (350°) about 30 minutes. Serve with Marsala wine sauce.

FARINA CAKE

(Torta di Farina e Uva Passita)

¼ cup farina
2½ cups milk
6 eggs, separated
2 tblsp. butter
¼ cup sugar
1 recipe white wine sauce (page 285)
¼ tsp. salt
½ cup almonds, blanched and chopped fine
4 drops almond extract
4 tblsp. seedless raisins

Cook farina with milk in double boiler until thick, add butter and cool. Beat egg yolks with sugar and salt; mix with cold farina, and add almond extract and raisins; mix well, and fold in stiffly beaten egg whites. Pour mixture into a buttered baking dish, and bake in a moderate oven (350°) about 45 minutes. When baked, dust with powdered sugar and serve with white wine sauce.

GENOESE CAKE

(Torta alla Genovese)

½ cup sugar
⅓ cup butter, melted
¾ cup pastry flour, sifted
3 large eggs (or 4 small)
½ tsp. vanilla
¾ tsp. baking powder

Combine sugar and eggs in the top of a double boiler over boiling water, reducing heat to keep water below boiling point; beat mixture with a rotary egg beater about 15 minutes, or until eggs become very light; remove from heat, add melted butter slowly with vanilla, and fold in baking powder and flour sifted together. Pour into two layer cake pans, and bake in a moderate oven (350°F.) from 20 to 30 minutes.

CAKE MARGHERITA

(Cassata alla Margherita)

1 sponge cake (page 291)
½ cup sugar
½ lb. glazed fruit, chopped
2 lbs. Ricotta cheese
2 squares bitter chocolate, chopped fine
2 tsp. almond flavoring

Sieve Ricotta three times, mix in sugar, chocolate, and flavoring; blend and set aside in refrigerator until needed. Cut sponge cake into three layers; spread half the Ricotta filling on bottom layer and remainder on second layer; top with third layer and set in refrigerator.

FROSTING:

1 egg white
1 tsp. lemon juice
1½ cups powdered sugar

Beat ingredients together, adding more sugar if needed to make a creamy consistency. Spread frosting over cake, and decorate with glazed fruit. If desired, sprinkle with pistachio nuts. Serves 10 to 12.

See also pages 292-293.

CAKE MARIA

(Pane di Maria)

8 eggs, separated
1⅓ cups flour
1¼ cups sugar
2 tblsp. water
2 tsp. lemon rind, grated
2 tsp. vanilla
¼ tsp. salt
powdered sugar

Mix together ½ cup sugar with flour. Beat egg yolks; mix in water and lemond rind and beat lightly, add vanilla, and beat in flour gradually. Beat egg whites until foamy, add salt and remaining sugar; beat until stiff, and fold into flour mixture. Pour batter into a 12-inch cake pan, and bake in a moderate oven (350°) about 45 minutes. When baked, invert on rack to cool. When ready to serve, sift powdered sugar over cake.

CAKE MARIANA

(Torta alla Marianna)

2 cups butter
2 cups sugar
10 eggs, well beaten
sugar
½ tsp. salt
4 slices candied citron peel
4 cups flour

Cream butter and sugar, add eggs a little at a time, and fold in sifted flour and salt; pour into a greased baking pan, sprinkle with sugar, and bake in a pre-heated oven. When batter has set, place thin slices of citron peel on top without removing pans from oven; bake about 1 hour in a moderate oven (350°F.).

NEAPOLITAN CAKE

(Torta alla Napolitana)

3½ cups cake flour
1 cup sugar
2 cups almonds, blanched and ground
¼ tsp. salt
1 cup butter
5 egg yolks
rinds of 2 oranges, grated

Cream the sugar and butter and add egg yolks and salt, then work in flour, almonds, and orange rind until mixture becomes a smooth dough. Knead the dough into a roll the size of a rolling pin, wrap in wax paper and leave in refrigerator for 1 hour. Remove roll and cut into 12 equal slices, then roll each slice out to about a 7-inch round. Place rounds of dough in buttered layer tins, trimming to fit, and prick well all over with a fork. Bake in a moderate oven (350°) to a delicate brown. When baked, remove to a flat surface and cover with wax paper to cool. Pile in tiers on a cake plate with jelly, marmalade or cream filling between each layer. Frost entire cake.

ROSE CARINO POTATO CAKE

(Torta di Patate alla Rosa Carino)

6 eggs, separated
½ cup potato flour
½ cup cake flour
1 tsp. baking powder
1 cup sugar
1 tsp. vanilla

Beat egg whites stiff, add ½ cup sugar and beat again. Beat egg yolks until a lemon color, add ½ cup sugar and beat until thick; fold in egg whites, and add flour, baking powder and vanilla. Bake in a torte pan in a pre-heated oven (350°) about 20 minutes. Cool.

FILLING:

2 cups sugar
8 tblsp. cornstarch
2 lbs. Ricotta cheese
1 chocolate almond bar, chopped
2½ cups milk
1 tblsp. vanilla
4 tblsp. candied fruit
pistachio nuts

Scald milk, add sugar, cornstarch and vanilla; cook until a thick custard; cool and add Ricotta, candied fruit and almond bar, mixing well. Split the cooled cake into two layers, and spread with filling, having a generous portion on top. (If filling is too thick, dilute with a little milk to a custard consistency.) Decorate top of cake with pistachio nuts.

RUM CAKE

(Torta al Rum)

¼ lb. butter
1 cup brown sugar
4 eggs, separated
1 cup flour
1 tsp. baking powder
1 large can mixed fruit
1 cup sugar
rum

Melt the brown sugar and butter in a heavy skillet, and cover with the fruit. Beat egg yolks and granulated sugar together, add flour and baking powder alternately with beaten egg whites. Pour this batter over fruit and bake in a moderate (350°) oven for 30 minutes. When baked, remove from oven, invert on a cake dish, and pour rum over it. Serve with almond sauce as follows:

ALMOND SAUCE (Salsa di Mandorle):

2 egg yolks
1 cup powdered sugar
1 tsp. almond extract
⅛ tsp. salt
½ pt. heavy cream

Beat yolks, salt, and sugar together, and add almond extract. Fold in the whipped cream and serve over rum cake, plain cakes, puddings, etc.

HOT MILK SPONGE CAKE

(Cassata di Latte)

1 cup flour, sifted
3 eggs, beaten thick
2 tsp. lemon juice
1 tsp. baking powder
1 cup sugar
6 tblsp. hot milk

Beat eggs about 10 minutes until thick; gradually add sugar, lemon juice, flour and baking powder sifted together, and milk, then mix quickly until smooth. Turn into an ungreased tube pan, and bake in a moderate oven (350°) about 35 minutes. Remove from oven, and invert pan until cooled. When cool, sift powdered sugar over cake.

NOTE: This cake can be baked in an 8 by 8 inch cake pan in a moderate oven (350°) about 25 minutes, if preferred.

PASTRY SHELL

(Cannoli)

1½ cups flour
1 tblsp. cocoa
1 tblsp. sugar
¼ tsp. salt
½ tsp. baking powder
2 tblsp. Spry (shortening)
½ cup wine
pistachio nuts, ground

Mix flour, cocoa, sugar, salt and baking powder, work in the Spry, then add wine a little at a time; knead well. Take a piece of the dough the size of a nickel and roll it very thin, then put this loosely around a 3-inch long stock that is 1-inch round, and pinch ends together. Deep fry in Spry or Crisco, and when nicely browned, remove carefully and place on brown paper to cool. Carefully remove sticks from pastry by pushing gently through so as not to break the pastry.

FILLING:

3 lbs. Ricotta cheese
2½ cups milk
8 tblsp. cornstarch
1 tblsp. vanilla
1 cup semi-sweet chocolate chips, ground
2½ cups sugar

Bring milk to a boil over a slow flame, mix in cornstarch and sugar combined, and add milk. Allow to cook for 30 minutes, then set to cool. Beat the cheese until creamy, add cornstarch custard, and ground chocolate, then beat until fluffy. Fill the pastry shells on both ends, dip ends in ground pistachio nuts and top with powdered sugar. Cannoli can be kept indefinitely in a cool place and filled as needed.

NOTE: Make pastry sticks to roll dough on by cutting an unpainted broom handle into 3-inch lengths.

CAKE MARGHERITA

(Cassata Margherita)

sponge cake (see page 291) **wine custard (see page 271)**

Split sponge cake into 3 layers. Place bottom layer on a cake platter and spread with zabaglione, one sliced orange and a sprinkle of sliced almonds. Repeat this process with the 2nd and 3rd layers, piling the remaining zabaglione attractively on the top layer. Whip a pint of heavy cream and cover sides of cake, then place a mound on top and sprinkle candied orange peel, citron peel and sliced almonds over top. Decorate platter with remaining whipped cream, and arrange candied fruit in clusters. Serve cake in wedges.

NOTE: Except for the whipped cream, this cake can be prepared a day ahead of your party.

See also page 289.

PUFF PASTE

½ cup cold water
2 cups flour
1 cup sweet butter

Cut 1/3 cup of butter into flour with sufficient water to hold ingredients together; place on a lightly floured board and roll into a square sheet about ¼-inch thick. Spread 2/3 of the dough with ¼ of the softened butter, fold into 3 layers with butter between each layer, and roll dough to ¼-inch thickness; again spread with ¼ of the butter, fold and roll as before; repeat process of buttering, folding and rolling, then spread remaining ¼ of butter over dough, fold and chill about 1 hour before using as directed in recipe using puff paste, then bake at once. This paste can be wrapped in wax paper and chilled 24 hours, if desired.

GENOESE PASTRY

(Torta alla Genovese)

¼ cup butter
½ cup sugar
½ cup almonds, blanched
4 egg whites
2 egg yolks
1 cup flour, sifted
½ tsp. vanilla
1 tsp. lemon juice

orange juice and water
powdered sugar
apricot jam
puff paste (see above)

Cream sugar and butter. Pound almonds with a little orange juice and water to a paste, add to creamed butter and sugar; mix and add whites of 2 eggs one at a time, and egg yolks separately, then stir in flour and vanilla, and mix well. Line a pie plate with a rich puff paste, pour in mixture, and bake in a moderate oven (350°F.) about 20 minutes. Remove from oven, and spread a layer of jam on top. Make an icing of remaining egg whites, lemon juice, and sufficient powdered sugar to thicken; spread over jam. Serve cold.

MOM'S CREAM TARTS

(Cassatelle alla Madre)

2 eggs
¼ tblsp. sugar
½ cup tepid water
2 lbs. flour
¼ cup Marsala wine
6 tblsp. butter
2 tsp. almond flavoring
1½ tblsp. baking powder
pinch of salt

Cream eggs, butter, and sugar; add flavoring, salt, flour, baking powder, and the water; then knead well. Add the wine a little at a time, while kneading; then set aside in cool place for about 30 minutes.

CREAM FILLING:

2 lbs. Ricotta cheese
2 squares bitter chocolate, melted
2 tblsp. chopped citron
2 tsp. anise flavoring
½ cup sugar
¼ cup grated orange peel
1 tblsp. grated lemon peel
peanut oil for deep frying

Mix Ricotta and sugar, then add the flavoring, lemon and orange peel, chopped citron, and chocolate, blending well, until a custard consistency. Add a little milk if not moist enough. Place in refrigerator until needed.

Cut dough into several sections, and roll on lightly floured board until very thin. Cut small discs about 3 inches in circumference, and fry in deep oil until a golden brown. Drain on brown paper, and cool. When cold, fill each disc with the cream filling, then place another disc on top and sprinkle with powdered sugar.

OPEN JAM TARTS

(Crostata di Marmellata)

Line a flat baking dish with a very short pastry, and fill with marmalade or jam. Cut remaining pastry into strips, and arrange in a lattice pattern over filling. Bake and serve hot or cold. (See pastry recipe on page 167.)

COTTAGE CHEESE TORTE

(Torta di Ricotta all'Italiana)

½ cup cake flour
¼ tsp. salt
½ cup butter
1 tsp. baking powder
½ cup sugar
1 egg, beaten slightly

Combine flour, salt, baking powder, sugar, butter, using egg for liquid. Handle like pie crust. Line a 5-inch deep torte pan with the crust.

FILLING:

1½ lbs. Ricotta cheese
1½ cups sugar
5 egg yolks
¼ cup flour
¼ tsp. nutmeg
2 tblsp. butter, melted
rind of 1 lemon, grated
juice of 1 lemon
5 egg whites, beaten stiff
2 tblsp. cream

Sieve Ricotta twice, add sugar, egg yolks, flour, nutmeg, butter, lemon rind and juice; mix well, and fold in egg whites and cream. Pour mixture into crust, bake 5 minutes in a hot oven (425°) and reduce heat to moderate (350°); bake about 30 minutes or until firm. Serves 12.

FILBERT TORTE

(Torta di Avellana)

4 eggs, separated
⅔ cup filberts, ground
⅔ cup sugar
1 scant cup flour

Beat egg yolks with sugar until thick; add flour, nuts and fold in stiffly beaten egg whites. Pour mixture into a buttered and floured torte pan, and bake in a slow oven (325° F.) about 45 minutes. Cover cake with a plain or chocolate icing.

CHOCOLATE FILBERT TORTE

(Torta di Nocciole Ciocolata)

6 eggs, separated
1 cup sugar
⅔ cup sweet chocolate, grated
6 tblsp. breadcrumbs, sifted
sweetened whipped cream to taste
⅔ cup filbert meats, grated
2 tsp. baking powder
¼ tsp. salt
1 tsp. vanilla

Beat egg yolks until thick and light, and add sugar slowly, while stirring; add chocolate, breadcrumbs, nut meats, baking powder, salt and vanilla, and beat until smooth; fold in the stiffly beaten egg whites. Bake in two buttered layer pans in a moderate oven (350°) about 30 minutes. Serve as a two layer cake with whipped cream filling and topping.

PINENUT TORTE

(Torta di Pignoli)

¾ tsp. salt
1 small stick cinnamon
1 qt. milk
½ cup white corn meal
½ cup pinenuts, blanched
⅓ cup sugar
1 tblsp. butter
2 eggs, well beaten
1 egg yolk
powdered sugar

Combine milk, salt, and cinnamon stick in the top of a double boiler; bring to boil, and stir in corn meal slowly; cook 2½ hours. Chop pinenuts coarsely. Remove cinnamon stick from corn meal mixture, and stir in sugar, butter, nuts and eggs. Line a shallow, buttered pan with thinly rolled pastry (see recipe on page 167); brush with beaten egg yolk, and fill with corn meal mixture. Bake in a moderate oven (350°F.) until brown. Sprinkle with powdered sugar, and slice when cool.

ENGLISH CUSTARD CAKE

(Zuppa Inglese)

2 cups milk, scalded
½ cup sugar
⅓ cup flour
¼ tsp. salt
4 eggs, separated
1 sponge cake (see page 291)
1 white cake
rum
red wine
vanilla

Mix sugar, flour and salt; add hot milk gradually and beat until smooth; pour over slightly beaten egg yolks, stir and cook until a thick custard; cool and flavor with vanilla. While custard is cooling, cut cakes into ½-inch slices; soak sponge cake in rum and the white cake in red wine until well soaked. Line the bottom of a 9-inch torte dish with a layer of the rum soaked cake; spread with the cooled custard, and cover with a layer of wine soaked cake spread with custard; repeat process until ingredients are used and there is a topping of cake. Beat egg whites into a stiff, sweet meringue and cover whole cake, making sure the sides are well covered. Serves 12.

NOTE: The secret of this dessert lies in using plenty of good liquor to soak the cakes, because if you are not tipsy after eating, it is not good. For an extra special occasion, add pieces of citron to the custard.

Ice Cream and Ices

The original ice cream soda originated in Italy, when the Roman Emperors used to send their slaves up the Appennines for snow to cool their fruit juices on hot summer days. A tall tumbler of shaved ice or snow was covered with the ruby red juice of the pomegranate, and sipped by the Caesars. They called this a granata, and it was the progenitor of our present day ice or ice cream.

FIG CREAM

(Crema di Fichi)

1 tsp. gelatine
1 cup figs, cut up
¼ cup filberts, chopped
½ tsp. almond extract
¼ cup powdered sugar
⅓ cup syrup from preserved figs
⅛ tsp. salt
½ pt. cream, whipped

Soak gelatine in fig syrup, and dissolve over hot water; add cut figs, filberts, salt and almond extract; chill and stir until light. Fold in the whipped cream with powdered sugar added, and freeze without stirring.

FIG AND ALMOND CREAM

(Crema di Fichi e Mandorle)

canned figs with syrup
toasted almonds, shredded
vanilla ice cream (page 301)

Rub figs with syrup through sieve; chill. Fill parfait glasses half full of vanilla ice cream, cover with some of the syrup, and add another layer of ice cream. Serve sprinkled with the almonds.

ITALIAN CREAM

(Crema Italiana)

- 1 pt. milk
- 3 tblsp. sugar
- 1 pkg. gelatine
- 3 egg whites, beaten stiff
- 3 egg yolks
- pinch of salt
- 1 tsp. almond extract

Dissolve gelatine in a little cold milk. Combine milk, egg yolks, sugar and salt in the top of a double boiler, and cook until custard is thick enough to coat a spoon; add gelatine, and cook until thick; cool. Fold egg whites into cold custard with flavoring, and pour into sherbet glasses to set. Serve covered with maraschino sauce (see recipe on page 285), and topped with a maraschino cherry. Serves 4.

LEMON CREAM

(Crema di Limone)

- 7 eggs, separated
- grated rind and juice of 2 lemons
- 7 tblsp. powdered sugar
- 1 glass white wine

Beat egg yolks with powdered sugar until thick; add grated rind and juice of lemons, beat again, and place in a double boiler with wine; cook, stirring until mixture thickens; cool. Beat egg whites with 2 tblsp. powdered sugar until stiff; mix with yolk cream, and chill. Serve very cold. Serves 4.

NOTE: This cream may be made the day before using, but do not add egg white until 1 hour before serving.

PURPLE DELIGHT

(Crema Deliziosa)

- ½ cup grape jam
- ¼ tsp. salt
- 1 cup heavy cream, whipped
- 2 tblsp. lemon juice
- ⅔ cup milk

Beat jam until smooth, stir in lemon juice and salt, and gradually add milk, while beating; fold in whipped cream, and freeze. As mixture begins to set, beat again, and freeze until firm. Serves 6.

FIGS MARIA

(Fichi alla Maria)

lady fingers, split (page 282)
ripe figs, peeled and quartered
maraschino sauce
vanilla ice cream
Marsala wine
powdered macaroons

Line individual bowls with lady fingers; add a layer of ice cream, a layer of figs; sprinkle with wine, cover with maraschino sauce (see recipe on page 285) and dust with macaroons. Serve bowls in plates of cracked ice.

CHOCOLATE FOAM

(Crema di Ciocolata)

Make a simple syrup of the water and sugar, and add to the chocolate which has been melted in a double boiler top, mix, then cool. When cool, beat in the whipped cream slowly and flavor with rum. Freeze, but not too hard. Serves 6.

1 lb. unsweetened chocolate, grated
1 cup water
rum
1 cup sugar
1 pt. heavy cream, whipped

PLUM FOAM

(Spumoni di Susine)

1 cup syrup from plums
¼ cup sugar
½ cup grape juice
8 plums, canned
¼ cup water
sprinkle of powdered sugar

Combine syrup, plums and sugar in a saucepan, bring to a boil, and remove plums. Add water and grape juice to the syrup, and freeze. To serve, sprinkle plums with powdered sugar, place in individual glasses, and cover with the frozen mixture. Serves 4.

BISCUIT GLACE

(Biscotti Invetriati)

1 cup sugar
⅓ cup water
8 egg yolks, beaten
½ tsp. lemon extract
1 tsp. vanilla or liqueur
1 qt. whipped cream

Cook sugar and water together 3 minutes, add to egg yolks gradually while stirring; cook over hot water until mixture coats a spoon, then add flavoring and beat until cold. Fold in whipped cream lightly, and fill molds; pack in ice and salt, and freeze 2 hours. Makes 2 quarts.

ORANGE ICE

(Granita di Aranci)

6 oranges
1 qt. water
2 cups sugar

Peel and slice oranges thin; lay in a dish and sprinkle with sugar; let stand 4 hours to make a rich syrup. Drain well. remove pulp, and add water; mix well and pour into freezer. When half frozen and it looks like wet snow, fill small glasses and serve at once. Makes 2 quarts.

APPLE ICE

(Gelato al Pomo)

1 qt. sweet cider
3 cups sugar
1 pt. orange juice

Mix ingredients well and let stand 3 hours. Stir thoroughly and freeze until hard. Keep packed in ice and salt until needed. Makes 2 quarts.

COFFEE ICE

(Granita di Caffè)

Make triple strength coffee and add sugar to taste. Freeze and beat to a mush, then freeze again. Beat to a mush again and serve plain or with whipped cream that has been flavored with vanilla.

LEMON ICE

(Granita di Limone)

1 ¼ cups sugar
grated rind of 2 lemons
1 pt. water
juice of 4 lemons

Make a syrup of the sugar and water, add lemon rind and boil 5 minutes; cool and add lemon juice. Freeze, beat to a mush and freeze again. Serves 6.

STRAWBERRY ICE

(Granita di Fragole)

1 ½ cups strawberry juice
3 cups sugar
2 tblsp. lemon juice

Mash and cover with sugar enough strawberries to make 1½ cups juice; let stand for several hours. Strain, add lemon juice and water, and freeze until mixture has a snowy, frothy look. Serve in tall glasses. Makes 2 quarts.

NOTE: Raspberries can be used in same manner.

TANGERINE ICE

(Granita di Mandarini)

juice and pulp of 3 tangerines
peel of 2 tangerines
1 tsp. gelatine
1 ½ tblsp. lemon juice
⅓ cup orange juice
½ cup sugar
1 ½ cups water

Combine sugar, peel, gelatine and water in a saucepan and stir until sugar is dissolved; boil 3 minutes and cool. Add juice and pulp of tangerines, orange juice and lemon juice; rub through a sieve and freeze.

ALMOND ICE CREAM

(Gelato di Crema alla Mandorle)

1 ½ cups milk
½ cup sugar
dash of salt
½ cup cream, whipped
½ cup almonds, blanched, roasted and chopped fine
1 tsp. gelatine
1 tsp. flour
1 egg, separated
½ tsp. almond extract

Combine a cup of milk with gelatine in the top of a double boiler and scald, stirring until gelatine has dissolved; mix in sugar, flour and salt, and stir until thickened, then cover and cook 10 minutes. Beat egg yolk slightly, mix with remaining ½ cup heated milk, and add to milk in double boiler; cook 1 minute, stirring constantly. Strain and chill, then beat until very light. Beat the egg white until stiff, mix in the whipped cream, and fold both into the custard with the almond extract and almonds; freeze. Serves 6.

For Vanilla Ice Cream use vanilla extract instead of almond.

COFFEE ICE CREAM

(Granita di Caffè)

1 qt. heavy cream
3 oz. coffee, freshly roasted whole beans
6 eggs
1½ cups sugar
whipped cream

Combine 1 pint of cream with coffee beans in a double boiler, cover and let infuse an hour over warm water; strain through a fine cloth into the remaining cream, and heat to a boil; add eggs and sugar, and cook until a thick custard. Cool and freeze. Serve with whipped cream. Serves 8.

CHOCOLATE ICE CREAM

(Gelato di Crema Ciocolata)

¼ cup boiling water
½ stick cinnamon, crushed
5 squares unsweetened chocolate
dash of salt
6 eggs, beaten
1½ cups sugar
1 qt. cream
whipped cream

Cover cinnamon stick with boiling water and let steep about 30 minutes; pour off clear liquid, and work it into the chocolate that has been melted over hot water and kept warm. Combine eggs, salt, sugar and cream in the top of a double boiler and cook until thick; add spiced chocolate and mix, then cool and freeze. Serve with whipped cream. Serves 8.

NOTE: For chocolate caramel ice cream, add 3 tblsp. caramel flavoring in place of cinnamon.

FROZEN PEACHES

(Granita di Pesca)

12 large ripe peaches
2 cups sugar
whipped cream
2 cups water
flavoring as desired

Slice peaches fine, mix with sugar, water and flavoring; stir 5 minutes, and freeze. Serve topped with whipped cream. Serves 8.

PEACH SHERBET

(Sorbetto di Pesca)

1 qt. peach pulp
3 cups sugar
1 pt. orange juice

Mix ingredients; let stand 3 hours, place in freezer and freeze hard. Makes 2 quarts.

NOTE: Any fruit, such as pineapple, orange, lemon, strawberries, raspberries with currants, grape with cherries, or plum may be used. They are all used without water, and make sherbet rich in body and luscious in taste.

PLUM CREAM SHERBET

(Sorbetto di Crema di Susina)

1½ cups milk
3 tblsp. sugar
½ cup cream, beaten stiff
scarlet food coloring
½ tblsp. gelatine
1 cup canned plums
dash of salt

Soak gelatine in ½ cup of milk; add remaining milk, scalded with sugar; chill. Drain plums, stone, and fold into the gelatine with whipped cream; add salt with food coloring, and freeze.

FRUIT FOAM

(Spumoni)

1 qt. milk
4 tblsp. cornstarch
5 egg yolks
1¼ cups sugar
⅛ tsp. salt
3 tblsp. chopped almonds
2 tblsp. candied pineapple, chopped fine—or any candied fruit or peel
6 maraschino cherries, chopped fine
½ cup powdered sugar
½ cup heavy cream

Blend cornstarch with a half cup of milk until smooth, using the top of a double boiler. Add rest of the milk, egg yolks and 1¼ cups of sugar and cook for about 10 minutes or until thick, then stir in chopped almonds and set aside to cool. When cool, freeze until firm, but not hard. While custard is freezing, beat the cream, adding the powdered sugar and whipping until thick. Add cherries and fruit, blend, then place in refrigerator to chill.

Use chilled jello molds and line about 1-inch thick with frozen custard, fill the hollow with cream filling, cover with more custard and wrap wax paper over molds and set to freeze. Makes 2 quarts.

PEACHERINO SUNDAE
(Gelato di Crema con Pesche)

sliced peaches
1 slice of orange, cut in half
ice cream (page 301)
whipped cream

Fill sherbet glass half full of peaches; sprinkle with sugar, cover with ice cream, and top with whipped cream. Serve garnished with the orange slice. 1 serving.

ICED TORTONI
(Granita di Tortoni)

6 egg yolks, beaten
1 pt. heavy cream, whipped
6 lady fingers, separated
1 pt. cream
vanilla flavoring
1 cup sugar
2 tblsp. maraschino liqueur
⅛ lb. candied cherries, halved
red wine

Sprinkle separated lady fingers with wine. Soak cherries in maraschino liqueur. Scald the pint of cream in a double boiler, stir into the egg yolks and sugar, and let cook until thick, stirring constantly; cool, add vanilla, fold in whipped cream, and freeze firmly. Fill a mold with alternate layers of lady fingers, frozen cream and cherries topped with whipped cream; seal tightly, and bury mold in salt and ice for 3 hours.

TUTTI-FRUTTI ICE
(Gelato di Tutti-Frutti)

1 cup pistachio nuts
4 oz. candied cherries
4 oz. candied apricots
1 qt. orange sherbet
(see under Peach Sherbet)
4 oz. candied orange peel
maraschino syrup
1 qt. pineapple sherbet

Soak nuts and fruit in enough maraschino syrup to cover until soft. Spread one pint of pineapple sherbet in a thin layer in the bottom of a 2-quart mold that is set in a mixture of ice and salt. Add fruit and nuts, diced, to the orange sherbet and pack a portion of it onto the layer of pineapple ice. Fill mold, alternating the remaining sherbet, to a little above the top, then press lid tightly. Seal joints with a strip of muslin, pack mold well in ice and salt. Freeze for 3 hours. Makes 2½ quarts.

BISCUIT TORTONI

(Biscotto Tortoni)

No. I

½ cup sugar
⅛ cup water
3 egg yolks
¼ lb. macaroons, crushed
1 tsp. vanilla
1 cup cream, whipped
¼ lb. marshmallows, cut
dash of salt

Boil sugar with water until syrup spins a thread when dropped from spoon. Pour syrup slowly onto lightly beaten egg yolks in top of double boiler and cook, stirring constantly until mixture coats the spoon. Add vanilla, whipped cream and marshmallows and all but 3 tablespoons of crushed macaroons. Pour in soufflé cups, sprinkle with macaroons then place in freezing compartment until ready to serve.

No. II

2 eggs
2 cups heavy whipped cream
½ cup powdered sugar
½ teaspoon vanilla
2 tblsp. sherry wine
½ cup macaroons, crushed

Beat the egg yolks with sugar until thick and lemon colored, add the vanilla and sherry. Fold in the egg whites, whip the cream until thick then gently add and stir in the crushed macaroons, saving 3 tablespoons for top trim. Pack in attractive paper cups and cover with crushed macaroons. Place in freezing compartment until firm. Serves 6.

No. III

¾ cup granulated sugar
½ cup water
6 egg yolks
2 tsp. gelatin soaked in
  2 tblsp. cold water
2 tsp. vanilla
1 pint heavy cream
¾ cup chopped blanched
  almonds
¾ cup powdered macaroons

Cook sugar and water for 4 minutes after boiling point is reached (to form a thin syrup). Pour slowly over the beaten eggs. As soon as blended add the soaked gelatin and stir until dissolved, cook until mixture thickens slightly. Fold into stiffly whipped cream along with vanilla and macaroons and nuts. Fill small paper cups, sprinkle top with macaroon crumbs. Place in freezing unit of refrigerator. Freeze until firm without stirring. Fills 12 cups.

MERINGUE

(Meringa)

2 cups sugar
½ cup water
½ tsp. liqueur
6 egg whites

Cook sugar and water in a saucepan, stirring until sugar is dissolved. If drops of moisture form on sides of pan, wipe away with a damp cloth. Cook without stirring until syrup will spin a long thread from tip of spoon. Remove from heat, flavor with liqueur, and set pan in a bowl of cold water. Beat egg whites until stiff and pour into syrup, then beat the mixture to a cold, smooth paste. This meringue is used in making fancy small cakes, meringue shells, decorations, or to combine with whipped cream and ices. In fact, the Italian chef with a pastry bag and tube, plus imagination and patience, performs magic with this paste, which is first cousin to our boiled frosting.

DATE MERINGUES

(Meringa di Datteri)

3 egg whites, stiffly beaten
1⅛ cups powdered sugar
½ cup dates, pitted and chopped fine
½ cup almonds, blanched and chopped fine
4 drops bitter almond extract

Add sugar gradually to the egg whites, then add dates and almonds. Rub almond extract onto heavy brown greased paper; drop spoonfuls of the meringue onto the paper, shaping as desired. Bake in a slow oven (250°) about 45 minutes.

CHAPTER FOURTEEN

Breads

MIXING DOUGH FOR ITALIAN BREAD

(Pane Italiano)

The basic ingredients for Italian bread are flour, yeast, salt and sufficient lukewarm water to hold them together. If desired a few tablespoons of sugar may be added.

For a stiff dough, mix ingredients, using water sparingly; knead by folding edges of dough toward center, press down and away with palms of hands, turning dough around and around as you knead until it no longer sticks to the hands or board, handling dough lightly the while. When dough is smooth and elastic, try working in about ¼ cup of olive oil to impart a delicious nutty flavor to bread. Dough is ready when smooth and elastic; this can be ascertained by poking your finger into the dough to see if it springs back smoothly.

For a sponge dough, mix about a cup of lukewarm water with the yeast and salt, then beat in part of the flour; continue adding flour and beating after each addition until you have a spongy dough. Add more water, if needed. Knead as described above.

Let dough rise at room temperature, free from drafts. This can be made certain by covering dough with a blanket. As dough rises, punch down once and let rise again.

Shape loaves by dividing dough into equal parts, and placing them in loaf tins that have been rubbed with olive oil; let rise again to double in size, then bake.

Bake loaves in moderate oven about 1 hour, or until bread shrinks from sides of pan.

BASIC BREAD RECIPE

(Ricetta Fondamentale)

¼ cup olive oil
1 cake yeast
1 tblsp. salt
6¼ cups flour
2 cups or more lukewarm water

Fill bowl with flour, make a well in center and add water, salt, and crumble yeast in with hands; mix thoroughly and add olive oil; knead until elastic and pliable, cover and set to rise. When dough has risen to double in bulk, punch down and knead well; let rise again. Form dough into two loaves; place in oiled bread pans to rise again, then bake in a moderate oven (350°F.) about 1 hour, or until bread shrinks from sides of pans.

CHRISTMAS BREAD

(Panettone Natalizio)

½ yeast cake
¼ cup sugar
lukewarm milk
1 cup butter
4 eggs
2 cups cake flour
1 tsp. vanilla
½ tsp. salt
2 tblsp. candied citron, chopped
¼ cup seedless raisins
2 tblsp. almonds, shredded
2 tblsp. candied orange peel, chopped

Crumble yeast with 1 tsp. sugar and dissolve in ¼ cup lukewarm milk, and let rise until light and bubbly. Cream butter with remaining sugar. Break eggs into a measuring cup and fill with lukewarm milk to make one cup; beat slightly. Sift flour and salt together and mix with fruit, then stir into creamed butter and sugar mixture alternately with eggs and milk; add risen yeast and beat to a smooth batter. Flavor with vanilla. Butter a tube pan and sprinkle bottom with almonds; pour in batter, cover and let rise overnight. Bake in a moderate oven (375°F.) for about 1 hour.

FRUITED CHRISTMAS BREAD

(Panetone Natalizio)

2 cups milk, scalded
1 cup sugar
1 cake yeast
6 cups flour
5 tblsp. shortening
2 eggs, well beaten
1½ tsp. salt
½ cup raisins
½ cup citron, sliced thin
1 cup walnut meats, chopped coarsely
1 tsp. nutmeg
1 egg, beaten slightly

Cool milk to lukewarm, crumble in yeast, add 2 cups of flour and beat well. Cream shortening with sugar, add eggs and beat well; add milk mixture with salt and remaining flour; knead and cover; let rise in a warm place about 1½ hours.

Work in remaining ingredients, and knead on floured board until smooth and elastic. Place in a greased bowl, rub with olive oil, cover, and let rise until double in bulk; knead again, and shape into loaves not too large. Arrange loaves on a cookie sheet, brush over lightly with lightly beaten egg, and let rise until double again. Bake in a moderately hot oven (400°F.) for 15 minutes, then reduce heat to 350°F. and bake for 25 minutes. Makes 2 large or 4 small loaves.

CORN MEAL, ONION, AND GARLIC BREAD

(Pane di Granturco con Cipolle ed Agli)

½ cup olive oil
1 onion, minced
1 clove garlic, minced
4 cups hot water
¾ tblsp. salt
⅛ tsp. pepper
1 lb. yellow corn meal
½ cup Parmesan cheese, grated
1 cup seedless raisins, parboiled
½ cup pinenuts
½ cup walnuts, chopped

Brown onion and garlic in hot olive oil, add hot water, salt and pepper, and bring to a quick boil; add corn meal, stirring until smooth and thickened. Remove from fire and stir in the cheese, pinenuts, walnuts and raisins, drained and dried; mix thoroughly, then pour into a well greased baking dish and bake in a moderate oven (350°F.) for about 30 minutes. Serve as hot as possible. Serves 6.

EASTER BREAD

(Pane di Pasqua)

4 cups flour
¾ tsp. salt
½ cup sugar
1 tblsp. citron, chopped fine
1 tblsp. angelica, chopped fine
4 egg yolks
1 tblsp. orange peel
½ cup white raisins
½ (scant) cup butter, melted
2 yeast cakes
1 cup lukewarm milk

Scald milk and cool to lukewarm; pour over crumbled yeast and stir until yeast is dissolved, then beat in the egg yolks and gradually add flour seasoned with salt and sugar, mixing well after each addition. Mix butter and fruit, and combine with dough; turn out onto a floured board and knead until smooth and elastic. Place in a large bowl, cover with a wet towel and let rise until double in bulk. Set the bowl in a pan of hot water so dough will rise fast. Divide dough into small loaves and place them in greased loaf pans, brush with melted butter and let rise again over a pan of hot water, until double in bulk. Brush tops with egg yolk with a little milk added, and bake in a moderate oven (375°F.) for about 35 minutes. Let cool before slicing. Makes 2 loaves.

EASTER BREAD EGGS

(Torta Pasqualina)

Make a bread dough using recipe for Christmas bread (page 308) or fruited Christmas bread (page 308), and form into shapes of lambs, or other animals; roses or baskets. Place hard-boiled eggs in centers or in positions desired, using strips of dough to form picture desired; bake in a moderate oven (350°F.) for about 25 minutes. When cool, frost and decorate with colored candy or sugars. The children will find eggs easier to eat when served in this festive manner on Easter Sunday morning.

EASTER SURPRISE BREAD

(Pane Sorpresa Pasqualino)

9 cups flour
2 tsp. salt
1 tsp. cinnamon, ground
1 tsp. grated lemon rind
6 eggs, beaten
½ cup nut meats, ground
4 cups sugar
1¾ cups butter, melted and cooled
1½ yeast cakes
¼ cup lukewarm water
¾ cup lukewarm milk
6 eggs, hard-boiled

Sift flour and add cinnamon, salt and grated rind. Stir butter, nuts and sugar into the eggs and blend thoroughly until smooth. Crumble yeast into lukewarm water, and add egg mixture, blend well, then combine with flour mixture gradually, stirring constantly for about 15 minutes. Set aside, covered, and allow to rise to double in bulk, then knead down two or three times and let rise again. Form into 3 loaves, reserving a little dough for later use. Place 2 of the hard-boiled eggs in center top of each loaf, and cover with 2 strips of the reserve dough about the size of a banana. Let rise again in a warm place until each loaf is double in size. Brush tops with egg yolk and bake in a moderate oven (375°F.) for about 30 minutes. Makes 3 loaves.

FRIED BREAD

(Pane Fritto)

My mother was a very busy woman, for there were eleven of us, not counting my Pop, to wash and iron for as well as to bathe and to feed. It required many a short-cut to keep her hungry brood fed. Consequently, if her batch of bread wasn't baked when we dashed home for lunch, she would quickly make fried bread for us. She would take a loaf (see basic bread recipe on page 307) before baking and cut it into slices, roll in sesame seed and fry in deep olive oil. When these were brown and crisp, she would arrange them on a platter, sprinkle with sugar and serve them hot. Mm-mm-muh! were they good! I didn't notice any of the grown-ups lagging when fried bread was served, either. Try it with a glass of fresh milk. I'll guarantee you will enjoy it.

GARLIC BREAD

(Pane all'Aglio)

¼ cup garlic oil
½ cup Parmesan cheese, grated
1 loaf Italian bread (see page 307)
paprika

Cut loaf into thick slices about 2/3 through; spread generously with garlic oil and sprinkle with cheese, top with dashes of paprika. Cover loaf with brown paper bag and bake in a slow oven (325°F.) for about 20 minutes. Serve hot.

GARLIC BREAD CHUNKS

(Bocconcini di Pane all'Aglio)

Slice a loaf of Italian bread (see page 307) into 2-inch slices; brush generously with garlic oil and toast on both sides; then sprinkle well with grated Parmesan cheese. Serve warm in a gayly lined bread basket with any meal and watch it disappear!

GENOESE BREAD

(Pane alla Genovese)

1 ¾ cup cake flour
2 cups powdered sugar
¼ tsp. salt
4 eggs
2 tblsp. brandy
1 cup butter, softened

Mix all ingredients together well, except butter; work in butter gradually. Pour batter into a buttered and lightly floured pan to about ¼-inch thickness. Bake in a moderate oven (350°F.) about 45 minutes.

ITALIAN SWEET BREAD

(Pandolce all'Italiana)

1 cup butter
1 cup sugar
6 eggs
2 cups flour, sifted
¼ cup candied fruit peel, shredded

Cream butter in a warm bowl, add sugar gradually and beat mixture until light and creamy. Add eggs two at a time, beating mixture after each addition; stir in flour. Butter a long, narrow pan, and place layers of batter and fruit alternately until ingredients are used up. Bake in a hot oven (375°F.) for about 45 minutes.

NEAPOLITAN BREAD

(Pane alla Napolitana)

1 egg, well beaten
½ lb. almond paste
rind of 1 orange, grated

Combine orange rind with almond paste and mix well; divide into pieces the size of a walnut, roll lengthwise to about ½-inch thickness, and braid three together. Brush over with beaten egg and bake in a moderate oven (375°F.) for about 45 minutes. Slice while warm.

ONION BREAD

(Pane alla Cipolla)

2 cups onions, coarsely chopped
salt and pepper
2 cups flour, sifted
3 tsp. baking powder
3 egg yolks
¼ cup olive oil
¼ cup Spry (shortening)
¾ cup cold milk
1 cup thin sour cream

Sift flour with baking powder and salt; sift again and cut in shortening as you would for baking powder biscuits, then stir in milk to make a soft dough. Turn dough onto a lightly floured board and knead; roll out to ½-inch thickness. Fry onions in olive oil until soft and transparent, stirring constantly; season and turn mixture into a shallow baking pan. Place rolled out dough over onions. Beat together sour cream and egg yolks, season and spread over dough. Bake in a very hot oven (450°F.) for 12 to 15 minutes. To serve, cut into individual servings. Serves 15.

NOTE: Individual breads can be made if desired by using small, individual size baking pans.

PISTACHIO NUT BREAD

(Pane di Pistacchio)

2⅓ cups flour
1 tblsp. baking powder
¼ cup brown sugar
¼ cup sugar
¼ cup chocolate, unsweetened (powdered)
melted butter for brushing tops
¾ cup pistachio nuts, blanched and chopped
1 egg, well beaten
1 cup cold milk
2 tblsp. butter, melted
1 tsp. anise seeds, warmed

Combine chocolate with flour and sift together, add baking powder, salt and sugars; sift over nuts and anise seed, mix. Combine egg, milk and butter, mix and stir into the flour mixture; blend thoroughly and turn into buttered loaf pan. Bake in a moderate oven (350°F.) for about 45 minutes. The flavor is improved if used a day after baking.

SESAME SEED BREAD

(Pane al Seme di Sesamo)

5 lbs. flour
3 tblsp. salt
sesame seeds (optional)
2 yeast cakes
warm water
olive oil

Sift flour into a large bowl, make a well and place salt and yeast in center with enough warm water to mix thoroughly; knead until elastic and pliable, rub with a little olive oil, cover and set to rise. When double in bulk, punch down and let rise again, then shape into loaves and place in oiled bread pans to rise again; bake in a moderate oven (350°F.) about 1 hour.

NOTE: When using sesame seeds, roll the loaves in the seeds before placing in the pans. Sesame seeds add a lovely, nutty flavor to your bread.

BREAD STICKS

(Grisini)

No. I

Make a bread dough (using basic bread recipe on page 307), and roll dough to about ⅛-inch thickness, cut into 6-inch pieces about 1-inch wide and roll lengthwise into long thin sticks. Roll sticks in coarse salt and a few caraway seeds, then let rise until double in size. Place sticks on a cookie sheet about 2-inches apart, and bake in a hot oven (425°F.) for about 20 minutes. Place a large flat pan filled with water on bottom of oven to give breadsticks crustiness. Should make about 5 dozen breadsticks.

No. II

1 cup milk, scalded
¼ cup butter
1½ tblsp. sugar
½ tsp. salt
1 cake yeast
1 egg, separated
3¾ cups flour

Cool milk to lukewarm, add butter, sugar, salt, yeast, well beaten egg whites, and flour; knead well, and let rise. Punch dough down and roll lengthwise into pieces about 12-inches long and the width of your finger. Place sticks on a floured cookie sheet about 2-inches apart; brush tops with beaten egg yolk, and bake in a hot oven (400°F.) until brown and crisp.

FUGACCIO

(Fogaccia per Antipasto)

Make a soft dough (using basic bread recipe on page 307), and roll out to a ¾-inch thickness, then lay in a well-oiled pan. Spread olive oil generously over the top, then sprinkle with coarsely chopped onions, pushing the pieces well into the dough. Sprinkle with salt and pepper, then let rise to double in bulk; bake in a fairly hot oven (425°F.) for about 30 minutes until well browned. Fugaccio should look rough and bubbly. Serve hot, cut into squares or wedges.

PIZZA DOUGH

(Pronounced Peet-za)

(Pasta per Pizza)

olive oil
1 cake yeast
1 tblsp. salt
6 1/4 cups flour
2 tblsp. shortening
2 cups or more lukewarm water

Fill bowl with flour, make a well and add the water with yeast added and salt; mix thoroughly and add the melted shortening, then knead until elastic and pliable. Spread a little olive oil over dough and knead a few minutes, then flatten to thin cakes the size of pan or pans to be used. Use any of the fillings suggested below.

FILLINGS FOR PIZZA

(Ripieni per Pizza)

No. I

Using the basic pizza recipe above, flatten dough to very thin cakes the size of pan to be used, and brush with olive oil. Cover with the following fillings:

1/2 lb. garlic sausage, chopped
2 tblsp. olive oil
1/2 lb. fresh mushrooms, sliced
3 tomatoes, cut and peeled

Cook sausage and mushrooms in hot olive oil for about 5 minutes, then sprinkle over dough, adding tomatoes, and press into dough. Bake in a moderate oven (350°F.) for about 45 minutes.

No. II

1/2 cup olive oil
1 lb. Mozzarella cheese, sliced
1 tsp. oregano
8 fresh tomatoes, cut up
1 onion, chopped
salt and fresh pepper

Scatter tomatoes and onion over dough brushed with olive oil; lay sliced cheese over all, brush again with olive oil and season. Bake in a hot oven (425°F.) for 25 minutes or so.

No. III

Drain oil from 2 small cans anchovy fillets, and press them into dough that has been brushed with olive oil; scatter with chopped tomatoes, season and add sliced olives. Bake in a moderate oven (350°F.) for about 45 minutes.

No. IV

¾ lb. ham, cut into 1-inch pieces
sprinkle of basil
1 cup Parmesan cheese, grated
4 tomatoes, peeled and cut up
salt and pepper to taste
olive oil

Brush pizza dough with olive oil, scatter ham and tomatoes over top, season and sprinkle well with cheese and olive oil. Bake in a moderate oven (350°F.) for about 45 minutes.

PIZZA WITH MOZZARELLA CHEESE

(Pizza con Mozzarella)

¼ cup olive oil
3 cups tomatoes, peeled and diced (or canned)
1 cup Parmesan cheese, grated
basil, oregano
1 clove garlic, minced (optional)
1 lb. Mozzarella cheese, coarsely shredded
salt and cayenne pepper

Make a bread dough (using basic pizza recipe on page 315), and flatten to very thin cakes the size of the pan or pans to be used. Brush tops with olive oil and cover with partly drained tomatoes, sprinkle with Mozzarella cheese, salt, pepper, oregano and basil. Add minced garlic, if desired, then sprinkle generously with Parmesan cheese; bake in a hot oven (425°F.) for about 20 to 30 minutes or until browned. Serve in wedges piping hot. Delicious with wine!

SICILIAN PIZZA

(Pizza Siciliana)

2 lbs. flour
2 tsp. salt
2 cups warm water
16 anchovy fillets
2 cakes yeast
¼ cup olive oil
2 lbs. tomatoes, peeled ana cut up
1 cup Parmesan cheese, grated
½ cup Romano cheese, cubed
1 large onion, sliced

Dissolve yeast in warm water. Place flour in a large bowl or on bread board, make a well in center and pour in the yeast and water and mix well; add a tblsp. olive oil and knead. Set aside to rise until double in size, then place in a well greased pie pan or cookie sheet. Make indentations in the dough with fingers and insert anchovies, cubed cheese and tomatoes here and there. Bake in a hot oven (425°F.) for about 30 minutes, then lower heat and bake 15 minutes to brown. While still warm, cover with grated cheese and sprinkle with olive oil. To serve, cut in wedges. Makes 2 medium sized pizza.

CHEESE ROLLS

(Involti di Cacio)

1 ½ cups flour
3 tsp. baking powder
½ tsp. salt
paprika
3 tblsp. shortening
½ cup milk
¾ cup sharp cheese, grated
2 pimentos, chopped

Mix flour, baking powder, salt, paprika and shortening together, stir in milk gradually making a biscuit dough. Roll dough out to an approximate 8 by 12 inches, sprinkle with cheese and pimento. Roll as a jelly roll, and bake in a hot oven (450°F.) for about 30 minutes or until browned. Serves 8.

PARMESAN ROLLS

(Involti alla Parmigiana)

1 cup Parmesan cheese, grated
4 tsp. baking powder
¼ cup shortening
2 cups flour
1 tsp. salt
⅔ cup milk

Mix cheese, flour, baking powder and salt; cut in shortening, add milk and mix quickly. Knead a few minutes on a lightly floured board, and pat out to ½-inch thickness; cut and place on greased cookie sheet about 2-inches apart to crust on all sides. Bake at once in hot oven (450°F.) for 12 minutes. Makes about 18 biscuits.

NOTE: The above recipe can be used as a crust for vegetables, meats or fowl by rolling dough to ¼-inch thickness to cover casserole to be used; press edges of dough to dish, cut opening in center to allow steam to escape.

CHAPTER FIFTEEN

Offerings of Mother Earth

Have you ever spent a day in the country, and returned home laden with the free offerings of Mother Earth? A book from the library will acquaint you with the many greens, herbs and fruits you can obtain just for the price of a little effort. The following pages will help you in the preparation of a few of them. Burdock, for instance, when picked young and fresh, is far superior to spinach. It has a flavor much like asparagus, and is a burr-like fruit that looks like a pie-plant, except that burdock has a wider stalk and a very large leaf.

BURDOCK LEAF SOUP

(Zuppa di Bardana)

2 cups water
2 tblsp. olive oil
salt and pepper to taste
1 ½ lbs. burdock leaves
1 clove garlic, minced
Parmesan cheese

Wash leaves and trim burrs from outer edges; drain, and cook in boiling, salted water until tender. Add remaining ingredients, and heat through. You will find this a treat if lightly sprinkled with grated Parmesan cheese.

BURDOCK MEAT SUBSTITUTE

(Sostituti per Carne)

1 ½ to 2 lbs. burdock stalks
2 tblsp. Parmesan cheese, grated
2 eggs, beaten
¼ cup olive oil
1 cup breadcrumbs
1 tsp. oregano
salt and pepper to taste

Wash burdock stalks, remove burrs, and parboil in salted, boiling water about 10 to 15 minutes. Mix breadcrumbs, cheese and seasoning. Cut stalks into 4-inch lengths; dip in eggs and then in breadcrumb mixture; fry in hot olive oil until a golden brown. Serve either hot or cold. Serves 6.

BOILED DANDELIONS

(Dente di Leone Bollite)

Wash dandelion greens thoroughly, and boil in a large amount of salted, boiling water until tender, approximately 10 minutes. Drain, season and sprinkle with olive oil. Garnish with chopped, hard-boiled egg.

DANDELION SALAD

(Insalata di Dente di Leone)

Pick a mess of dandelion greens in early spring before they begin to blossom. Wash thoroughly and remove roots; sprinkle with salt and pepper, and toss in garlic oil and wine vinegar.

DANDELION SOUP

(Zuppa di Dente di Leone)

Cook as in boiled dandelions, but do not drain off liquid. Season with olive oil or butter, salt and pepper to taste. Serve with toasted garlic bread croutons.

DANDELION SPAGHETTI

(Spaghetti con Dente di Leone)

Combine boiled dandelions with cooked spaghetti, season with salt and pepper, sprinkle with olive oil and Parmesan cheese.

FENNEL

(Finocchio)

Fennel, which resembles a stalk of celery, grows wild in many parts of the United States. The stalks can be quartered and eaten as celery; the green feathery ends are good in soups, stews or with spaghetti (see page 61).

GRANADILLA

(Passiflora)

The granadilla is of the passion fruit family, and can be picked in the spring or early summer. The fruit grows 6 to

12 inches long, and though it is round it looks to be four-sided; the thick rind is a yellow-ish green filled with flattened seeds, each enclosed in a sack of juice. A very refreshing drink is made by straining the juice, and adding water with sugar. Chill, and serve as a fruit-ade.

MUSTARD GREENS

(Mostarda)

Mustard greens can be found in most any open field in early spring. Wash greens well, remove roots and yellow flower, and cook in a goodly supply of boiling, salted water until tender. Drain off most of the water, season with salt and pepper, and sprinkle with garlic olive oil.

MUSTARD GREEN PATTIES

(Pasticcini di Mostarda)

3 eggs, beaten
¼ cup flour
salt and pepper to taste
¼ cup Parmesan cheese, grated
2 lbs. mustard greens
¼ cup olive oil

Cook mustard greens in boiling, salted water until tender; drain. Combine eggs, flour, cheese, seasoning with mustard greens, and form into patties; fry in hot olive oil until a golden brown.

PURSLANE

(Portulaca)

The young, tender leaves and shoots of this common garden weed make excellent greens. They can be used raw, in salads, boiled or fried. Cook in the same manner as dandelions.

ST. JOHN'S BREAD

(Caruba)

St. John's Bread grows on trees in California, and is edible just as picked, however, the flavor is improved if roasted in a hot oven (450°F.) about 15 minutes. It makes an excellent, nourishing sweet for children in place of candy.

WILD STRAWBERRIES

(Fragole di Montagna)

There is nothing more delicious than the tiny, fresh wild strawberry. Use them on a shortcake, crushed over vanilla ice cream, or served just plain with sugar and cream.

CHAPTER SIXTEEN

Menus

THE FEAST OF ST. JOSEPH

(As celebrated by the Sicilians)

The Feast of St. Joseph is celebrated on March 19th, and for this great day preparations are made weeks in advance by the Sicilians.

An altar is erected at the end of a large room against a background of white satin and baby's breath, and in the center is placed a life-size statue of St. Joseph holding the hand of the Baby Jesus with the proud Mother watching them. Tall white tapers and waxy white Easter lilies surround the statues.

A long table the length of the room is laden with food of every description.

A group of people is selected from poor families and orphans to represent the Holy Family; an elderly man to represent St. Joseph, a 16-year old girl to take the part of the Blessed Mother, a 2-year old boy to perform as the Infant Jesus, and a number of little girls to act as Angels. All are clothed in white with crowns of gold stars.

The Holy Family and Angels take their places at the table, with St. Joseph sitting at the head facing the altar; alongside him is his Staff made of bread. The Madonna sits at the right of St. Joseph, and the Infant Jesus on his left is seated on a white satin cushion in the place of honor, with the Angels seated all around.

After the Holy Family are seated, the priest enters and blesses all before him; then the little boy, taking the part of the Infant Jesus, who has been taught to bless all around him with his two fingers, raises his hand in benediction, thereby giving the signal that dinner will start.

First, one segment of orange is served to each at table, followed by lentil soup, spaghetti Milanese, fish, frittata, artichokes, burdock, finocchio, olives, pickles, salads, cheeses, eggs, vegetables, fruits, cookies of every description, breads in many shapes and styles, such as braids, fish, baskets, horns of plenty, flowers, fruits and vegetables, and a large Cross. Finally, confetti with almond, confetti with liqueur, wines and milk are served at the end of the feast by the Holy Family. Now the guests, who have been praying and singing religious songs, are invited to eat, continuing the festivity until a late hour. The guests leave laden with food and memories of a great day.

A TYPICAL ITALIAN MENU FOR ONE DAY

BREAKFAST

(Prima Colazione)

Bread, Butter and Honey
Coffee with Hot Milk

LUNCH

(Colazione)

Anchovies and Black Olives
Spaghetti al Burro
Scaloppine with Zucchini
Formaggio Gorgonzola
Red Wine
Finocchi dipped in oil
Frutta
Caffè Nero

DINNER

(Pranzo)

Antipasto
Minestrone Soup
Pollo con Funghi
Romaine Salad
Biscuit Tortoni
White Wine
Fritto Misto
Bread Sticks
Caffè Nero
Strega

RECOMMENDED DINNERS

No. I

Antipasto
Buttered Asparagus with Cheese Sauce
Watercress Salad
Fruit and Cheese
Paradise Soup
Deviled Chicken
Chocolate Spuma
Coffee or Wine

No. II

Antipasto
Minestrone
Ravioli
Veal Spinchoni

Garlic Bread
Romaine Salad
Zucchini
Cannoli
Coffee
Wine

No. III

Antipasto
Cannelloni Stuffed with Clams
Lamb with Mint Jelly
Tossed Salad
Zuppa Inglese
White Wine
Coffee

No. IV

Antipasto Platter
Bread Sticks
Garlic Bread
Stuffed Tuffali
Fried Chicken
Tossed Salad
Chilled Marsala
Fruit and Nuts
Coffee and Brandy

No. V

Spaghetti with Broccoli Sauce
Tossed Salad
Wine
Veal Braccioli
Garlic Bread
Fruit or Cookies

No. VI

Ham and Veal with Wine
Ravioli with Tomato and
  Mushroom Sauce
Fillet of Sole in Wine
String Beans with Tomatoes
Lemon Cream
Wine
Roast Beef
Romaine Salad
Cheese and Nuts
Fresh Fruit
Demitasse

No. VII

Veal Samuelo
Endive Salad
Biscotti
Wine
Peter's Favorite Cauliflower
Warmed Bread
Coffee

No. VIII

Gnocchi No. III
Veal Roast
Mixed Salad
Chestnut Pudding
Wine
Spinach Maria
Garlic Bread
Coffee

No. IX

Spaghetti with Broccoli Sauce
Simple Romaine Salad
Fruit or Cookies
Wine
Veal Braccioli
Garlic Bread
Coffee

No. X

Spaghetti Shells with Meat Sauce
Lemon and Orange Salad
Violet Cream
Wine
Garlic Bread
Coffee

No. XI

Kidney Bean Soup
Veal Scaloppine
Buttered Noodles
Steamed Artichokes
Tomato Salad
Garlic Bread
Bowl of Fruit
Wine
Coffee

No. XII

Spaghetti with your favorite sauce
Garlic Bread
Spinach Salad
Purple Delight
Coffee

No. XIII

Zucchini in Cheese Sauce
Romaine Salad
Garlic Bread
Veal Parmesan
Boiled Artichokes
Sweet Dumplings
Wine
Coffee

No. XIV

Veal Anchovy
Broccoli with Lemon
Artichoke Salad
Garlic Bread
Fruit
Wine
Coffee

No. XV

Macaroni with Ricotta
Rosa's Favorite Eggplant
Tossed Garden Salad
Green Peas
Garlic Bread
Spumoni
Coffee
Veal Roast with Eggplant
Anchovy and Caper Salad
Cheese
Wine
Toasted Garlic Bread
Fruit
Coffee

No. XVI

Gnocchi No. II
Meat Balls in Tomato Sauce
Mixed Vegetable Salad
Toasted Garlic Bread
Fruit
Cheese
Wine
Spaghetti with Anchovy Tomato Sauce
Beef Scaloppine
Bean and Chestnut Loaf
Sliced Oranges and Apples
Cookies
Marsala Wine

No. XVII

Rice Balls
Chicory Salad
Stuffed Breast of Veal
Steamed Spinach
Warm Bread
Coffee or Wine

No. XVIII

Minestrone No. IV
Spinach
Torta Margherita
Fritto Misto
Salad alla Marchesa
Coffee or Wine

No. XIX

Antipasto
Chicken Diavolo
Chocolate Foam
Paradise Soup
Fried Zucchini
Cheese
Chilled White Wine
Endive Salad
Coffee
Strega

HOLIDAY DINNERS

No. I

Antipasto
Lasagne Imbottite
Roasted Chestnuts
Chilled Marsala Wine
Roast Kid
Stuffed Artichokes
Mixed Nuts
Bread Sticks
Mixed Salad
Spumoni
Demitasse
Anisetta
Lentil Soup
Spaghetti alla Eleanor
Individual Meat Rolls
Artichokes with Mushrooms
Broiled Italian Sausages
String Bean Salad
Salt Sticks
Roasted Chestnuts
Macaroons
Red Wine
Fruit
Café Royal

No. II

Pizza Wedges
Spinach and Egg Soup
Sliced Turkey with Peas
Baked Fish
Fritto Misto
Marsala Wine
Fruit and Cheese
Filbert Torte
Coffee
Vermouth

No. III

Minestrone
Rigatoni with Grace's Favorite Sauce
Escarole Salad
Rose Carino Potato Cake
Chilled Wine
Stuffed Artichokes
Toasted Garlic Bread
Anisetta
Demitasse

No. IV

Antipasto
Minestrone
Roasted Squab with Mushrooms
Rabbit Stew
Rice Balls
Chilled Red Wine
Tossed Salad
Assorted Cheese
Bread Sticks
Zabaglione
Benedictine
Demitasse

No. V

Antipasto
Broiled Italian Sausage in Wine
Stuffed Mushrooms
Romaine Salad
Fruit Bowl with Cheese and Nuts
Chilled Marsala
Ravioli with Tomato Sauce
Fried Eggplant
Warm Bread
Demitasse
Cognac

EASTER DINNER

(Pranzo di Pasqua)

Antipasto Platter
Lasagne Imbottite
Fried Artichokes
Lemon and Orange Salad
Cassata Margherita
Chilled Wine
Veal Rolls
Eggplant with Tomato Sauce
Mixed Nuts
Garlic Bread
Easter Bread
Coffee
Cookies
Liqueur

CHRISTMAS DINNER

(Pranzo di Natale)

Antipasto
Rice Milanese
Broiled Sausages
Stuffed Artichokes
Turkey with Chestnut Dressing
Steamed Escarole
Tossed Salad
Pizza
Champagne
Holiday Bread
Chestnuts served at Christmas-time by Mom
Spumoni
Cookies
Confetti
Caffe Espresso
Liqueur

ST. JOSEPH'S DAY DINNER

(Pranzo di San Giuseppe)

Lentil Soup
Spaghetti alla Milanese
Cheese Platter
Anchovy Salad
Pane di Spagna
Fruit Bowl
Chilled Wine
Asparagus Milanese
Lima Bean Salad
Assorted Breads
Chestnuts and Mixed Nuts
Cookies
Bread Sticks
Baked Mackerel
Boiled Carrots
Red Bean Salad
Candies
Cassata Margherita
Caffè Espresso
Liqueur

PIZZA PARTY

Pizza with Mozzarella Cheese
Marsala Wine
Coffee

NOTE: Pizza should be torn apart with hands, forgetting table manners, and wolfed down while hot.

FESTIVE SUNDAY BREAKFAST

Eggs Francesca
Cream Puffs with Ricotta Filling
Caffè Espresso
Holiday Bread
Fruit Bowl
Brandy

TO SERVE 100 SPAGHETTI DINNERS

Spaghetti and Meat Balls
Bread, Butter or Garlic Bread
Tossed Green Salad
Wine, Coffee

* * * *

20 lbs. spaghetti
2 gals. tomato paste
20 lbs. beef, ground
6 lbs. breadcrumbs
1 tblsp. garlic salt
3 ozs. fennel seed
12 heads lettuce
1 qt. wine vinegar
6 ozs. oregano
2 tblsps. pepper
12 loaves bread
3 lbs. coffee
2 lbs. sugar
1 box salt
3 lbs. Parmesan cheese, grated
20 lbs. pork, ground
3 bunches parsley, minced
3 ozs. dry basil
3 lbs. onions, grated
4 heads endive
3 cups olive oil
½ cup salt
2 lbs. butter
4 qts. cream (half and half)
4 gals. wine

TO SERVE 1000 SPAGHETTI DINNERS

Spaghetti and Meat Balls
Hot Bread with Grated Cheese
Tossed Salad
Coffee

* * * *

200 lbs. spaghetti
6 lbs. salt
6 lbs. Parmesan cheese, grated

TOMATO SAUCE

10 gals. tomato paste
1 6-oz. can garlic salt
1 box salt
½ lb. basil
5 lbs. onions, grated
⅛ lb. fennel seed
½ lb. oregano
¼ lb. mint leaves

MEAT BALLS

60 lbs. beef, ground
30 lbs. veal, ground
5 lbs. Parmesan cheese, grated
2 lbs. salt
½ lb. oregano
10 lbs. onions, grated
30 lbs. pork, ground
25 lbs. breadcrumbs
15 bunches parsley, chopped
¼ lb. pepper
½ lb. basil
15 doz. eggs

Fry meatballs in 1 qt. olive oil, using what is left over in the tomato sauce.

SALAD

1½ case No. 5 lettuce
4 doz. bunches green onions
½ gal. olive oil
1½ lbs. salt
½ lb. mint leaves
25 lbs. tomatoes
3 doz. bunches celery
1 gal. wine vinegar
½ lb. oregano

INCIDENTALS

100 loaves bread
25 lbs. coffee
10 lbs. sugar
10 lbs. butter
24 qts. cream

LUNCHEONS

No. I

Rice Soup with Grated Cheese
Anchovy Salad
Garlic Bread
Cookies
Red Wine

No. II

Broiled Fish with Parsley Sauce
Hot Chunks of Bread
Tossed Salad
Fruit
Wine

No. III

Veal Scaloppine
Endive Salad
Frozen Peaches
Tender Green Peas
Wine
Cheese

No. IV

Rice Balls
Crema di Pistachio
Wine
Tomato Salad
Coffee

No. V

Gnocchi
Cheese
Veal Roast
Spinach Salad
Cookies
Coffee
Wine

No. VI

Spaghetti with Meat Sauce
Smothered String Beans
Cream Puffs with Ricotta Filling
Beef Scaloppine
Bread
Coffee

No. VII

Celery Almond Soup
Sliced Orange Salad
Cookies
Chicken Hunter's Style
Garlic Bread
Marsala Wine
Broccoli
Coffee

No. VIII

Tomato Polenta
Tossed Green Salad
Cookies
Broccoli
Lima Beans
Garlic Bread
Coffee

No. IX

Broiled Halibut
Rum Cake
Buttered Noodles
Romaine Salad
Warm Bread
Wine
8 tblsp. Italian pulverized coffee

CHAPTER SEVENTEEN

Miscellaneous

CAFFE ESPRESSO

6 cups boiling water
1 lemon peel
Coffee
sugar to taste

Add coffee to water with lemon peel; boil 3 or 4 minutes, and remove lemon peel. Pour into demitasse cups, and let each guest sweeten to taste. Makes 10 cups. (Italian coffee is very black and is sold in almost every Italian store.)

NOTE: Serve a small glass of Cognac with the Caffè Espresso for thorough enjoyment.

COFFEE FOR 40 SERVINGS

1 lb. coffee, ground fine
1 egg
sugar
8 qts. boiling water
1½ pts. cream (or 1 qt. milk)

Mix coffee with just enough water to moisten; add egg, and let stand several hours. Place coffee in a bag, tie tightly and drop into boiling water; cook 5 minutes, and turn off heat; let stand. Remove coffee bag and add cream. Serve.

HOT CHOCOLATE

(Cioccolata)

1½ oz. bitter chocolate
4 tblsp. sugar
few grains salt
1 cup boiling water
3 cups milk, scalded

Melt chocolate in a small saucepan over hot water, add sugar, salt, and boiling water, gradually, stirring the while. When smooth, place directly over fire and boil 1 minute; add milk, and beat with an egg beater. Serves 4.

HINTS

Are you so afraid of offending that you pass up two of Nature's most valuable foods? The onion and garlic are two of the best seasoners for vegetables and meats. Any good dietitian will tell you that their vitamin content is important to health. Garlic does not stink, it just smells strong. Both of these vegetables can be eaten without fear of offending if you will just chew and swallow a sprig of parsley, the forgotten vegetable, directly after eating. Parsley is also an excellent breath sweetener after heavy drinking.

* * * *

When using herbs in soups to be removed later, tie in little bags for easy handling when soup is done.

* * * *

Cooking with garlic: In making sauces, try cutting the garlic clove in half and frying it in olive oil until a golden brown, then remove from sauce and you will have a delicate flavor. When making salads, there are two ways of introducing the garlic flavor: one is to cut a clove of garlic in half, and rub the cut surface around the inside of the salad bowl; the other is to peel and mash 3 cloves of garlic in a pint of olive oil, and let marinate for later use.

* * * *

Italian ham: Prosciutto cotto is a cooked ham ready to serve with antipasto or any way you wish. Prosciutto crudo is a raw, smoked, reddish brown ham resembling dried beef. This, too, is sliced paper thin, and may be used as an antipasto, but it is mainly used in cooking.

* * * *

Tomato sauce: This can be made with either canned tomato paste or fresh tomatoes. When tomatoes are plentiful in the summer, don't miss making a batch of fresh tomato sauce for future use, as it will save you money. However, in the wintertime, it is cheaper to buy canned tomato paste.

* * * *

Plain macaroni, spaghetti or noodles may be used to "stretch" left-over meats or poultry. Not only does this device increase your servings, but it gives a varied menu.

* * * *

Egg Noodles, served with any gravy as a sauce, may be used in place of potatoes.

* * * *

To dispel cabbage odors, wrap 3 slices of stale bread in cheesecloth and place on top of cabbage, while cooking, covered.

* * * *

To drain artichokes well after cooking, turn them upside-down.

* * * *

A pair of scissors in the kitchen serves many purposes, such as cutting up vegetables, soft bones, sticky foods, etc. Dip blades in and out of hot water while working, and the food will not adhere to blades.

* * * *

To keep toast crisp: Cut buttered toast diagonally, and overlap pieces forming a square. Do not stack one slice on top of the other.

* * * *

To make rice fluffy and white: Add one teaspoonful of lemon juice to each quart of water used to boil rice.

* * * *

For economy, buy large quantities of olive oil and wine vinegar, transferring small amounts to bottles for every day use, and storing the remainder on a low shelf, where it will keep indefinitely.

* * * *

To prepare cinnamon brandy for use over sauces, add 3 ounces of bruised cinnamon bark to a bottle of Italian brandy, and let ferment about 2 weeks.

* * * *

To clear cloudy wines, add 4 or 5 leaves of ground ivy to each bottle, and set to clear.

* * * *

To make lovage cordial, steep fresh lovage seeds in brandy with sugar. This is used as a liqueur, and is also helpful in curing colds—so they say.

English Names with Italian Translation

Almonds .... Mandorle
Almond Crisp .... Croccante di Mandorle
Anise .... Anice
Anchovies .. Accuighi or Alici
Apple .... Mela or Pomo
Artichokes .... Carciofi
Asparagus .... Asparagi
Basil .... Basilico
Bass .... Pesce Lupo
To baste .... Pillottare
Bean .... Fave or Fagioli
Beef .... Bue
Beef Rolls .... Braccioline
Birds .... Uccelletti
Black .... Nero
Blanket .... Coperta
Boiled .... Bollito
Bow Knots .... Farfallette
Bread .... Pane
Breaded .... Pannato
Bread Sticks .... Grisini
Breast .... Petto
Broiled .... Arrostito
Brown .... Bruna
Burdock .... Bardana
Cabbage .... Cavoli
Cake .... Torta or Cassatta
Candied .... Candite
Candy .... Torroni
Capers .... Capperi
Capon .... Cappone
Cardamon .... Cardamono
Carrots .... Carote
Casserole .... Casseruola
Cauliflower .... Cavolfiore
Celery .... Sedani
Cheese .... Formaggio
Cheese Rolls .... Involti di Cacio
Cherries .... Ciliegia
Chestnuts .... Castagne
Chestnut Sweet Bread .... Pondolce di Castagne
Chicken .... Pollo
Chick Peas .... Ceci
Chicory .... Indivia
Chocolate .... Ciocolatta
Cinnamon Sticks .... Cassia
Clams .... Vongolle
Cloves .... Garofani
Codfish .... Merluzzo
Coffee .... Caffè
Collards .... Trunzo
Compote .... Composta
Cooked .... Cotto
Cooked Water ...... Acquacotta
Cookies .... Biscotti
Corn .... Frumento
Corn Meal .... Polenta
Crab .... Granchio
Cream .... Crema
Cream Puffs .... Spinge
Cup Cakes .... Torticelli
Curled .... Arricciato
Custard .... Spuma
Cutlets .... Costolette
Dandelion Salad .... Insalata di Denti di Leone
Dates .... Datteri

Devil .... Diavolo
Dinner .... Pranzo
Drunk .... Ubbriacato
Duck .... Anitra
Dumplings .... Gnocchi
Easter Bread .. Pane di Pasqua
Easter Nests .. Nidi di Pasqua
Eel .... Anguilla
Eggplant .... Melanzana
Eggplant Relish .... Caponatina
Eggs .... Uova
Escarole .... Scarola or Lattuga Arriciata
Fennel .... Finocchio
Festive .... Festivo
Figs .... Fichi
Filberts .... Avellane
Fillets .... Filette
Filling .... Ripieno
Fish .... Pesce
Fisherman .... Marinaro
Flounder .... Passara
Frances .... Francesca
Fresh .... Fresco
Fried .... Fritto
Fried Bread .... Pane Fritto
Fritters .... Fritelle
Frogs .... Ranocchi
Fruit .... Frutta
Fruited Christmas Bread .... Panetone Natalizio
Garden .... Giardino
Garlic .... Aglio
Garlic Bread .... Pane All'Aglio
Grace .... Grazia
Granadilla .... Passiflora
Gravy .... Sugo
Green .... Verde
Grilled .. Al Ferro or Ai Ferri
Ham .... Prosciutto
Hamburger ...... Hamburghese
Head .... Testa
Hearts .... Cuori
Herbs .... Erbe
History .... Storia
Home .... Casa
Homemade .... Casalinga
Hot .... Caldo
Hunter .... Cacciatore
Ice Cream .... Gelato di Crema
Jack .... Giacomo
Kid .... Capretto
Kidney .... Rognone
Kitchen .... La Cucina
Knuckles .... Garretti
Lady Fingers .... Savoiardi
Lamb .... Agnello
Large .... Largo
Large Meat Balls .... Polpettoni
Large Platter .... Granpiatto
Leg .... Gamba or Coscia
Lemon .... Limone
Lentils .... Legume
Lettuce .... Lettuga
Liquid .... Liquida
Little Hats .... Capelletti
Live (infinitive) .... Vivere
Liver .... Fegato
Loaf .... Formato
Lobster .... Aragosto
Lunch .... Colazione
Macaroni .... Maccheroni
Mackerel .... Sgombro
Man .... Uomo
Manner .... Modo
Marie .... Maria
Marrow Bones .... Osso Bucco
Mayonnaise .... Maionesa
Meat .... Carne

Meat Balls .... Polpette
Meat
Substitutes ...... Sostituti per Carne
Meringue .... Miringhe
Milk .... Latte
Mint .... Menta
Mixed .... Mista
Mock .... Finta
Mushrooms .... Funghi
Mustard .... Mostarda
Noodles .... Lasagne
Nuts .... Noci
Offerings of Mother
Earth .... Doni di Madre Terra
Oil .... Olio
Onion .... Cipolla
Oranges .... Aranci
Oven .... Forno
Oysters .... Ostriche
Paradise .... Paradiso
Parmesan .... Parmigiana
Partridge .... Pernice
Patty .... Focaccia
Peaches .... Pesche
Peas .... Pisselli
Pepper .... Pepe
Pheasant .... Fagiano
Pickled .... Salamoia
Pie .... Pasticcio
Pineapples .... Ananassi
Pinenut Clusters .... Pignolate
Pinenuts .... Pignoli
Pistachio .... Pistacchi
Plain .... Semplice
Platter .... Granpiatto
Pork .... Maiale
Pot .... Marmitta
Potatoes .... Patate
Potted .... Invasato
Pounded .... Pestate
Prunes .... Susine
Pudding .. Pasticcio or Budino
Purslane .... Portulaca
Quail .... Quaglia
Rabbit .... Coniglio
Raw .... Crudo
Recipe .... Ricetta
Red .... Rosso
Relish .... Saporoso
Rice .... Riso
Ring of
Plenty .... Anello di Abbondanza
Roast .... Arrosto
Roe (Dried) .... Caviale
Rolled .... Involto
Romaine .... Romana
St. John's Bread .... Caruba
Salad .... Insalada
Salmon .... Salamone
Salt Sticks ...... Bastoni di Sale
Samuel .... Samuele
Sardellen .... Sardelle
Sauce .... Salsa
Sausage .... Salsiccia
Seashells .... Conchiglie
Sesame .... Sesamo
Sherbet .... Sorbetto
Shrimp .... Gamberitti
Skewers .... Spiedo
Skillet .... Padella
Slices .... Fette
Small Garden ...... Giardinetto
Small Meat Balls .. Polpettini
Soup .... Zuppa
Spareribs .... Costole
Spinach .... Spinacci
Spread .... Pasta
Squab .... Piccionetto
Squid .... Calamaretti

Steak .... Bistecca
Steamed .... Affogato
Stew .... Stufato
Stock .... Base
Story .... Storia
Strawberries .... Fragole
Stuffed .... Ripieno
Sugared Chestnuts .... Castagne Zuccherate
Surprise .... Sorpresa
Sweet-sour .... Agrodolce
Tarragon .... Tarragonese
Tartar Sauce .... Salsa di Tartaro
Tarts .... Cassatelle
Tenderloin .... Filletto
Thick .... Gruese
Thin .... Fino
Toast .... Crostini
Tomato .... Pomidoro
Tongue .... Lingua
Toothsome .... Al Dente
Top Hats .... Cappe
Tripe .... Trippa
Trout .... Trotto
Tuna .... Tonno
Turkey .... Tacchino
Two Colors .... Due Colori
Variations .... Variazioni
Veal .... Vitello
Vegetables .... Verdura or Legume
Venison .... Selvaggina
White .... Bianco
White Mountain ...... Monte Bianco
Wild Strawberries .... Fragole di Montagna
Wine .... Vino
Wine Pastry .... Dolce al Vino
Yellow Flat Beans ...... Lupini

Cheeses

Belarno, rich, table
Bitto, mild, table
Caciocarnallo, rich, flavoring
Cacio Fiore, sweet, table
Formaggini, pleasant, dessert cheese
Gorgonzola, very pungent, dressing, antipasto
Hard Cheese, mild, grating
Inconestrato, very sharp, grating
Mozzarella, mild, table cheese
Parma, medium sharp, grating
Parmesan, medium sharp, grating
Pecorino, tangy, grating
Provoloni, mild, table cheese
Ricotta, mild, cottage cheese
Romano, tangy, grating
Salamana, delicate taste, a spread
Scamozza, mild, grating or table
Scanno, burnt taste, served with fruit
Stracchino, soft fresh mild, table

GRATED CHEESE—Sprinkle over soups, meats, stuffings, egg dishes, vegetables. Try it in breadings for meats. You will find the flavor an added delight.

Herb Hints

ALLSPICE—Use in stews, soups, fish, meats and gravies.

ANISE SEED—Exciting in cookies, rolls, tomato sauces and fish sauces.

BAY LEAF—Lends itself to stews, sauces, gravies, meats, fowl and game.

BORAGE—To season cucumbers, string beans and green salads.

BALM—Do try in broiled fish, meats, salad and sauces.

BASIL—Famous in all tomato dishes, soups, sauces, egg dishes, steaks and game. Do try some minced with grated cheese for that festive, appetizing spaghetti dish.

CELERY SEED—For stews, baked potatoes, stuffings, fish and meats.

CELERY SALT—Soups, salads, roasts, potatoes and vegetables.

CARAWAY SEED—Potatoes, pork and fowl.

CUMIN—Cookies, eggs, cheese dishes, soups and meats.

CELERY LEAVES—For a constant companion in endless recipes that call for celery.

CARDAMON—Do try just a pinch in cookies, pastry and after dinner coffee.

CASSIA—Try it in place of cinnamon. Excitingly different.

CAYENNE—For eggs, fish, meats and sauces. Use sparingly.

CHIVES—Adds color and flavor to most any dish.

DILL—Try in sauces, potatoes, beans, lamb, veal, fish and do try it as a garnish.

DILL SEED—For all lentil soups.

FENNEL SEED—Sauces, meats, fish, eggs, soups, breads and pizza.

GARLIC—Sauces, soups, breads, roasts, egg dishes, fowl, fish. Do try garlic bread with your Antipasto. To give pork roast a delicious flavor, split a clove of garlic and rub over the roast. Remember, just a trace will enhance the flavor without offending.

MARJORAM—Wonderful pounded into roasts, cutlets, and when added to casseroles, salads, cheese dishes and omelets.

MINT LEAVES—A breath of fresh flavor in salads, cream soups, roasts, pork, lamb, and minced in grated cheese. In your next roast cut slits here and there and insert a sprinkling of salt, pepper and mint. Try a few leaves when boiling potatoes.

MUSTARD SEED—Sauces, gravies and fowl.

OREGANO—Spaghetti dishes, salads, baked potatoes, meats, stews. Try sprinkling over potatoes while basting. A sure treat.

PARSLEY—Do try in meat loaf, sauces, stuffing, soups, egg dishes and, of course, as a beautiful garnish.

ROSEMARY—A great meat herb, beef, lamb, veal, stews, fried potatoes. It is strong, so use it sparingly for a treat.

SAVORY—Perfect for lentils, stuffings, rich stews and egg dishes.

SAFFRON—Soups, rice dishes, fish and fowl.

SESAME SEED—Breads, cookies and candies.

SORREL—Do try in place of lemon juice.

TARRAGON—Adds zest to hot and cold fish dishes, chicken and most any sauce.

THYME—Springle a pinch in any dish and taste a delightful surprise.

TURMERIC—Excellent with roasts and egg omelets.

TABASCO—Use lightly to enhance egg dishes, gravies, sauces, salad dressings, seafoods and soups.

Don't let your adventure stop. Keep exploring and you will delight in the many herb treats.

Index